GAMP VC

**Dedicated to
John and Vera**

A.M. Beasley
Please Return

GAMP VC

The wartime story of maverick submarine commander Anthony Miers

BRIAN IZZARD

Haynes Publishing

First published in November 2009

A catalogue record for this book is available from the British Library

ISBN 978 1 84425 725 6

Library of Congress catalog card no 2009928031

Published by Haynes Publishing,
Sparkford, Yeovil, Somerset BA22 7JJ, UK
Tel: 01963 442030 Fax: 01963 440001
Int.tel: +44 1963 442030 Int.fax: +44 1963 440001
E-mail: sales@haynes.co.uk
Website: www.haynes.co.uk

Haynes North America Inc.,
861 Lawrence Drive, Newbury Park, California 91320, USA

Designed and typeset by Dominic Stickland
Printed and bound in the UK

CONTENTS

Chapter 1

BALL OF FIRE

The Royal Navy had taken on a cadet who would turn out to be 'a ball of fire', one of its most colourful and controversial officers. As his career progressed, Anthony Cecil Capel Miers was seen as 'totally loyal, outstandingly keen, fearless, hot-tempered and incautiously outspoken'. His language was paint blistering. *The Times* would say of the short, stocky officer with a penetrating glare: 'No one could be indifferent to his presence, or doubt his courage; he was not always easy to deal with and he was not always right in his judgements or his decisions. But his impulses were so often warm and generous that while his energies might raise the temperature of the affairs that he was engaged in, they also created wide tolerance and great loyalties.'[1]

However, men would dread his volcanic eruptions, which for those on the receiving end might culminate in a black eye, close arrest or the sack. For someone really unlucky, it was all three. But when the fire-eater cooled down he could be charm personified. Miers did not bear grudges; a man put under close arrest at lunchtime would probably find himself free by teatime as if nothing had happened. And no one who came into contact with his fists ever made a formal complaint. When he was in command, Miers was fiercely loyal to his crew, regarding them as untouchables. If discipline were necessary, he would administer it. There were, of course, men who sought a calmer life and went out of their way to avoid him. Interestingly, his 'best friend', his brother Ronald, appears never to have been a target of his temper, nor were children, who found him great fun.

Miers joined the navy in 1925 as a special entry cadet, aged 19. By January 1928 his uniform displayed the single gold ring of a sub-lieutenant.[2]

For a man who went on to become one of the greatest submarine commanders of the Second World War, it is remarkable that early in his career he never had any intention of going beneath the waves. Reluctantly, he found himself being pointed towards a submarine course at Fort Blockhouse, Gosport. There were two things worrying him. He was not a natural when it came to the technical world and would cheerfully admit later that he had come 'bottom in engineering', though that did not stop him making sure others were highly proficient. The second point, perhaps more significant, was that he felt that a submarine posting would not allow him so much opportunity when it came to his beloved sports, especially rugby. As an officer in, say, a destroyer there would be more scope.

Lieutenant-Commander Harry 'Joe' Oram had recently taken up the post of instructional officer to the Submarine Service when Miers arrived at Fort Blockhouse for the three-month course in May 1929. Oram had enjoyed two years in command of the submarine HMS *L16*, carrying out routine patrols in the Mediterranean from her base at Malta, but the idea of teaching young officers the basics appealed to him. He wanted his trainees to do well, noting: 'As I came to know men better through sharing the submarine life with them I discovered that most people are far more intelligent than circumstances allow them to demonstrate. Much talent is wasted. This comes about for a number of reasons, notable among which are deficient systems of tuition and failure to recognise a man's true potential.'

Miers found himself with other sub-lieutenants or junior lieutenants, who were split into classes numbering between 10 and 15 on a course covering the general operation of submarines, diving, electrics and administrative work. The instructors had been carefully chosen for their ability in specialist fields, but Oram soon saw that some of his students were struggling.

'It was not until I found myself engaged in amiable conversation with a bright but disheartened young sub-lieutenant at teatime one Friday afternoon that I hit upon the reason,' he said. 'I happened to enquire how he was getting on with his engineering course to which he admitted, rather shamefacedly, "Well, sir, I'm afraid I'm making rather heavy weather of it".

'None of his compatriots was within earshot and, on realising he had a sympathetic listener, he vouchsafed his worries. Having just come out of the classroom he had all his books and papers with him and it only took a little gentle encouragement on my part for him to illustrate what he meant by turning to some of his most recent work. No wonder the poor chap was in extremis. I felt deep sympathy with him. His notebook contained page after page of elaborate drawings of the innards of a diesel engine. They were meticulous in their accuracy and wonderfully neat and tidy in their execution. It was all highly professional stuff but did not advance this poor sub-lieutenant's general understanding of the diesel engine one iota.

'He clearly recognised this shortcoming and was somewhat confused as to what was expected of him. His recapitulation of this highly specialised information in visual form was of an impressive standard and earned him praise from his instructor but left him very far from being able to diagnose simple malfunctions or predict the likely consequences of a fault, should it arise, at sea.'

Was this Miers, the sub-lieutenant who would come 'bottom' in engineering? Over the weekend Oram wrestled with the problem of presentation and on the Monday morning called a meeting of his instructors. It was decided there was no point in trying to teach engine design. They would also simplify engine maintenance because future COs would be able to rely on engine room artificers to carry out the skilled work. The officers needed only a basic understanding. Oram also made the electrical course easier by dispensing with pages of complex circuit diagrams and coming up with his own teaching tool, a large board with wires, switches and lights. Light on, right answer. Light off, wrong answer. He got the desired results.

If Miers had been worried about failing the examination at the end of the course, Oram's attitude would have reassured him: 'It was rarely that we failed anyone. There is little point in requiring a man to go through three-months' intensive work learning about an area entirely new to him if, at the end of it, he has been unable to grasp the basic principles.'

Before the final examination the young officers were sent on a three-week trip in a submarine to give them experience of a routine patrol. Oram had his own training submarine, HMS *L12*, but because the intake on this particular course was large a second submarine, HMS *L14*, was also used.

The boats left Haslar Creek, close to Fort Blockhouse, for the west coast of Scotland. Miers was with Oram in *L12*.

The sub-lieutenant was extremely superstitious and perhaps he was right to be so. Three of the five submarines he trained in or served in before the outbreak of the Second World War would end up being involved in disasters. He was about to have a lucky escape.

On the morning of 9 July, *L12*, with *L14* astern, was in the Irish Sea off the north coast of Pembrokeshire, heading home after a successful training exercise. Visibility was moderate to good when another submarine, HMS *H47*, was spotted returning to the base at Gosport, HMS *Dolphin*. It seems incredible that two submarines on the surface more than two miles apart in daylight and aware of each other's presence should collide, but that is what happened. Oram was officer of the watch before handing over to his navigating officer. At this time there was no reason for concern, although *H47* was on a converging course. Oram went below, checked a chart and headed to the wardroom for breakfast, a large plate of bacon and eggs. But before he had time to cut through a slice of bacon the alarm bell sounded and seconds later he was back in the conning tower.

On the bridge he saw 'a great solid slab of submarine dead ahead'. He ordered the watertight doors shut and ten seconds later *L12* ploughed into *H47*'s port side almost amidships, impaling herself some 2ft. 'From a perfectly normal morning at the end of a rather pleasant cruise, the situation had changed in minutes to one of appalling catastrophe,' said Oram.

H47 listed to starboard and sank quickly, dragging the still-embedded *L12* with her, bow first at an angle of about 50 degrees. Oram managed to shut the upper conning tower hatch before water engulfed the bridge and he and six others were swept overboard. He was swimming when *L12* suddenly broke free and surfaced – with a man clinging to the wire that runs fore and aft from the periscope standards. This was the remarkable escape of Stoker Petty Officer Henry Hicks.

The man made his way to the bridge where he found Miers, who assumed he was a member of *L12*'s crew. The sub-lieutenant was baffled when Hicks insisted he had come from *H47* and thought the man was in a state of shock.

Later an *L12* crewman, unnamed, reported a conversation he had with the bedraggled Hicks: 'I had never seen him in my life before. I knew all the crew of the *L12* by sight and this man was not one of them. I went over to him. He looked as if he had been washed up by the sea.

'"Where the hell have you come from?" I asked.

'"You've just sunk us," he said.

'"Us?" I stared at him. "Who's us?"

'"The *H47*."

'"The *H47*?" He must have thought me stupid, the way I repeated everything he said. "Then where's everybody?" I was looking over the side for survivors.

'The man from *H47* pointed. "Over there," he said.

'I looked and could just make out little blobs in the water, about half a mile away. Then I began to understand. We had hit *H47* almost amidships. Our bows had penetrated about two feet and she had sunk in a few seconds. And she had taken us down with her. She had dragged our bows down forty feet or more until her weight released us, and we came up again. Or rather our bows came up because our stern must have been sticking up in the air. Because we had a lot of sternway on, we had evened off about half a mile away from the scene of the collision.

'Our captain had reached the bridge only a few seconds before the collision. He had been swept overboard, together with everyone one else on the bridge, including several of our training class officers. They were the blobs in the water that I could see swimming for their lives – they with any other survivors from the *H47*.

'This still did not explain how this one man had managed to change boats. In a few breathless, graphic sentences he told me. He was Stoker Petty Officer Hicks, and he had been relieved just before the collision. He had gone on the bridge for a breather before breakfast. The only other person up top was the captain of *H47*, Lieutenant Gardner.

'Hicks had seen the *L12* approaching, and had actually looked over the side and watched our bows go right into the *H47*. He was a non-swimmer and, with great presence of mind, he jumped over the side and on to our bows and clung to the jackstay. The next moment he was submerged, but he clung on. He clung on to that jackstay while he was pulled down forty feet – and he was still clinging when our bows surfaced, bringing him up half a mile away from the scene of the collision.

'"I was just hanging there like a piece of washing on the line," he told me. It was the most remarkable escape I had ever heard of.'

Crewmen of *L12* were confused when their boat levelled off. They thought she had sunk to the bottom. When the depth gauge gave a reading of 7ft, they tapped it. Then, to their relief, they realised that they were on the surface. Seawater had poured in before the lower conning tower hatch could be shut, contaminating the batteries and producing so much chlorine that gas masks were needed in the control room and crew space. The first lieutenant called up to Miers on the bridge to ask if he knew the whereabouts of the captain and was surprised to learn that Oram was now in *L14*.

The trailing submarine had picked up the survivors, but only three of the 22 crew of *H47* were alive, including the captain, Lieutenant Robert Gardner. *L12* lost three men. The submarine went to Milford Haven for temporary repairs before continuing to Gosport.

Miers had gone on a training exercise and learnt a brutal lesson on how not to lose a submarine and most of the crew. In the years ahead he would prove a hard taskmaster when it came to efficiency and following orders. Incompetence would not be tolerated. Only the highest standards were acceptable. And it would not take much to set off that short fuse.

It emerged that *L12* had changed course to allow *H47* to pass ahead, but a message to this effect was not given to Oram, who would have gone back to the bridge. The navy had a 'rule of the road' etiquette that senior officers should get priority, a sort of 'No, no, after you, old chap'. Oram was a lieutenant-commander and *H47*'s captain was a lieutenant. *H47* appears to have forgotten about this until the last moment, suddenly slowing down to give way but not allowing *L12* enough time to avoid a collision.

Oram, Gardner and *L12*'s navigator, Lieutenant Claude Keen, were court-martialled in Portsmouth soon afterwards. Keen, an officer in the Royal Naval Reserve, was the first to be tried. Found guilty of negligence, he was dismissed his ship, HMS *Dolphin*, and given a severe reprimand. Gardner, wounded at the Battle of Jutland at the age of 16, was found guilty of two of four charges but only reprimanded. Oram was cleared of hazarding his boat.[3]

Ten years later Oram had an even more dramatic escape in a submarine disaster that shocked Britain. He found himself in the role of an observer when HMS *Thetis*, one of the new T class submarines, went to Liverpool Bay for her first diving trial on 1 June 1939. The boat was still the property of the builders, Cammell Laird, and carried a number of the company's workers, as well as a navy crew and Admiralty officials, with a total complement of 103, twice the usual number. In the afternoon *Thetis* spent half an hour trying to dive without success. She was not carrying torpedoes and some of her torpedo tubes had been flooded to compensate for the lack of weight. It was decided to check two of the tubes. Soon afterwards the submarine lurched bow down and hit the bottom, with the control room depth gauge reading 128ft. Someone had opened one of the tubes, but its bow cap was also open and water poured in, flooding two compartments. Thetis could not surface.

Later the crew managed to angle the boat so that her stern was sticking out of the water, but rescuers did not arrive on the scene until the following day, when those in the crowded submarine were running out of air. Oram was one of only four men to leave the aft escape chamber alive. The remaining 99 perished.[4]

After he was cleared over the disaster involving *L12* and *H47* in 1929, Oram was given command of a new submarine, HMS *Regulus*. The boat and her crew were lost in December 1940 after leaving Alexandria for the Adriatic. She was probably mined in the Strait of Otranto, between Italy and Albania. Oram's first submarine command, *H31*, vanished a year later in the Bay of Biscay. She, too, is thought to have hit a mine. In 1986 Oram died peacefully, aged 91.

Miers passed the submarine course, much to the annoyance of a close friend who had been desperate to join the service but could not get himself picked.

Chapter 2

KILLED IN ACTION

A nthony Miers was 7 years old when German shells killed his father during the First Battle of the Aisne on 25 September 1914, less than six weeks after the outbreak of the First World War. One of the family's favourite photographs shows Anthony and his brother Ronald, who was four years older, leaving the officers' quarters at Edinburgh Castle. Ronald, in school uniform, is striding along purposefully, with the shorter Anthony, wearing a kilt and a rather large cap, at his side, looking up earnestly. The picture was taken shortly before Captain Douglas Nathaniel Carleton Capel Miers, of the Queen's Own Cameron Highlanders, the old 79th Highlanders, marched out of Edinburgh Castle with the 1st Battalion to go to war.

The regiment was feeling patriotic and optimistic: 'On Wednesday, 12th August, the 79th, completed to full war strength with about 700 army reservists, who had answered the call to arms as Camerons always do, marched out of the historic castle of Edinburgh for the seat of war, a sight that has thrilled the people of the capital from time immemorial.'[1]

It was Captain Miers's third major campaign, and he had always experienced a degree of good fortune. During the reconquest of Sudan in 1898 he took part in the Battle of The Atbara, when the 1st Camerons led the brigade attacking the Dervish army of Emir Mahmoud. Three years later, in the Second Boer War, he escaped unhurt when bullets riddled his valise as he slept in a bivouac while on operations in the Transvaal.[2] But he soon realised that his latest conflict was different from anything he had encountered before.

On 14 August 1914 the Camerons sailed from Southampton to Le Havre, where French troops on the quayside sang *God Save The King* in broken

English, and the Scots made 'feeble' cries of *Vive La France!* With pipes and drums leading the way, the Camerons marched to a rest camp at Gonfreville-l'Orcher, near Harfleur, about six miles from the docks. But soldiers were already suffering: 'The heat was great and some of the men, untrained as yet in carrying full equipment, fell out on the way. The French people were very cordial, offering the soldiers fruit, wine and beer, not the most recommended forms of nourishment for a marching regiment.'

The camp was filling with men from other regiments, and thousands of locals turned up to see them. During the night a thunderstorm drenched the camp and it rained throughout the day 'turning the ground into a swamp, and giving the British Army a foretaste of the mud it was to know so well later on'.

By the end of August German forces were sweeping across north-east France and heading for Paris. The British Expeditionary Force and two French armies were in retreat. The French government and about 500,000 civilians fled Paris. Then the French commander-in-chief, Joseph Joffre, and the BEF's Sir John French decided on a counter attack, and 6 September saw the start of the Battle of the Marne, which raged for several days and split two German armies.

The Camerons played a part in this battle, and one of the wounded, Lance Corporal Richard George, a Glaswegian, gave a clear picture of what the men were experiencing. 'Saturday, Sunday and Monday was pretty preliminary, but at dawn on Tuesday we went out to meet the Germans in force, and we swept them back, getting eight guns and about 600 prisoners,' he said. 'The ground was very soft with the rain, and the only cover we could get was the stooks of corn standing in a field. We lay behind the corn and potted away, but the German artillery slogged away at a terrific rate, and it didn't stop even when their own men came in close to us.

'We got it very rough, and a Cameron beside me went out to help an officer who was badly wounded, but as he reached him he dropped. Our fellows were falling all round, and at about ten o'clock in the morning I got my share. Throughout the day fighting on that part fell off, and I lay on the ground till dark, when another fellow who saw I wasn't able to move came over to make me a bed of straw and get me comfortable. But before he got my bed made a bullet got him through the spine, and he tumbled in a heap. He was stone dead.

'I was lucky to get out of it, for the Germans were firing upon our ambulance men. Now and again a German or two would come over the field, and those of us who had been hit shammed dead, or soon there wouldn't have been any need for shamming. The enemy had snipers lying among our wounded, and that night, when stretcher-bearers came out to carry out the officer I spoke about, three of the stretcher-bearers were shot.

'It was Wednesday morning before I was picked up by a picket of the Coldstream Guards, and as I had been out since Monday night, you can bet I thought they were a long time coming.'[3]

The Battle of the Marne forced the Germans to retreat, but the price had been high, with some 250,000 French and nearly 13,000 British casualties. German losses were about 250,000. With the enemy on the run, hopes grew that it might be a short war. The pursuit, however, was slow. Allied soldiers were exhausted, enduring long marches, constant shelling and appalling weather. Captain Miers, who was 39, would mount tired men, the company piper among them, on his horse.

The German First and Second Armies withdrew to high ground overlooking the River Aisne, an ideal defensive position. The Allies launched the First Battle of the Aisne on 12 September. British troops crossed the river and attacked the Germans at Vailly. Sir John French was optimistic and acknowledged 'gallant' attacks on the 13th and 14th.

The British soldiers were trying to fight their way up slopes, but the Germans were in well-defended positions using heavy artillery and machine guns to great effect. The breakthrough never came, and the Germans began extending their lines towards the North Sea. It was the beginning of long years of trench warfare.

By 23 September Captain Miers, surprisingly, found himself in temporary command of the 1st Camerons, because of the toll among officers. Despite his responsibilities there was time to write an 'in the field' letter to Major Seymour Clarke, who had taken over as editor of the regimental magazine, *The 79th News*: 'As you know, I am *not* [his italics] able to give you any information worth having, and you will have seen the lists in the papers.

Poor Alfred Maitland [a major and former editor of *The 79th News*, who was killed in action on 14 September] did his duty nobly, and I feel his loss more than I can say. I am in command at present, but we expect to have the colonel back again very soon.

'We have been considering a plan of each officer sending periodically a copy, or extracts, from his diary to the depot, where, we thought, they could be collected in a file, each officer having a separate envelope. This would then enable someone at the end of the war to make a record from those diaries of officers who give their permission for them to be used, which, I should think, would be given by every officer. Several diaries were lost on the 14th. MacKinnon [Second Lieutenant Alexander MacKinnon] had a very complete one for my company, which, I fear, is lost. We have had hardly any information about the missing. A few identity discs have been sent in to us, which accounts for some as being killed, but only one officer, i.e. Maitland's. Until the battle is over we shall not get any more definite information. I suppose this is the longest battle on record; it started on the 12th (or 11th) and is still going on. I must end up now, and I hope you are all flourishing.'[4]

The loss of friends, the new type of warfare and the physical battering must have seemed a world away from the one he had recently inhabited. In July, the month before the outbreak of war, he had been in charge of the guard at Holyrood Palace, dining with King George V and Queen Mary. Then, ceremony was everything. On 23 September he was facing the demands of the rain and the mud, the bullets and the shells, the challenges of leadership and courage.

Captain Miers, born at Methven, Perthshire, in 1875, was a distinguished looking officer, mild mannered and reflective. He had followed his father into the army after being educated at The Oratory School in Edgbaston, Birmingham, then regarded as the Catholic Eton. His father, Capel Henry Miers, had been born and brought up in Glamorgan on the family estate in the Swansea Valley. As a younger son Capel Henry was free to seek adventure elsewhere, and joined the Royal Canadian Rifles as an ensign in 1860. He took part in the suppression of the Fenian Raid of 1866, when a band of Irishmen from the United States tried to 'liberate' Canada. Three years later he transferred to the Cameron Highlanders, rising to the rank of lieutenant-colonel. For nearly a century the Miers family had a remarkable record of service with the Camerons.[5]

Captain Douglas Miers joined the regular regiment from a militia battalion in 1896. He distinguished himself in the Boer War, seeing action at the Vet River and Zand River in the Orange Free State and at Wittebergen and Ladybrand in the Orange River Colony. He was Mentioned in Despatches by Lord Roberts. He was also awarded the Royal Humane Society's bronze medal after saving a drowning lieutenant of the Royal Artillery who had tried to swim across the Vaal River. 'At great risk, Captain Miers went in and with difficulty saved him,' said the citation.

In 1901, soon after returning from South Africa, he married Margaret Annie Christie, a Scot with 'a very strong character'. The ceremony was at St Mary's in Cadogan Street, Chelsea, a Roman Catholic church, with a reception at the nearby Hans Crescent Hotel. The couple had a brief honeymoon in Brighton, Sussex, before going to Gibraltar.[6] Thirteen years of peaceful postings lay ahead.

On 25 September 1914, at about 7am, Captain Miers received a shrapnel wound to his arm. The 1st Camerons were still facing an enemy entrenched above the River Aisne. Captain Miers was standing on top of a trench close to a village identified in the regimental records as Beaulne when one or two shells burst near him. A private was also hit. Both men went to the battalion's headquarters, which was in a nearby limestone cave, to have their wounds seen to by a medical officer. Captain Miers decided to go to a hospital set up at Verneuil Château to have his wound dressed, and had just stepped out of the cave when more shells started falling. He delayed his departure. At 7.30am two huge shells exploded, one on top of the cave and one at the entrance, bringing down the roof and tons of stone. Captain Miers probably died instantly. Twenty-eight soldiers, including four officers, were also killed. The regimental records note: 'Friday, 25th September 1914 will always be remembered in the Cameron Highlanders as a day of sudden and crippling disaster.'

That night a shocked Sir John French visited the cave 'to tender his sympathies'. Bandsman Henry Rosher was one of only four men to escape alive. 'Several shells fell near us then, when all of a sudden, a big shell must have fallen on top of the cave as I never heard any explosion, but we were all buried,' he said. 'When I came to I found my head sticking out of the earth, but could not move. Two men came to help me and eventually about 10am I got out.

'We were still under heavy fire, but we tried to dig the others out. We reported to the brigade camp, and they sent out a party of the Scots Guards to help, but the shellfire was too hot. In the evening a party of engineers was sent to dig the others out, but only succeeded in getting Lieutenant Meiklejohn's body out, and Corporal Mitchell, who was still alive but badly crushed. No others had been got out up to Friday night, when I left for the front base. I feel absolutely sure that all inside the cave were killed.'[7]

The regiment's War Diary for the 27th states: 'Major Hill of the HLI [Highland Light Infantry] took over temporary command of the battn. Lieut Meiklejohn buried by RAMC [Royal Army Medical Corps] in grave 48 at the Château Verneuil. Capt Miers and Lieut Crocket buried in cemetery at Bourg. Stone erected with names engraved. Left Bourg at 8.30pm for trenches at Vendresse and relieved the South Wales Borderers.'

Captain Miers's war had lasted less than two months. Already the battalion was so short of officers that three out of four companies were being led by second lieutenants. In a letter to his widow, Captain Ewen Brodie gave more detail about events leading up to the disaster:

The 25th, the date of his death, was a sad one. Our battalion was sent at 1am the morning of the 24th to relieve the Black Watch on a ridge north of Verneuil and west of a little village called Beaulne. Your husband was commanding the regiment. The ridge was rather an isolated one, and we held the top of it. C company, under me, was right in the front holding trenches; to my right was B company under Allan Cameron in a wood in the valley; D company was to the left rear of C company; then came headquarters, and in rear in support, A company.

On the 24th we were heavily shelled and lost some men by shellfire in the trench immediately to the right of headquarters. Your husband gave orders this trench should not be held on the 25th. On the 25th we were heavily shelled again, some hundreds of rounds must have burst on the ridge. At 7am your husband got a slight flesh wound in the arm and decided to have it dressed, and said he would be back in the afternoon. He sent a message to Allan Cameron, who was next senior, to that effect. Before your husband could get away, heavy shellfire again started, so he delayed going. Allan Cameron, however, came straight to headquarters. Just as Allan got to the trench a high explosive shell burst on top of the trench and blew it in. The trench was really a small cave, of which there are many in this district, as there are a large number of underground stone quarries. This cave contained the headquarters staff and signallers. The shell burst on top of the cave, and another one at the mouth of it, and brought down some tons of heavy stones; death to all must have been instantaneous. It took us three nights to dig out the cave to get the bodies out. We could only work at night in the dark as the place was heavily shelled by day. We buried the officers at Bourg. We as a regiment deeply deplore their loss, and I have lost a most kind and able captain.[8]

The First World War would see many families of Cameron Highlanders left to grieve. The regiment lost 367 officers and 5,615 other ranks.[9]

Captain Miers was not the only member of the family to be killed during the First World War. His brother Lieutenant-Colonel Maurice Colin Capel Miers was badly wounded on 12 July 1917 shortly before the Third Battle of Ypres, only two days after taking command of the 8th Battalion Somerset Light Infantry. He died on 9 August, aged 35.[10] But tragedy had visited the family before. Another brother, Captain Ronald Hill MacDonald Capel Miers, was killed in treacherous circumstances during the Second Boer War on 25 September 1901. He was a subaltern in the Somerset Light Infantry, attached to the South African Constabulary with the acting rank of captain. In the February he had been wounded but recovered quickly. He was noted for his toughness, a fine athlete who became army middleweight boxing champion.[11] He was a follower of Eugen Sandow, a pioneering bodybuilder of the Victorian era.

Sandow, a Prussian originally named Friederich Wilhelm Mueller, had started by performing strongman stunts in sideshows. His popularity grew and he toured Europe and went to America. Women would go backstage after performances to pay to feel his flexed muscles. He also had a serious side about nutrition and developing a healthy body. He wrote books on the 'perfect' physique, including one called *Strength And How To Obtain It*, and ran a mail-order business selling exercise equipment. One of the recipients of the Sandow gold medal for excellence was Ronald Miers, just the kind of person a young Anthony would have looked up to, a man's man. Anthony inherited his uncle's love of sport and would himself become a very physical person.

In September 1901 Ronald Miers had taken to riding out with a white flag to Boers of the Heidelberg Commando to try to persuade them to surrender, stressing that further fighting was pointless. Many of the men wavered under his arguments, so the Boer command decided to send a group of men led by Solomon van As to capture him. On the day of his death Ronald Miers was checking on three blockhouses, about a mile apart from each other, near Heidelberg. A corporal of the South African Constabulary gave a detailed account of the 'most dastardly and cold-blooded murder'. At 8.45am on 25 September the corporal, unnamed, was at the middle blockhouse and looking through his field glasses when he spotted seven or eight mounted Boers about 5 miles away. He saw that they had a 'white object', which as they came nearer was clearly a white flag. Then the Boers dismounted and talked among themselves. A cat-and-mouse game ensued. The Boers kept moving moving forward and then halting. Some of them disappeared. Three men approached to within two miles of the blockhouse waving 'the white flag in an eager and persistent manner'.

The corporal saddled up, taking his bandolier, rifle, field glasses and a white flag made up of handkerchiefs, and rode out to meet them, stopping about 500 yards from the group when they showed no sign of continuing their approach. After waiting a quarter of an hour the corporal headed 'leisurely' back to his blockhouse. Another corporal, a 'pig-headed Irishman and a bit of a pro-Boer', decided to go out to the three men, believing they were simply afraid of 'the kind of reception we will give them'. He rode off in his shirtsleeves – unarmed. The Boer with the white flag went to meet him 'without hesitation', and the Irish corporal spoke to all the men for about ten minutes, returning at a canter.

At this point Ronald Miers arrived on his favourite grey mare, with his brown and white spaniel alongside. He was told about the reluctant Boers. The Irish corporal said the three men wanted an assurance from an officer that if they surrendered they would not be forced to fight against their countrymen, 'as they had heard to be the case', because it meant certain death if they were captured. The officer decided to ride out towards the Boers. The first corporal noticed that he was leaving without his carbine and bandolier and shouted after him: 'Won't you take your carbine and bandolier with you, sir?' The answer: 'No thanks, I've got my revolver.'

The corporal reported: 'These words were the last I was destined to hear from the lips of this splendid officer and thorough gentleman.' At about 1.15pm the Boer with the white flag rode to meet Ronald Miers, who, like the Irish corporal, went on to see the other two men. The group dismounted and talked for between five and ten minutes. Then a shot rang out. Soldiers watching from the nearest blockhouse 2 miles away saw the officer's grey mare bolt. The three Boers rode off 'helter skelter'.

The first corporal took another soldier with him to the spot. 'For I knew that should our poor officer be merely wounded, I should be quite incapable alone of bringing him in,' said the corporal. 'He was a heavy man being of an exceptionally strong and athletic build. I came across the body . . . It was his dog that first caught my eye. The faithful animal was sitting near him. It was a never to be forgotten sight that met my eye – so sad and maddening beyond description. It would be quite impossible for me to describe my feelings.

'I dismounted and went up to him, and as soon as I saw his face, which was quite purple, I knew he was dead. However, I was loath to acknowledge the sad reality, and I took hold of his arm and shook it gently, at the same time calling him by name. All I could say was "My God". The poor fellow had been stripped of everything except his shirt and a charm that he wore round his neck. The fact of seeing him thus ignominiously treated was enough to make one cry with rage at not being able to get hold of the devils who had done this inhuman work.'[12]

The war in South Africa ended on 31 May 1902, and the following month the young Solomon van As was put on trial in Heidelberg for the murder of Ronald Miers. From his cell Van As wrote to his parents: 'I must tell you that I am in prison because I fought against the enemy like one of the bravest heroes.' He told his girlfriend, Nelly Nortje: 'I trust that the Dear Lord will bring us together again even if it is not on this earth . . . Love of my heart, I perish of pain and despondency. I die of sorrow . . . My heart is broken.'

A few days later he was executed by a firing squad from Ronald Miers's regiment, the Somerset Light Infantry. Van As had claimed that he killed the officer in self-defence. The court did not believe him. Another Boer, Louis Slabbert, was found guilty of being an accomplice and sentenced to penal servitude for life, but this was commuted to five years.[13] Anthony's brother Ronald was named after the gallant captain, who was 25 at the time of his death. From an early age Anthony and Ronald were conscious of the sacrifices that their family had made on the field of battle. They would come to dread one particular day every year – 25 September. Their father was killed on 25 September 1914 and his brother Ronald had died on 25 September 1901. During his life the superstitious Anthony would make sure that every 25 September remained a quiet day. When he was commanding the submarine HMS *Torbay* in the Mediterranean in 1941 there was no question of going into battle on 25 September. Even that date is missing from his war patrol report.

Black cats, walking under ladders and the colour green were also things to be taken seriously. He would never buy or wear anything green, a centuries-old superstition, particularly among actors in the world of theatre. He would become a keen theatregoer. Nor did he like 13 people sitting at a table and would count the number. It was not unknown for an extra chair to be placed at a table and occupied by a teddy bear.[14]

After her husband's death, Margaret Miers, who was 39, could have been forgiven if she had lost her way. She was, however, an 'extremely determined' woman. One had to get on with life. Anthony would learn a lot from his mother. Mrs Miers had already experienced a lot of tragedy. Her parents were dead when she married, and she had lost two children in infancy, a boy and a girl, who were victims of tuberculosis linked to milk that had not been pasteurised. Alone, she was faced with bringing up her sons Anthony and Ronald, a younger daughter, Rosemary, and a baby boy,

David, who was six months old when his father died. Financially, she needed to be careful. Although her husband left her an estate valued at £14,667, a reasonable sum in those days, her war widow's pension was only £100 a year. Mrs Miers saw two injustices, which she pointed out to the War Office. The pension was based on her husband's rank, and he had been a captain for nearly 14 years. She complained that she was getting the same amount as the widow of a captain who had been recently promoted. And she expressed dismay that her husband, who was in command of a battalion at the time of his death, had not been awarded the Distinguished Service Order. Surprisingly, Captain Miers was not even Mentioned in Despatches. Less than four months after the death of her husband, Mrs Miers faced another tragedy. Her son David died of pneumonia at their temporary home in Edinburgh. He was ten months old.

Within a short time Mrs Miers set off on something of a nomadic life, and her remaining children would not know a permanent home. She left Scotland and headed south, choosing to stay at hotels or boarding houses in London and Folkestone, Kent, which were often cheaper than renting a property. Anthony would buy his first home when he was in his 50s after leaving the navy.

To boost her income Mrs Miers dabbled in stocks and shares, checking prices daily. Usually, she would stake 2s 6d at a time, but her instinct was good and the investments grew. She was able to take her children on holiday to the fashionable French resort of Deauville. The youngsters would spend much of the day playing on the beach. Mother would pop into one of the casinos, and winnings went towards the cost of the holiday.[15]

Captain Miers had long ago mapped out the future for his sons. The eldest would join the army, preferably his regiment, and Anthony would have a career in the Royal Navy. Anthony, born at Birchwood, Inverness, the home town of the Camerons, on 11 November 1906, was 'immensely proud' of his father. He seems to have been happy with this arrangement. So his first school was Stubbington House, a few miles from Portsmouth, which specialised in coaching pupils for naval cadetships. The school, founded by the Reverend William Foster in 1841, produced a number of admirals and several winners of the Victoria Cross. Scott of the Antarctic was a pupil before joining the navy in 1881, aged 13. Robert Falcon Scott is said to have described his times there as among the happiest of his life.

After his early years at Stubbington House, Anthony went to The Edinburgh Academy, but he was not there long when his mother thought of sending him to The Oratory School in Edgbaston, which his father, uncle Ronald and brother Ronald attended. Mrs Miers, however, was not that impressed with The Oratory. Her son Ronald had learnt 'nothing whatever' there, coming away with only one lasting memory – that of being 'stabbed by an Italian', though this may be apocryphal. She also had to consider her finances, and decided that Anthony should go as a foundationer to Wellington College at Crowthorne, Berkshire, the school for the sons of heroes. This would give him an almost free education. With Queen Victoria's blessing, the college had opened in 1859 as a charitable educational institution for the orphan sons of army officers, in memory of the victor at Waterloo.

Mrs Miers arranged an interview with the Master of Wellington and, with Anthony in tow, she took the train to Crowthorne. The Master was William Wyamar Vaughan, 'a great woolly bear of a man with a disconcertingly truculent growl'. One of Vaughan's cousins observed: 'He was one of those men whose entry into a room makes a difference and who stamp themselves ineffaceably upon the tablets of the mind.'[16] In Mrs Miers he seems to have met his match. She was a woman who could walk into a room and make a difference. In the years ahead, her son would have a similar presence. Mrs Miers started the interview by saying: 'Wellington is the school for the sons of heroes. My son is one and I would like you to take him.' The Master said the college would consider the boy when a place became available. Mrs Miers replied to the effect: 'Well, that's fine. I'm not in any hurry.' She remained seated and took out her knitting. Vaughan soon realised that she was not going to leave without a firm offer.

Thus in 1920, at the age of 13, Anthony started at Wellington – and prospered. Vaughan liked straightforward people and probably admired Mrs Miers's boldness. He had been appointed Master ten years earlier. Unlike his predecessors, he was not a scholar or a theologian, and was seen as Wellington's first 'professional' head. He stressed the importance of individuality, and valued integrity, courage, enthusiasm and hard work, all things that would appeal to Anthony. There was one area, however, that the energetic teenager would have found himself at odds with the Master. Vaughan did not like 'excessive athleticism'. Nevertheless the boy who took to sport 'as soon as he could breath' still found himself in ideal surroundings. He enjoyed rugby, cricket and athletics, and also developed a passion for squash and tennis. The 'natural' rugby player went on to play for London Scottish and the United Services, and was given a trial for Scotland. There is a story that when he was not picked for a United Services team to play London Scottish at Portsmouth, he got himself into the London Scottish side and scored the winning try. But there was a question mark over his integrity on the field, with 'anything above a blade of grass getting kicked'.[17]

Winning was everything. He would have the same attitude when he was a naval officer at war. As a submarine commander, he went out of his way to find crew members who were good at sport, and was suspicious of those who did not play anything. Such odd behaviour would be recorded in his confidential assessments of junior officers, even those who shone in other areas. One lieutenant, he noted, 'does not play games well but is a keen rider and first-class shot'. Another lieutenant had 'no proficiency at games other than boxing at which he is an expert'. One officer had 'a fine physique'. Perhaps he was thinking of his murdered uncle, Captain Ronald Miers, the sportsman who had so enthusiastically embraced Victorian bodybuilding.

When he was director of the Royal Navy Submarine Museum, Commander Richard Compton-Hall wrote: 'One of the traditional teachings of English public schools is that a man must always play the game, and that he should be a good loser if the game goes the wrong way. Anthony Cecil Capel Miers, of Scottish fighting stock, attended excellent schools and played games well but most emphatically, he never became a good loser. He was fiercely competitive and determined, from his youngest years, to win – whatever and however.'[18]

He was still playing squash and tennis in his 60s, and once confessed that he might have been categorised 'School of McEnroe' – after John McEnroe, the three-times Wimbledon champion, who was the scourge of umpires.

At Wellington, Anthony did reasonably well in the classroom. His favourite subject was history. In the summer of 1921 Vaughan, who could be a terror, left to go to Rugby and was replaced by one F.B. Malim, a stern, dignified figure. Malim described himself as an 'impenitent Victorian'. The classical scholar was a fine public speaker, and boys held him in awe.

In the aftermath of the First World War there were constant reminders of the sacrifices that had been made. Anthony was one of many boys who had lost their fathers. And Wellingtonians had not been slow in answering the call to duty – 3,350 fought for their country and 597 of them died. Their bravery was recognised many times. Five won the Victoria Cross. There were 302 awards of the Distinguished Service Order and 336 awards of the Military Cross. Nearly 1,000 were Mentioned in Despatches. A monument to the fallen by Sir Edwin Lutyens was unveiled in the college chapel on 24 October 1922.

Graham Stainforth went to Wellington at the same time as Anthony, ending up as the Master from 1956 to 1966. He recalled: 'We were in the same form and sat opposite each other at the bottom of the dormitory table. In those gilt-edged days when traditionally the unbroken rhythm of feudal community life was grooming us for empire . . . squealers [junior boys] knew their place. When the Jally-Ho [servant] put the vegetables on the table we had to fight for them and pass them straight up our side, being beaten if we helped ourselves on the way. Forty years later when I described our confrontation to the Queen she said she needed only one guess as to who won.'[19]

Anthony was at the college for four years, becoming a prefect and a sergeant major in the OTC. In his last year, 1924, he was in command of the squad that won the inter-house drill competition.

There was a setback, however, when he tried to join the navy. Initially, he was turned down after failing an eyesight test. He was short-sighted in one eye. But the navy had not reckoned on the battling Mrs Miers. She had got her son a place at Wellington College and would do everything in her power to ensure that he joined the service. And so he did. He went to the training ship HMS *Thunderer* at Portsmouth. The 22,200-ton *Thunderer* had been one of the battleships at Jutland.

Anthony left Wellington with a prediction ringing in his ears. One of his tutors, Alexander Wallace, who went on to become Dean of Exeter Cathedral, said that his energetic charge would either face a court martial or win the Victoria Cross. He would manage to do both.

He came up with a solution when eyesight tests arose in the future. He would go to army doctors rather than navy ones because they were less strict. When it came to reading the chart with letters in decreasing sizes he would use his good eye first, covering up the other one, and pass the first part of the test. Then with the sleight of hand worthy of a member of The Magic Circle he would pretend to do it the other way round but, in fact, continue to use his good eye. The army doctors never noticed, which did not say a great deal for their eyesight. It was one of his favourite stories. And anyway, as he would have pointed out, only one good eye was necessary for a submarine periscope. One eye had sufficed for Nelson.[20]

Chapter 3

CAPTAIN OF HMS *TORBAY*

In August 1929, a month after the disaster involving *L12* and *H47*, Sub-Lieutenant Anthony Miers was posted to a bizarre submarine, HMS *M2*, the navy's first – and last – submersible aircraft carrier. There were four M class boats, although one was scrapped before completion. They were built using K class hulls and had a striking feature, a 12in gun weighing 60 tons located in front of the conning tower. The guns had been removed from an old battleship.

HMS *M1* was completed shortly before the end of the First World War and *M2* and HMS *M3* appeared in 1920, but they never saw action, probably to the relief of their crews. The idea was that the submarine would rise close to the surface with the gun barrel just visible, open fire and then disappear. Critics pointed out that the huge gun might have done more damage to the submarine than an enemy target. The submarine's effectiveness was also called into question when it emerged that the gun could not be reloaded under water. In 1927 *M2* had her gun removed and replaced by a watertight hangar for a two-seater biplane with folding wings and floats. The idea this time was that the plane would be used for spotting targets. It could take off on a ramp using a catapult and be winched back on its return. The submarine might, however, be forced to spend a dangerous amount of time on the surface. Miers served in *M2* from August 1929 until April 1931, and during this time he was promoted lieutenant.

Ten months later *M2* sank with the loss of all 60 people on board. The boat had sailed from Portland for a routine exercise. *M2* was heading for West Bay, 15 miles west of Portland Bill, when she vanished. The captain of a merchant ship reported seeing a submarine dive stern first. *M2* was found more than a week later, lying at a depth of about 100ft, with her stern buried in sand. It appears that her captain had been going through the stages of launching the seaplane. But as the submarine rose to the surface at an angle the hangar doors and an access hatch to the hull were opened too soon, and water rushed in. A salvage operation was abandoned after more than ten months.

M1 was also lost during an exercise. In November 1925 the boat was with other submarines, including *M3*, minesweepers and depot ships, off the south coast of Devon. She dived and was not seen again until September 1967. A Swedish collier, *Vidar*, taking coal from Cardiff to Stockholm, had been shaken by a heavy blow. The vessel saw the warships exercising and the crew thought they had experienced the shock from the firing of 'submarine bombs'. In the Kiel Canal, the captain learned that a British submarine was missing and reported what had happened. Later *Vidar* was inspected in dry dock and traces of paint from *M1* were found on the stem. In 1967 the submarine was found by chance when a salvage vessel was searching for the wreck of a torpedoed ship. Only *M3* survived without mishap. She was successfully converted into a minelayer but ended up being sold for scrap in 1932.

Miers went from *M2* to HMS *H28* as first lieutenant, based at Harwich. The boat was used for training young officers, similar to the role of Oram's *L12*. The first H boat had been launched in 1915 and there were 36 in the class. They had the distinction of serving in both world wars, although by the 1930s they were considered obsolete and most of them were scrapped. Apart from a minor collision with a steamer in the Bruges Canal in 1929, *H28* survived unscathed until 1944 when she was sold for scrap.

In 1933 Miers fulfilled one of the prophecies of his old tutor Alexander Wallace. He was court-martialled. At the time Miers was away from submarines and serving in the fishery protection vessel HMS *Dart*, based at Devonport. He was charged with attempting to strike a stoker. One report said that on returning to the gunboat at about 1am on 5 February he became involved in a heated argument with the rating over a football match. The stoker may have made deprecatory remarks about Scottish players.

Miers certainly lost his temper and he spent the early hours pacing the deck with another officer wondering what to do next. That day he apologised to Stoker John Jenkins and reported the incident to his commanding officer. Miers and Jenkins gave evidence at the court martial but, according to the report, neither man could give any reason for the quarrel. On behalf of Miers, Paymaster Lieutenant-Commander Royston Johnson pointed out that had he not reported the incident it would never have come to light. 'It is greatly to his credit that his sense of duty was so strong as to compel him to reveal the matter,' he said.

Miers was dismissed his ship, severely reprimanded and put on half pay for one month.[1] After the trial it emerged that he had received 'a severe knock' while playing rugby hours before the offence. A note went on his service record: 'It is possible that the effect of this knock may have left Lieutenant Miers in an abnormal condition from which he had not recovered when he returned to his ship.'[2] His mother told him not to worry about the court martial. She pointed out that Admiral Beatty had experienced run-ins with authority and these had not affected his career.

A few months later he was sent to the other side of the world to join the China Station. He arrived in the enveloping heat of Hong Kong with a growing reputation as a 'ball of fire'. He was first lieutenant of the relatively new R class submarine HMS *Rainbow*, part of the 4th Submarine Flotilla, with HMS *Medway* as the depot ship. It was here that he acquired the lower-deck nickname Gamp – after Charles Dickens's character Mrs Gamp in *Martin Chuzzlewit*. Mrs Gamp carried a bulky umbrella with 'particular ostentation', and she was so popular with her Victorian audience that Gamp became a common expression for umbrella. Miers would often appear in the conning tower of *Rainbow* with an umbrella to ward off tropical storms.

Miers's nickname became more relevant when it emerged that he had once whacked a sailor over the head with an umbrella. The man was on watch and failed to salute the officer on his return from leave. There was another nickname, Crap, which was usually used by officers. The origin of this name is not clear. It could have been a play on one of his names, Capel, or 'because he gave out a lot of crap'.[3]

The first lieutenant did not particularly like Hong Kong. He enjoyed a good time, but he found the colony's social whirl distracting. Nor was he that fond of snipe and duck shooting, which was the passion of many officers when the fleet sailed north to Wei-hai-wei for the summer months to escape the heat and humidity of Hong Kong. Some senior officers, he felt, were 'rather useless'. Miers was focused on two things: the efficient running of *Rainbow* and 'tons' of sport in the shape of rugby, football, cricket, water polo and tennis.

In April 1935 a new captain arrived on board *Rainbow*. There are submariners who lovingly know every bolt, pipe and gauge on their boat. Miers, the reluctant engineer, was not one of them. The captain asked his first lieutenant to take him on a tour of *Rainbow*, fore and aft. At the end of the inspection, he turned and said: 'You don't seem to know much about how this submarine works, Miers.'

The first lieutenant replied: 'I may not, sir, but your submarine will win every trophy going for efficiency and sport.'[4] The captain went away satisfied. He was Lieutenant-Commander John 'Jackie' Broome, who made headlines in 1970 when he successfully sued historian David Irving over claims about the destruction of Artic convoy PQ17 in 1942.

Miers endeavoured to get as many sportsmen as possible to make up *Rainbow*'s crew. An interview with one able seaman, Paddy Dale, went something like this.

Miers: 'Do you play sports, Dale?'

Dale: 'Yes, several.'

Miers: 'Do you play rugby?'

Dale: 'I do, sir.'

Miers: 'Football?'

Dale: 'Yes, sir.'

Miers: 'Cricket?'

Dale: 'Yes, sir, love it.'

Miers: 'Can you fight?'

Dale: 'Of course.'

Miers: 'Do you think you could fight me?'

Dale: 'I could eat you for breakfast, sir.'

Miers: 'Excellent, Dale, well done. Welcome aboard.'

One day *Rainbow* crewmen were scheduled to play a game of water polo against a team from the submarine HMS *Phoenix*. A large, outspoken sub-lieutenant called Grace, who claimed to be related to the famous cricketer, was in the *Phoenix* team. He and Miers had a similar outlook: win at all costs. Grace, however, was on the wrong side – and Miers happened to be the referee. The sub-lieutenant was warned about ducking opponents' heads, but carried on doing it.

Miers shouted: 'One more foul, Grace, and you're out of the bloody water.'

Naturally, Grace committed another foul and was banished. *Rainbow* won the match. Under the shadow of the mother ship *Medway*, *Rainbow* and *Phoenix* were tied up alongside each other, and later a still-furious Grace appeared on the bridge of his submarine. He shouted across: 'I say *Rainbow*, is your fucking first lieutenant aboard?'

A head appeared in *Rainbow*'s conning tower. It was Lieutenant-Commander Broome. 'No, he fucking well isn't,' he said. 'Report to my cabin immediately.'

Grace, who had experienced a number of run-ins with authority, apparently left the Submarine Service shortly afterwards, returning to general duties.

Miers continued to see that *Rainbow* did everything possible to collect prizes for best submarine. George Pickup, a 'sparker' in *Phoenix*, recalled: 'He was very proud of his boat. Out of his own pocket he had all the overhead pipes in the control room covered in what appeared to be nickel plating. It looked beautiful. The pipes normally needed much elbow grease to maintain by the control room sweepers. Now they only needed a quick rub with a damp cloth. We couldn't imagine our Jimmy [first lieutenant] doing that. We in *Phoenix* were jealous of the bright work in *Rainbow*.'[5]

A month after Broome took over as captain, a new fourth hand appeared, Sub-Lieutenant Hugh Mackenzie. He was nervous about meeting Miers, who was 'already known throughout the Submarine Service as a very redoubtable, fierce and dynamic character'. The first lieutenant lost no time in carrying out a 'rigorous interrogation of my antecedents'. Mackenzie was lucky. Like Miers, he had been born in Inverness, with family links to the Queen's Own Cameron Highlanders. He would go on to distinguish himself in the Second World War, commanding the submarines HMS *Thrasher* and

HMS *Tantalus* and winning the Distinguished Service Order and Bar and the Distinguished Service Cross. In the 1960s he was appointed Flag Officer Submarines and Chief Polaris Executive, retiring as Vice-Admiral Sir Hugh Mackenzie. But in 1935 he was facing the challenge of serving under Miers and Broome, also a character hard to please.

'*Rainbow* was a happy ship, reflecting the spirit that ran through the whole flotilla,' Mackenzie recalled. 'They were cheerful, sparkling times. Our captain was a talented games player of the same calibre as his first lieutenant. It was inevitable that there was a clash of personalities between the two. They seldom saw eye to eye and at times were at daggers drawn. Despite this they were united in their efforts to make *Rainbow* the most efficient and smartest submarine in the flotilla – some task. With ten other lieutenant-commanders in command, all vying for promotion and their brass hats, competition was severe.'

Mackenzie was given the tasks of navigator and correspondence officer, which had problems of their own. Broome was 'as meticulous over the handling of official letters as he was on other matters when on the bridge or in the control room at sea'. As for navigating, the fishing grounds off the coast of China could be a nightmare, with junks failing to observe rules and cutting across the submarine's bows, believing that 'devils' in pursuit would end up on the foreign vessel.

Rainbow, however, could make a mess of things without the presence of junks. One morning an exercise in carrying out a torpedo attack on the depot ship *Medway* would not go right, and a row broke out between Broome and Miers.

'For some unknown reason a satisfactory trim [the balance of the submarine] could not be obtained,' said Mackenzie. 'As *Medway* approached and the attack progressed, *Rainbow* continued to flounder about with conning tower awash, half way between the desired periscope depth and the surface. Fury enveloped the control room. The classroom in *Dolphin* had not prepared me for anything like this. I stood transfixed, as inconspicuous as possible, trying to keep out of the line of fire as battle raged between the captain and first lieutenant.

'This lamentable display of how things should not be done ended with some acid signals from Captain (S) in *Medway*, but no doubt, thus to be able to see a submarine throughout its attack, it was great entertainment to the flotilla wives, and others from the fleet, embarked in the depot ship for passage to Wei-hai-wei.'

Rainbow also went north to the cooler base, but at the end of August headed back to Hong Kong to spend three months in dry dock for work on her main ballast tanks. Miers made sure that everything went smoothly. The Chinese were impressive workers, doing eight-hour shifts without tea breaks. And there was plenty of sport for the crew.

When *Medway* and the other submarines and wives returned to Hong Kong, the social life 'exploded', with cocktail parties, dinners and dances. Mackenzie noted that there were many attractive girls in the colony. 'It was a hectic life and temptingly easy to burn the candle at both ends, leading to dire physical and financial consequences,' he said.[6]

Miers had girlfriends, but they continued to take third place after *Rainbow* and sport. One man who put a girlfriend first was Lieutenant Richard Dyer, whom Mackenzie had replaced. 'I cannot say that I loved Miers, but I did have much respect for his integrity, together with admiration for his thoroughness,' said Dyer. 'We had many a sparring match, which of course he mostly won. They were principally concerned about my behaviour ashore, where I was strongly chasing a nice young woman, often to the detriment of my duty aboard. Need I say more to Miers's reaction? However, when the crunch came and we were determined to marry, he then did all he could to ensure a first-class wedding, presents and send-off.'[7]

Early in 1936 the flotilla left Hong Kong to visit different parts of the China Station. The trip took in Malaya, Borneo and Singapore and also the Dutch East Indies and the Philippines, with submarines making individual visits. *Rainbow*'s first port of call was the Rajang River in northern Borneo, where she spent four days. For several officers the highlight of the visit was a feast at a Dayak long house. Fortunately, 'girls of stunning beauty, topless and clad only in colourful sarongs fastened about their waists' were able to provide some distraction from the many shrunken human heads hanging from pillars supporting the roof. But Miers's spell in the Far East was nearing its end and he was about to make the big leap – a command of his own, HMS *L54*.

Rainbow did not survive the Second World War. She was sunk with the loss of everyone on board after leaving Alexandria for a patrol off Calabria on 23 September 1940. The submarine was in collision with the Italian merchant ship *Antonietta Costa*. It is not clear whether the ship deliberately rammed *Rainbow*, as the Italians claimed, or the collision was accidental. Up until 1988, it was thought that *Rainbow* had been lost in a spectacular surface duel with the Italian submarine *Enrico Toti*. New research showed the boat was, in fact, HMS *Triad*, which had sailed from Malta to join the 1st Submarine Flotilla at Alexandria. In the early hours of 15 October, five days after the sinking of *Rainbow*, the moon picked out the gloomy shapes of *Triad* and *Enrico Toti*, which both went to action stations as they headed towards each other. According to an account by *Enrico Toti*'s first lieutenant, Giovanni Cunsolo, *Triad* opened fire with her gun but the shells went over the Italian submarine, which responded with 'hellish' machine gun and rifle fire. *Triad*'s gun went silent as she closed to within four yards of *Enrico Toti*, just passing her stern. The Italian submarine changed course and found a better attacking position. She fired a torpedo, which failed to explode, but *Triad* received two direct hits from *Enrico Toti*'s 4.7in gun as she tried to dive. Cunsolo recorded: 'The submarine sinks. Then in a desperate attempt to escape she tries to surface stern-first, but soon after she disappears forever under the surface of the sea. The duel is over. A moment of silence hangs over the spectators in a salute between fighters. The entire crew of another submarine would never see light again, shut in a coffin of steel lying 3,000 metres at the bottom of the sea.'

Believing that he had sunk *Rainbow*, *Enrico Toti*'s captain, Lieutenant-Commander Bandino Bandini, said: 'From our conning tower we could see the *Rainbow* men and I could see clearly the commander, who was giving orders, wearing white overalls. It is always alive within me the memory of the heroic behaviour of *Rainbow*'s crew.' The battle had lasted between 30 and 45 minutes, and *Enrico Toti* was the only Italian submarine to sink a British submarine.[8]

When Miers took command of *L54*, based at HMS *Dolphin*, Gosport, in August 1936, it was more of the same – the efficiency of the submarine and sport, though without any of the frustration of working directly under a superior officer. Now he was the captain, giving all the orders. His reputation was well known in the Submarine Service, and many of the surface ships packing Portsmouth harbour were about to learn that they had a fierce competitor in their midst. Miers entered *L54* for the prestigious fleet athletics competition. The submarine was up against battleships and cruisers with large crews, offering plenty of choice when it came to picking teams. But Miers was 'an amazing man for detail'. He went through everything, noticing things that others would pass over. Miers studied the small print of the competition's rules and discovered that everyone who entered the mile got a point, even the person who came last. So the entire crew of *L54* were ordered to take part in the mile, collecting around 40 extra points. Against all the odds, the submarine snatched one of the top places in the competition and 'everyone was furious, thinking it was incredibly bad sportsmanship'.[9]

On the efficiency front, Miers was a winner again when *L54* was chosen to appear before King George VI at the Coronation Review of the Fleet off Spithead on 20 May 1937. That year the first medal ribbon appeared on his uniform – blue edged with one red and two white stripes, the Coronation Medal 1937. In a few years' time he would be displaying 'real' ribbons denoting courage.

Over the next two and a half years he was away from submarines. He was given a post on the old battleship HMS *Iron Duke*, a veteran of the Battle of Jutland, which was being used as a training ship, and he attended a staff course at the Royal Naval College, Greenwich. He was also promoted lieutenant-commander. When on leave he would often stay with his mother or his brother's family. After years of hotels and boarding houses the roaming Mrs Miers, known in the family as Daisy, 'although she wasn't anything like a Daisy', had settled down in Queen's Gate, central London. When her son visited, she would make sure there was an ample supply of beer, which in those days usually came in bottles with flip-up tops. Miers discovered that his mother's maid was helping herself to some of the beer, topping up bottles with water. Mrs Miers was furious – with her son. It meant that she had to get rid of the maid.

Miers's brother Ronald had followed in their father's footsteps, joining the Queen's Own Cameron Highlanders. In 1930 he married Honor Bucknill, daughter of a high court judge in India, Sir John Bucknill. They had two sons, Douglas and David, who would both serve in the Cameron Highlanders. Ronald was promoted captain in 1935 and for three years served as adjutant of the Liverpool Scottish. His son Douglas, then a young boy, remembers hair-raising car trips with his uncle, a favourite visitor, who owned a coupé.

Miers's driving was charitably described as 'determined'. He was particularly bad at roundabouts. But it was the other drivers who got the blame. He carried a pack of printed cards with the warning 'You are driving dangerously'. When drivers stopped to complain about his driving, they would end up receiving a broadside and a card. On one occasion Douglas was a passenger on a trip to deliver a gift to Miers's mother – a wardrobe 'which she didn't particularly want'. It was in the back of the coupé and lurched violently as Miers raced to make his delivery. At a roundabout there was major altercation with another driver – who was handed a card. Many years after retiring from the navy, Miers managed to damage around ten cars driving down a single street near his home in Roehampton, south-west London. Perhaps aggressive was a better description than determined.[10]

By January 1939 he was on the staff of the Commander-in-Chief, Home Fleet, Admiral Sir Charles Forbes. He remained in that post for the entire year and much of 1940. After the confines of submarines he found plenty of space on board the battleships HMS *Nelson*, HMS *Rodney* and HMS *Warspite*. War had been declared on 3 September 1939, but still he had not seen any action. For a man anxious for a frontline role it must have been a frustrating time. And he was not getting any younger. Admiral Sir Max Horton, who had distinguished himself as a submariner during the First World War, was put in charge of submarines in 1940, and he wanted young men to captain his boats. Horton, from his own experiences, knew the immense strain that wartime commanding officers faced, and he relieved a significant number of men who were over the age of 35, sending them to general service. Soon it would not be unusual to find lieutenants in their early 20s in command.[11]

Miers must have kept pushing for a submarine command. Surprisingly, on 12 November 1940, one day after his 34th birthday, he was given command of a new T class submarine, HMS *Torbay*, pennant number N79, a poignant reminder of his father and the Camerons, the old 79th Highlanders. More good news came on 1 January 1941 – he was Mentioned in Despatches.

The T class submarines, powered by diesel engines and electric motors, would prove to be highly successful in the war. They were 275ft in length and normal displacement was 1,325 tons, with a diving depth of 300ft. The boats packed a punch. *Torbay* had ten torpedo tubes. Six of them were in the bow and were reloadable. Two tubes were at the bow but outside the hull; they were not reloadable. Two further tubes were abreast of the bridge; their settings could not be altered at sea. A total of 16 torpedoes were carried. A 4in gun was mounted in front of the conning tower, and Miers would use this gun to great effect. The crew in wartime numbered 61. The T class submarines were built in three batches, and *Torbay*, a batch one boat, had been launched at Chatham dockyard on 9 April 1940. She was still being fitted out when Miers headed for Chatham. Captains of new submarines usually spent weeks or months liaising with dockyard officials and workers to ensure that everything went to plan. A standby crew was assembled, with accommodation in local barracks.

But there would always be time for some fun. One day, when leave was due, Miers challenged a sailor 'of immense physique', Edward 'Duchy' Holland, to a race to London by car. Holland, an electrical artificer, got off to a flying start, but Miers lost precious seconds when a dockyard goods train blocked his way. A torrent of abuse directed at the engine driver further delayed his departure. Holland won the race 'hands down'.

In the West End, Miers and Holland indulged in a spot of shoplifting. They visited a shop run by the newly formed WRVS. What happened next is best described by Alexander McCulloch, a *Torbay* crewman: 'The shop had stacks of knitted garments for the troops. In marched Gamp and Duchy. Gamp told the lady behind the counter that he was a submarine captain just about to put to sea and could she fix him up with something warm to wear on the bridge.

'In the centre of the shop was a bust with a beautiful thick sweater. Gamp asked her if he could have it as it looked about his size. She said she was sorry but he couldn't as it was an exhibition item knitted by Mrs Winston Churchill. He then pointed to some articles that were out of reach and, as she went up the steps to get them, Gamp whipped off the sweater and they scarpered pronto. He used to come down the conning tower, complete with cigar, saying "Mrs Winston Churchill knitted this for me".'[12]

Miers made a point of testing his crew. Frederick Rumsey, then a leading seaman, recalled: 'The usual familiarisation routine was carried out, looking round the boat while work was being carried out by the dockyardies. One thing was certain during that period – if Gamp passed any member of the crew at any time he would point at random to some pipes or leads or valves and demand to know what it was and what was its purpose. If you did not know you were given a strictly limited time to find out and to then report the correct answer. The whole crew were, without doubt, kept on their toes. The captain was a martinet and we were all, I think to some extent for one reason or another, somewhat nervous about going to sea with him in this boat. But one thing is certain – before *Torbay* underwent acceptance trials we all knew our boat, from the most senior to the most junior member of the crew.'

Whether Miers – 'bottom' in engineering – knew the true function of the pipes, leads and valves he was gesturing towards remains open to question, but it would have taken a brave man to attempt to bluff his way out.

Rumsey, who notched up 24 years' service, found Miers 'the most positive character that I came across in the whole of my time in the Royal Navy', including 'Cutts' Cunningham, the Commander-in-Chief, Mediterranean from 1939 to 1942. The leading seaman found himself having to be positive when Miers suddenly gave him a couple of days notice to take the examination for promotion to petty officer. To his surprise he passed. Miers obviously had faith in him, but he reflected later that it might have had something to do with an air raid on Devonport, when a direct hit on the petty officers' mess resulted in a high number of casualties. In an air raid on Chatham, a bomb exploded near *Torbay* when she was in dry dock, but there was no serious damage.

Shortly before the submarine headed to Scotland for trials, Miers arranged a commissioning party for his officers and dockyard officials. A special cake was baked, with *Torbay's* crest in icing, and it was left in a hut next to the dockyard's submarine office where the party was due to be held. 'Then it was found that somebody had nobbled the cake,' said Rumsey. 'It had disappeared and although it was rumoured that the engine room department might know something about it, the cake remained nobbled and the culprits undiscovered. You can imagine the rumpus.'[13] Only the plate and a few crumbs were left. Miers was furious and stopped leave for the entire crew. This did not go down well with McCulloch whose wife, six months' pregnant, lived in nearby Gillingham. 'You can imagine my thoughts of Gamp,' he said.

There was a new face among the officers, 20-year-old Lieutenant Paul Chapman, who had been appointed fourth hand and was only supposed to be on loan from HMS *H34*. He did not know that he was replacing someone who had been sacked by Miers. Two other officers would be shown the gangway before *Torbay* became operational. They say that opposites attract, and the introverted Chapman managed to get along with his extrovert captain, although it was never an easy ride. Fate would quickly promote him to second in command. Chapman died in 1994, aged 73, and the first paragraph of an obituary said: '. . . his greatest achievement in the eyes of his fellow submariners was to survive more than a year as first lieutenant of *Torbay* under the irascible Crap Miers . . .'[14]

Despite the great emphasis on efficiency, *Torbay* was lucky to emerge in one piece after her trials in early 1941, and Miers was fortunate to remain captain. From Chatham the submarine went to Sheerness in a snowstorm, tying up at a buoy with difficulty. Miers was keen on using the klaxon, which should have been reserved for emergencies. McCulloch said: 'It was a memorable bit of tying up at the buoy in that weather. Gamp ordered us off the casing in preparation for a trim dive. On taking up my position on the foreplanes, Gamp pressed the klaxon, shut the conning tower hatch and down he came – omitting to give the order to disregard the klaxon. Petty Officer Bert Rayner naturally smacked in the switches – he wasn't to know that it wasn't an air raid – and we tore away from the buoy. Gamp said to Jimmy [the first lieutenant, Paul Skelton, who would be sacked], "Are the motors running?" It was bloody obvious by the vibration of the boat. We surfaced, missing the cruiser HMS *Arethusa* by inches.'

In dashing away from the buoy *Torbay* damaged many fathoms of cable and was forced to return to Chatham to replace them. The cable was made in Scotland and there was a wait of several days, which pleased McCulloch: 'I managed to see my beloved before we finally left for the Holy Loch, but for me Gamp was out – kaput.'

Reaching the Holy Loch on the west coast after a trip round Scotland from the east, *Torbay* tied up alongside the depot ship HMS *Forth*. A busy time followed with day and night exercises, usually in Loch Long. The submarine would return to the depot ship after an exercise but on one occasion she anchored off Arrochar at the head of Loch Long and some men, including Rumsey, were allowed to go ashore.

'While the liberty men were ashore the weather changed suddenly and it became quite choppy,' said Rumsey. 'When the time came for the liberty men to return to the submarine the young AB who was duty boatman doubted the wisdom of doing it in the rather dilapidated dinghy we were using. As I happened to be the senior rating present I took charge, borrowed the boatman's torch and tried to signal to *Torbay* that due to the adverse conditions the boat was not returning to the submarine. Knowing that the captain was also ashore and in the Arrochar Hotel, I went to report to him. He took a dim view of events and he sent me back to the jetty and told me to wait for him.

'Shortly afterwards he arrived at the jetty and ordered everyone into the dinghy and off we set. One of the crutches in the dinghy was very loose in its socket, which made pulling on that particular oar very difficult, especially in those conditions. So I found myself crouching in the boat with the crutch lanyard wrapped around my hand trying to hold the crutch sufficiently firm for the oarsman to be able to put his weight behind the oar without it slipping out. By the time we reached *Torbay* I had a very sore hand.

'Up to the time that we reached the submarine and got everybody out of the dinghy and it had been tied astern, I had been taking the brunt of Miers's disgruntlement. But I had no sooner got below when I was told to report to the wardroom and there I found the captain, who by this time had discovered that I was not the duty boatman but had been a liberty man and had taken charge of the situation to the best of my ability. He then took the wind out of my sails by enquiring about my hand and telling me that he had not realised that I had been a liberty man and treating me to a tot of whisky.'

One day on exercise in Loch Long the submarine, at periscope depth, found a merchant ship at anchor in her path, and Miers decided to go under the vessel. He was unaware, however, that there was a tanker on the other side. *Torbay* went down 90ft and as she came up at an angle her bow net cutter sliced into the tanker's hull. Miers was climbing the conning tower ladder ready for surfacing when Chapman, peering through the periscope, realised a collision was inevitable and ordered full speed astern. His prompt action saved *Torbay* from serious damage.

Crewmen were thrown forward by the impact. As he picked himself up, Skelton, the first lieutenant, shouted: 'What the hell was that?'

Chapman said: 'We have rammed a tanker.'

Skelton: 'Poor old Crap. This will finish him.'

Later Chapman noted: 'There was severe trouble on the brew between them. But it was "Poor old Crap" and not "Serve the bastard right".'[15]

The tanker was beached and, according to McCulloch, she spewed out thousands of gallons of oil, which fouled many miles of beaches. But Chapman was not convinced the tanker had been badly damaged, and wondered if the crew beached her so that they could take a break from wartime duties.

When *Torbay* tied up alongside the depot ship Miers went on board to make a full report. 'In due course Miers returned to the boat and ordered lower deck to be cleared and so all hands gathered in the fore ends and he addressed us,' said Rumsey. 'I can't remember anything of that address except for him telling us that this boat and this crew would make him an admiral.'

So Miers displayed no loss of confidence. Perhaps he already knew the outcome. The collision was investigated and no charges were brought. But Chapman, the novice submariner, would question – privately – the judgement of Miers, the submariner with many years' experience. Off

Sheerness, *Torbay* surfaced close to a towed lighter, and Miers narrowly avoided ramming a ship at Parkestone Quay, Harwich. There had been a 'gentle submerged grounding' near Arrochar, and Miers was 'rescued from some confusion' in the Thames estuary near Tilbury. Chapman learned that Miers had a suspect left eye and had fiddled his eyesight tests, concluding that his superior experienced 'a ranger finder problem and erratic turning circle judgement'. Nevertheless it was time to go to war.

Torbay's first task was to help escort a convoy across the Atlantic to Nova Scotia, Halifax. This turned out to be an uneventful trip, rough and monotonous. When the Canadian navy took over the job, the submarine headed back to the Clyde. But Miers was keen to find the enemy.

'The return voyage was greatly enlivened at one stage when the captain broke W/T silence in order to send a signal requesting permission to hunt for U-boats when we had reached a known U-boat zone,' said Rumsey. 'The reply was in the negative at which the captain remarked, "Well, at least they now know where we are, and that should give us a chance". From that moment on no submarine anywhere had keener sets of lookouts on the bridge than did *Torbay*. However, nothing developed. Perhaps the heavy weather explained that, and eventually we arrived back in the Holy Loch. Part of the crew, including me, were given four days' leave.'

Rumsey's wife had found a room locally for herself and their baby son. One afternoon the family were on a bus travelling from Dunoon when the sailor saw a submarine travelling down the Holy Loch and then spotted *Torbay*'s pennant number, N79. He assumed the submarine was going to refuel off Greenock, and 'happily carried on with his leave'. When Rumsey reported back, he discovered that *Torbay* had, in fact, sailed for the Bay of Biscay on 22 March 1941 to join an 'iron ring' of submarines aiming to stop the German battlecruisers *Scharnhorst* and *Gneisenau* from breaking out of Brest and wreaking havoc on Atlantic convoys.

McCulloch was another crewman who had been on leave. He went down to Gillingham to meet his pregnant wife, whom he had been prevented from seeing after the cake for *Torbay*'s commissioning party vanished. Returning to Scotland, he learned about the submarine's sudden departure. 'I had missed *Torbay*,' he said. 'Hallelujah!'

McCulloch ended up 'having a lovely time' on a fishing boat. 'Upon my eventual return to Fort Blockhouse I found that Gamp had put the spoke in as to my qualifying for coxswain,' he said. McCulloch was sent on an electrical course at Roedean, the girls' school outside Brighton, which had been taken over by HMS *Vernon*, the torpedo and mine training establishment. He moved into a flat with his wife and newborn son. 'Gamp had done me a favour,' he said. 'Luck was still on my side as I was drafted up to Birkenhead to stand by *P212* [the new S class submarine HMS *Sahib*] and being a Scouser this was right up my street. Standing by *P212* was totally different from *Torbay*. We were a happy crew, spending many hours in the pub playing snooker and sinking gallons of ale.'

Snooker and beer would give way to the reality of war. *Sahib* went to the Mediterranean where she carried out a number of successful attacks, though one of them left the crew deeply shocked. On 14 November 1942, off the coast of Libya, the submarine sank the Italian steamer *Scillin*, which was carrying more than 800 prisoners of war, most of whom drowned. There had been no indication that the ship was carrying prisoners, and *Sahib*'s captain, Lieutenant John Bromage, was later cleared by an inquiry. On 24 April 1943, after sinking the transport *Galiola* off north-east Sicily, *Sahib* came under a sustained depth charge attack by Italian warships. The submarine was fatally damaged but managed to surface. Bromage gave the order to abandon ship and scuttled her. He was the last man to leave. As men swam away from the sinking boat they were machine-gunned by German planes.

McCulloch said: 'There was no hope of saving the boat and we were lucky to surface. We were ordered to abandon ship and, as luck would have it, the water was flat calm and lovely and warm. Three cheers were given as *Sahib* slid into the depths. Then more drama – two Junkers 88s dived down and machine-gunned us in the water.'

One man was killed but the rest of the crew survived the attack and were rescued by an Italian corvette. The immediate future was a prisoner-of-war camp.

When *Torbay* had been ordered to sail from the Holy Loch to the Bay of Biscay at a few hours' notice, half the crew, including the first lieutenant, Skelton, were on leave. Miers conducted a hasty recruiting campaign among sailors on board the depot ship and elevated the inexperienced Chapman, who had marked his 21st birthday days earlier, to first lieutenant, despite a number of raised eyebrows. No doubt the brush with the tanker – and Chapman's quick thinking – were fresh in Miers's mind. The captain wanted men who could take correct, split-second decisions. Officially, Chapman was still on loan. Skelton got the sack although he was considered good enough to go on a submarine command course. He died later in the war in a plane crash. But the sack was not reserved for officers. During *Torbay*'s first commission under Miers several senior ratings and 'lesser mortals' were replaced, including the coxswain twice.

Torbay had been part of the 'iron ring' in the often unforgiving Bay of Biscay for about two weeks when Miers received orders to go to the Mediterranean where the submarine was urgently needed for operations. It was just what he wanted. Keeping a watch for *Scharnhorst* and *Gneisenau* was a thankless task and, in the event, the battlecruisers remained bottled up in Brest until February 1942, never again menacing Atlantic convoys. On her way to her new base, Alexandria, *Torbay* stopped off at Gibraltar for supplies and a new engineer officer, Tono Kidd. Miers came under pressure to replace the 'green' Chapman with a more experienced man but he insisted on keeping him. Many of the ratings left behind when *Torbay* sailed at short notice from the Holy Loch ended up in the submarine HMS *Cachalot*. About three months after *Torbay*'s arrival in Alexandria *Cachalot* sailed in. The former *Torbay* men were given the chance to rejoin their old boat but they all declined. With some irony, they suffered the same fate as McCulloch.

On 30 July 1941 off Benghazi, Libya, *Cachalot* carried out a surface attack on what she thought was a tanker. The ship turned out to be an Italian destroyer, which rammed the submarine before she could dive. *Cachalot* was scuttled but all the crew, with the exception of a Maltese steward, were rescued, ending up as prisoners of war. One rating, Leading Seaman Cecil Osmond, had a bizarre encounter. He swam to the destroyer and was helped out of the water by an Italian sailor who said in English without any hint of a foreign accent: 'Hard luck, mate.' It turned out that the Italian owned a café in Cardiff. When war broke out, he happened to be visiting his parents in Italy and was called up.[16]

Chapter 4

WAR IN THE MEDITERRANEAN

Miers and *Torbay* went to the Mediterranean theatre at a critical time. The battle for North Africa was raging, with the Suez Canal and Middle East oil supplies as the big prizes. The British were heavily outnumbered at sea and on land. In 1939 Admiral Sir Andrew Cunningham had 45 warships in his Mediterranean fleet, against Italy's 183. There were only 12 submarines – the Italians possessed ten times that number. When Italy declared war in June 1940, the 1st Submarine Flotilla at Alexandria was reinforced with boats from the Far East. But these additions were old and large, and not suitable for the relatively clear and shallow waters of the Mediterranean. When submerged they were among the easiest submarines to spot from the air. The offensive against the Italians could not have got off to a worse start. Four of the boats were sent out on patrol and three of them were destroyed in less than a week, with the loss of 170 lives – HMS *Odin* was sunk by gunfire and depth charges in the Gulf of Taranto on 13 June 1940, HMS *Grampus* was depth-charged off Syracuse on 16 June and HMS *Orpheus* was depth-charged off Tobruk on 19 June.[1] HMS *Rorqual* was the submarine that returned and her captain, Lieutenant-Commander Ronald 'Dizzy' Dewhurst, would quickly gain a reputation as an aggressive submariner – like Miers.

Taking the fight to the enemy was not made any easier by an acute shortage of torpedoes. In the second half of 1940, 299 torpedoes were fired in action in the Mediterranean and elsewhere. As factories desperately tried to increase production, the total reserve of torpedoes fell below 100, and submarine commanders were told to ration their attacks. Added to this was the problem that not all torpedoes worked, some exploding prematurely, others failing to detonate. And the really awkward ones would fray nerves by circling and heading back to the submarine.[2]

After France's surrender on 25 June 1940 the Royal Navy was alone in the fight for control of the Mediterranean. On land, the picture was bleak. The Italians had a huge army in Libya and in September they invaded Egypt, which was held by a much smaller British force. Fortunately, the enemy was reluctant to push deep into the country. With reinforcements, British troops launched a counter attack in December, Operation Compass, throwing the Italians out of Egypt and driving 500 miles into Libya. Two months later two divisions had defeated ten Italian divisions and taken about 130,000 prisoners. The success persuaded Winston Churchill to remove a significant number of troops for the defence of Greece. It was the wrong decision. Major General Erwin Rommel and his Afrika Korps were descending on North Africa. And the Luftwaffe's Fliegerkorps X was sent to Sicily to attack Allied shipping. The British were forced out of Benghazi on 2 April 1941, and Rommel's rapid advance saw Tobruk surrounded on 10 April.

The year 1941 began badly for the Royal Navy. On 10 January the carrier HMS *Illustrious* was seriously damaged in an attack by 40 Stukas. The cruiser HMS *Southampton* was lost in another air attack and the destroyer HMS *Hyperion* sank after hitting a mine. But in February the submarine HMS *Upright* torpedoed the Italian cruiser *Armando Diaz*, and in March the navy scored a major victory, sinking three cruisers and two destroyers in the Battle of Matapan.

The Mediterranean was becoming a cauldron, the battle of the convoys, as both sides tried to move troops and supplies. On 23 April *Torbay* left Gibraltar on her first war patrol, heading for the east coast of Sardinia.[3] By 25 April she was on the southern approach to Cagliari and the following night entered her patrol area. Miers had a problem: 'Without knowledge of the enemy's habits it was difficult to judge whether the coastal shipping was more likely to keep in deep water to avoid possible minefields, or keep in shallow water perhaps inside protective minefields to minimise the risk of submarine attack.'

The next morning *Torbay* scented first blood – an unescorted merchant ship. But within half an hour the attack was broken off because of the long range and the small size of the target. Another ship, of about 2,000 tons, was sighted soon afterwards at a range of 2,000 yards, and the submarine closed at speed. Then a much larger ship, about a mile astern of the target, was spotted and the attack shifted. At a range of about 1,000 yards Miers gave the order to fire four torpedoes. Two missed and two did not even leave the tubes because of a mix-up with the torpedo gunner's mate.

Miers reported: 'The error in drill has been investigated and found to be a mistake on the part of the TGM who only joined the submarine in the evening before leaving Gibraltar and had no previous submarine experience. I am confident that no such mistake will occur in future.'

When Miers realised that his torpedoes had missed, he decided to surface and use the submarine's 4in gun. A plane was spotted about a mile away, following the torpedo tracks, and so he dived deep, changing course. That night *Torbay* picked a new area to patrol, hoping to sight ships from Naples, but for the next three days no vessels or planes were seen. The submarine went to another area, north of Sicily, and on 2 May saw two destroyers about 6 miles away, but an attack was not possible.

Only a plane and a trawler, probably anti-submarine, were picked up over the next few days. On 10 May *Torbay* was positioned off Navarin Bay ready to attack shipping, but the harbour was empty. That night the submarine surfaced and set course for her new base, Alexandria. Chapman was the officer of the watch on the night before they were due to arrive and he suddenly spotted a group of ships. Miers joined him on the bridge. *Torbay* increased speed and altered course, ready to launch a torpedo attack. Fortunately, the moon was able to reveal that the main targets were battleships of the Queen Elizabeth class. The attack was hurriedly called off. In his patrol report, Miers restricted himself to just 'sighted friendly forces'.

Not so friendly. As *Torbay* neared a destroyer screen she fired a recognition signal, a pyrotechnic grenade. The closest destroyer, HMS *Kingston*, replied by opening fire with machine guns. According to Chapman, Miers leaned over the bridge and roared: 'Don't be a cunt.' The firing stopped. Miers enhanced his reputation.[4]

In his report, he summed up: 'Although this was an unsuccessful patrol, it was of considerable value both in training and experience for the personnel of whom, when *Torbay* left home waters in March, a large number were making their first patrol in a submarine and some had previously never been to sea at all. In this connection it may be of interest to record that the commanding officer was making his first war patrol after an absence of three and a half years in submarines, and that the experience of the remaining officers, of whom the age of the oldest executive officer is twenty-one, was negligible. The keenness and zest of all on board, however, should promise better things in future.'

There were two other points about this patrol. The asdic failed early in the mission and a repair was carried out with difficulty using a 'Heath Robinson device'. And an American naval officer, Lieutenant-Commander Frank Watkins, was on board as an observer, although he carried out various duties. His presence was interesting because the United States would not go to war until after the Japanese attack on Pearl Harbor in December. 'The helpful and friendly attitude of Lieutenant-Commander Watkins was felt and appreciated by all on board,' said Miers.

Captain 'Sammy' Raw, in charge of the 1st Submarine Flotilla at Alexandria, commented on the patrol: '*Torbay* cannot yet be considered a fully efficient unit and there are no opportunities for submarines to work up on this station such as exist in home waters. I have every confidence, however, in Lieutenant-Commander Miers, who is an officer of great energy and enthusiasm, and I consider that credit is due to him for the way he has overcome many difficulties since leaving the UK.'[5]

On 28 May *Torbay* slipped away from Alexandria for her second patrol.[6] Eight days earlier, German paratroopers had descended on Crete and by 1 June, after savage fighting, the island was lost. The Royal Navy paid a heavy price as it evacuated some 16,000 troops. Without adequate air cover, it found itself at the mercy of the Luftwaffe. During the battle for Crete three cruisers and six destroyers were sunk and other vessels were badly damaged. More than 2,000 sailors died. The navy had already taken a pounding during Operation Demon in April, when more than 50,000 troops were evacuated from Greece, also without air cover 'because the aircraft simply did not exist'. This Dunkirk-style withdrawal took place less than two months after the navy had been given the task of landing the Allied expeditionary force in Greece 'at considerable risk' and then supplying it.[7]

For her second patrol *Torbay* was given a large hunting ground in the eastern Mediterranean, the Aegean. Raw sent a 'good hunting' message. 'So much may depend on your success,' he told *Torbay*.

On 1 June the submarine claimed her first victim, a caique flying the German flag. The sailing vessel, probably packed with explosives, was caught in the Doro Channel between the islands of Andros and Euboea. *Torbay* surfaced and five rounds were fired from her 4in gun. The second round caused a huge explosion, which blew the stern off. Miers reported: 'The occupants did not appear to be soldiers and were left in calm water with plenty of floating wood to support them.' That the survivors were spared is significant, in view of controversial claims decades later.

Torbay's first patrol had been largely uneventful, but this mission would be packed with incident. Two days later another caique was sunk by gunfire, this time off Mitylene. Again the survivors were spared. 'This caique was very well handled under fire and, by repeated tacking, made herself a very difficult target,' said Miers. 'Shortly before sinking, however, the crew signified their surrender and, as they did not appear to be German, were left afloat in the wreckage.'

Miers decided to position himself off the Turkish coast, close to the mouth of the Dardanelles, a gateway for shipping using the Bosphorus and the Black Sea. He needed to be careful because a lot of the shipping was neutral. There was also a natural hazard, strong currents that made staying submerged and manoeuvring difficult. On 6 June he launched his first successful torpedo attack on a major target, a Vichy French tanker, *Alberta*, which had orders to go to the Black Sea to pick up oil and take it to Italy. This is how Miers described the attack shortly before 1pm:

1242: *In position 246 degrees Cape Helles five miles, sighted 3,000-ton merchant ship bearing 200 degrees, six miles approaching Dardanelles. Commenced attack.*

1318 *Enemy altered course to enter straits. I was well placed on the enemy's port bow, a mile off track.*

1332 *Enemy, having misjudged the current, altered course to 070 degrees and put me in a dangerous position, as at this time Torbay was also feeling the full strength of the stream. Steering at slow speed was impossible and I was only about ten degrees on the enemy's bow running in.*

1333 *Went deep and turned to run out at full speed, hoping to have sufficient speed to maintain bearing on the enemy.*

1341 *Came to periscope depth on enemy's port quarter and chased at full speed on parallel course (070 degrees).*

1408 *Came level with enemy just inside territorial waters, but now the strength of the stream frustrated my efforts to get onto a firing course until the track was a very poor one (160 degrees).*

1412 *Decided to get immediately astern of enemy and fire on a track of 180 degrees.*

1415 *Fired one torpedo at a range of 1,200 yards, course 070 degrees, in position 229 degrees Cape Helles three and a half miles. Torpedo hit, obviously wrecking shaft and steering gear. Ship stopped, settled rapidly by the stern and appeared to be sinking.*

Later that afternoon, with *Alberta* still afloat, a second torpedo struck, but the ship failed to sink, probably because the explosion was in an area already flooded. According to Chapman, David Verschoyle-Campbell, the fourth officer, took a fix on the tanker's position and pointed out to Miers that she had been attacked in Turkish territorial waters. If the captain was concerned, he did not show it. *Alberta*, Miers suggested, must have been unlucky and hit a mine.

The next night the ship was still defiantly afloat, and Miers decided to board her. When *Torbay*, with Lewis guns manned on the bridge, went alongside she found *Alberta* deserted. Boarding parties were led by Verschoyle-Campbell, who recovered log books and charts, and Kidd, the engineer officer, who looked at the possibility of scuttling the ship, which was not feasible. In the end the tanker was set adrift.

In Alexandria, Raw noted: 'Although *Torbay* failed to achieve the destruction of *Alberta* at this stage the efforts made by the CO were most commendable and showed much forethought and determination. It must be remembered that this operation took place in full exposure of the searchlights at Cape Helles.'

On 9 June a Turkish tug put a line on board *Alberta* but gave up towing when *Torbay*, still watching her prey, fired another torpedo. The tanker was adrift again. An Italian destroyer arrived on the scene and the submarine dived. That night, with Miers determined to send the ship to the bottom, *Torbay* surfaced and fired 40 4in shells at the hull. Miers reported that the tanker sank, but according to Chapman she remained afloat although a total loss.

The next day, by contrast, Miers enjoyed a quick major success. It owed something to good fortune. *Torbay* was patrolling the same area off the Dardanelles when she spotted a convoy of six ships escorted by two Italian destroyers. Miers was about to attack when he realised he was too close to the leading destroyer – 50 yards. He held fire, selected a new target and sent three torpedoes, two of which found the other destroyer. The warship paid a fatal price for changing course.

Now it was *Torbay*'s turn to be hunted. She was targeted with depth charges – her first, dropped by the leading destroyer. Miers was pleased to see that his inexperienced crew came through the counter attack without problems. Soon afterwards *Torbay* went to periscope depth. It was Miers's day. He must have rubbed his good eye. In his sight was the Italian tanker *Giuseppina Ghiradi*, which had emerged from the Dardanelles loaded with oil. She sank quickly. With a destroyer and two motor anti-submarine boats trying to find him, Miers turned south.

Early on 11 June, *Torbay* found a caique carrying military stores, which she rammed. The Greek crew were allowed to take to a boat before the caique was destroyed. Returning to the area around the Doro Channel, the submarine encountered a large Italian schooner on course for Limnos, loaded with soldiers, ammunition and stores. After a chase the schooner was sunk. There were no survivors apparently. *Torbay*'s patrol ended on 16 June.

Miers said: 'This patrol was a splendid working-up for an inexperienced ship's company who had previously been prevented from getting together by unprecedented changes in complement . . . The slice of good fortune that we have enjoyed has acted as a tonic on the men who have previously had nothing more wholesome to think about than their ill-fortune in finding themselves in the Mediterranean instead of in the Clyde, unexpectedly and without their clothes or gear.

'Their morale is now high and, with a little more training, I have every hope that this crew will prove worthy of the high tradition of their new flotilla.'

Worthy of the high tradition of the new flotilla? Miers was getting a bit carried away, but there was no doubting the success of the patrol – two tankers, one destroyer, one schooner and three caiques.

When *Torbay* returned to Alexandria, Raw sent a message to the submarine, saying: 'I have just heard the full account of *Torbay*'s recent patrol. From previous reports and the enemy's distress signals I knew that *Torbay* had been active with her torpedoes. Now I hear that the gun and ram have also been very busy. I want to congratulate you, your officers and ship's company most heartily on a most successful and determined patrol which must have far reaching effects on the enemy's morale.'

In his official report, Raw thought the patrol had been 'brilliantly' conducted. 'Throughout the patrol the CO showed great determination, which is typified by his many and finally successful attempts to dispatch *Alberta*,' he said, adding: 'I consider *Torbay* to be a most useful addition to the 1st Submarine Flotilla and confidently expect that she will maintain this offensive spirit which is so valuable.'[8]

Admiral Cunningham was also impressed: 'This very ably conducted patrol inflicted considerable damage on the enemy. Great credit is due to Lieutenant-Commander A.C.C. Miers and the ship's company for reaching so high a standard of war efficiency at an early stage of their commission.'[9]

Chapter 5

NAZI PUBLIC ENEMY NO.1

HMS *Torbay* left Alexandria on 28 June for her third patrol.[1] Two days later she spotted and chased a laden caique of about 50 tons near the island of Falconera, west of Milos. The submarine surfaced and sank the vessel – not flying any colours – with gunfire. The crew of four were allowed to escape in a dinghy being towed astern. *Torbay* remained in the area and the next day she was forced to dive deep repeatedly to avoid enemy aircraft. It was an unpleasant time. The gyro compass was out of action and the diving compass was unreadable because of flooding.

On 2 July, north-east of Kea island, two merchant ships were sighted, escorted by a destroyer and a plane. The sea was like 'the proverbial mill pond' and Miers decided on a long-range attack, because any increase in speed might have given his position away. A spread of three torpedoes was fired at each merchant ship. One torpedo hit the leading ship, the 3,000-ton *Citta di Tripoli*, which sank. The destroyer dropped 18 depth charges in retaliation, but *Torbay* was well out of range.

The following day *Torbay* saw an anti-submarine trawler and started an attack. This, however, was called off because a heavy sea was running, and Miers feared that torpedoes set to a shallow depth would not run correctly. In the afternoon two large merchant ships without escorts appeared, but the range could not be closed in time.

Miers showed his ruthless streak early the next day in the northern approaches to the Doro Channel after chasing a caique loaded with German troops and stores, which probably included a large quantity of petrol. Gunfire started a fierce fire. 'Dived when it was obvious that the caique must sink, but remained in the vicinity to make sure,' Miers reported. 'The caique heeled over but the fire was extinguished and the survivors (about 30) clambered back and huddled together on the gunwhale that was out of the water. Just when it seemed that a few practice projectiles might profitably be fired to finish her off, the caique sank and, there being no boat serviceable, the occupants were soon drowned.'

A few hours later a schooner 'wearing the Nazi colours' approached the channel, heading straight for the submarine. 'The position was uncomfortably close to the land, but it was felt that the German flag could not go unpunished, hence gun action was ordered,' said Miers. 'The schooner was well filled with troops and stores and was of about 60 tons. Surfaced and sank the enemy with gunfire using both Lewis guns to destroy the boats and personnel in order to ensure a quick success in view of the proximity of land.'

Chapman would note: 'The troops were not allowed to escape – everything and everybody was destroyed by one sort of gunfire or another.'[2]

This patrol was different from previous missions. On board were two army commandos of the Special Boat Section (SBS), Corporals George Bremner and Jim Sherwood. The idea was to find them suitable targets on land to sabotage, using a folbot, a type of canoe with a wooden frame and canvas skin, as transport. Early on 5 July Miers thought he had found a place to attack, Syros harbour, with a power station, a foundry, workshops and warehouses as the backdrop.

'The weather was, however, unsuitable and deteriorated still further towards evening so that the decision was made for me, but I am bound to confess that, though their keenness was beyond question, I doubted whether the military had sufficient experience to ensure success in other than a plain ship demolition operation,' said Miers. 'Had there been two folbots so that an officer could have accompanied the expedition, the plan would have seemed more attractive, but I did not wish to jeopardise the future fulfilment of it, if thought worthwhile, by losing the element of surprise through initial "amateur bungling". There was, however, no sign of the harbour being put to military use although it has a potential value to the enemy.'

According to Chapman, Bremner, who would figure prominently in the

Torbay story, and Sherwood were manning the Lewis guns when the submarine launched surface attacks.

That evening *Torbay* spotted a submarine with a large conning tower 4 miles away off the southern coast of Mykonos. Miers thought at first that it was a French boat of the Dauphin class. It was, in fact, the Italian submarine *Jantina*, blissfully unaware that *Torbay* was closing in. Miers gave the order to fire a spread of six torpedoes at a range of 1,500 yards.

'Heard one fairly loud explosion followed ten seconds later by a tremendous double explosion which shook the submarine considerably, breaking the glass in both navigation lights and causing other minor damage,' he said. A quick look in the direction of the target showed 'an enormous upheaval of dirty coloured water'. *Torbay* dived deep after spotting a plane, but surfaced about half an hour later to find the air smelling strongly of fuel oil. *Jantina* had been destroyed.

There was an intelligence tip-off that the Vichy French tanker *Strombo* had sailed from Istanbul, and Miers headed to an area to the south-west to intercept her. At 0928 on 8 July, 7 miles off Cape Malea, *Torbay* spotted a 200-ton schooner flying the German flag and loaded with troops and stores bound for Crete. At 1122 the submarine surfaced to engage the enemy.

'After firing some rounds of Lewis gun but before actually opening fire with the 4in gun, sighted aircraft and dived,' Miers reported. 'Submarine was apparently unsighted. Schooner now turned westward to make for Kithera [Kythira] island and appeared to be manning some form of AA gun and grenades.'

Less than 20 minutes later *Torbay* surfaced and returned to the attack. 'Opened fire at point-blank range (the first round misfired owing to having got wet on diving and was thrown overboard). The enemy opened fire, their shots passing overhead and bursting in the sky, but this was short lived owing to the very accurate firing of the Lewis guns (manned by the navigating officer [David Verschoyle-Campbell] and leading signalman) which got off six pans without a single jam. A report from the starboard lookout of two aircraft caused the action to be broken off once more and the upper deck cleared for diving, but I delayed pressing the klaxon until I should myself sight the aircraft and not being able to do so after several minutes gun action was once more resumed. By this time the enemy personnel had been almost wholly destroyed by Lewis gunfire and it only remained for the schooner itself to be sunk with a few more rounds of 4in ammunition.'[3]

The 9th of July would prove to be a significant day. At 0220 *Torbay* spotted a caique, and as she turned to attack saw three more caiques and a schooner about 2 miles apart, all apparently heading towards Cape Malea from Crete. Miers was low on 4in ammunition and decided to use one well-aimed high explosive shell to stop the leading caique, clear the decks with fire from the Lewis guns, go alongside and blow the vessel up with TNT charges. Men on board this caique, flying the swastika and carrying soldiers, appear to have been confused about the identity of the submarine because they sent up a red flare as a recognition signal. A minute later they were left in no doubt. *Torbay* opened fire and the caique was quickly ablaze. The Lewis guns carried on firing until all those on board had been killed or forced to jump into the sea.

Twenty minutes later *Torbay* engaged the second caique. The crew took to the water and those remaining on board made signals of surrender, shouting 'Captain is Greek'. *Torbay* went alongside, with a boarding party on the casing. One of the commandos, Bremner, was keeping watch with a tommy-gun. He spotted a German soldier about to hurl a grenade and shot him. Those on board the caique pretended to be Greek until they were addressed by the navigating officer, Verschoyle-Campbell, in German. The treachery continued. Verschoyle-Campbell, armed with a pistol, then spotted a German soldier taking aim with a rifle and shot him. The prisoners were forced to launch a rubber raft and jump into it. A demolition charge was left to finish off the 100-ton caique, which was loaded with ammunition and petrol.

Miers reported: 'Submarine cast off and with the Lewis gun accounted for the soldiers in the rubber raft to prevent them regaining their ship and then set off in search of number three.'

The third target was the schooner. It took 45 minutes to catch up with her at full speed. *Torbay* opened fire on the vessel 'which fortunately was filled with petrol and explosives and was very quickly ablaze from stem to stern, with loud intermittent explosions'. A large pall of smoke rose from her until she sank. Only one caique from the convoy escaped. *Torbay* spent much of the rest of the day diving to avoid aircraft and then resumed the hunt for the Vichy French tanker *Strombo*. At 1445 on 10 July, she spotted the ship near the Kea Channel, escorted by a destroyer, which was zig-zagging half a mile in front. A long-range attack offered a better chance of remaining unseen, but Miers had only four torpedoes left and decided to go closer to increase the odds of a successful strike. He fired all his torpedoes at a range of 1,200 yards and two hit. Two minutes later the destroyer started dropping depth charges, 'some of which were extremely close and shook the submarine considerably'. The depth charges were being dropped singly. Miers was certain that if they had been dropped in patterns his boat would have been damaged on several occasions.

Strombo sank, but *Torbay* was not in the clear. She went deep and had a nerve-racking time hugging the coast of Makronisi as she tried to mask her sound. Two other destroyers joined the hunt, dropping a further 25 depth charges, making a total of 38.

Torbay survived the counter attack. With his torpedoes gone, and low on 4in ammunition, Miers decided to return to Alexandria. This was not an easy task. It was too dangerous to use the Kea or Doro channels because the moonlight was too bright. The destroyers were still lurking, and Miers needed to be patient until they got tired of searching. At this point a rumour circulated among some of the crew that the submarine might not escape and could end up being scuttled. If Miers considered this a serious option, he certainly did not put it down on paper. But as *Torbay* headed east and then south, she had a 'very nasty encounter' when a destroyer appeared out of the darkness on a direct course. As the submarine dived, the ship passed by on the starboard side unaware that she had found her quarry.

Torbay arrived at Alexandria on 15 July and heard the crew of the battleship HMS *Queen Elizabeth* cheering. She sent the message: 'If you were cheering us it was very much appreciated. Thank you very much.' The battleship replied: 'We certainly were.'

Like the second patrol, this had been a successful mission – claiming one submarine, one merchant ship, one tanker, three schooners and five caiques. In these two patrols *Torbay* had shown herself to be highly effective in surface gun actions, and Miers asked for an increased allowance of 4in ammunition 'in view of the policy of the enemy of transporting a quantity of their stores and personnel across the Aegean in caiques and schooners, and the essential need to destroy them . . .' He also asked for a tommy-gun, noting Bremner's effective use of the weapon.

'The value of this weapon in the hands of one of the embarked soldiers was fully shown when going alongside a caique filled with German soldiers on the night of 8th/9th July,' he said. 'Without it casualties might have been caused to the boarding party on the casing as well as damage to the submarine. Providing this cover at night with the Lewis gun from the bridge is not effective due to the darkness and it is impracticable to take the Lewis gun onto the casing. The tommy-gun is the ideal weapon for this purpose.'

Miers was keen on commando operations despite his reservations about sending off the folbot for an attack on Syros. 'It is considered desirable to carry out sabotage operations in occupied Greek territory, the numerous islands and the prevailing good weather should make the Aegean Sea an unusually profitable area. It is suggested that the accomplishment of one or two such operations would have a considerable effect on the enemy's morale and would put him to much trouble and expense to counteract it.'

Soon after getting Miers's patrol report, Raw, the captain of the 1st Flotilla, observed: '*Torbay* must now be Nazi Public Enemy No. 1 in the Aegean.' In his own report to the commander-in-chief, Cunningham, he commented: '*Torbay*'s patrol was again brilliantly carried out . . . Great credit is due to Lieutenant-Commander Miers for his offensive spirit, careful planning, accurate appreciation and happy ability of being in the right place at the right time. The operation against the convoy of caiques was a model of efficient destruction.'[4]

Miers's request for more 4in ammunition was turned down. It was 'impossible' to give him more until bigger stocks were received in Alexandria. However, Miers got his tommy-gun.

Cunningham was pleased with *Torbay*'s achievements. He told the Admiralty: 'This was a brilliantly conducted offensive patrol which inflicted severe damage on the enemy. These results are not obtained by chance, but by sound appreciation and careful planning, which together with his offensive spirit, render Lieutenant-Commander ACC Miers, Royal Navy, an outstanding submarine commander.'[5]

In 1989 the broadcaster and writer Ludovic Kennedy published his autobiography, which contained a highly controversial claim relating to the actions of 4 July and 9 July.[6] He alleged that 'a much-decorated officer who had risen to high rank' was responsible for 'an atrocity'. Kennedy's claim will be examined fully in a later chapter.

Chapter 6

THE GREAT ESCAPE

The crew of *Torbay* had a break of about two weeks before their fourth patrol. On 31 July Miers wrote in his log that he had been forced to 'admonish' his officers Chapman, Kidd and Verschoyle-Campbell, for failing to return from leave on time. Whether the captain contented himself with a verbal rebuke is not known. Swift punishment could have resulted in a black eye.

Two days later the submarine left Alexandria to patrol a new area, the Gulf of Sirte, mostly off Benghazi, and then the waters off south-west Crete.[1] The patrol lasted nearly three weeks, and *Torbay* would carry out a spectacular rescue mission.

Off Benghazi on 9 August, the submarine spotted her first possible target, an unescorted merchant ship of about 3,000 tons leaving the port. Closer inspection revealed that she was flying the Italian flag – and was carrying the markings of a hospital ship. There was a list of approved Italian hospital ships, but this vessel appeared to be less than half the size that she should have been. The enemy was known to use 'hospital ships' to carry war supplies.

Miers was immediately suspicious: 'In view of the enemy's shameful record of abuse of every known privilege of war among civilised peoples the temptation to fire was great and, in the main, the spirit of the ship's company seemed to favour no quarter being given, but in the end the dictates of humanity traditional to the Royal Navy prevailed and I reluctantly broke off the attack.'

In light of Ludovic Kennedy's claim many years later, this was an interesting observation.[2] Miers decided to follow the ship and stop her after dark for inspection. She was on course for Messina, Sicily, and increased her speed to about 12 knots. A boarding party was assembled with orders to take the ship to Malta. But Miers had made up his mind to sink her anyway if she was not properly illuminated at night. Before he could do anything *Torbay* was forced to dive and make a long detour to avoid enemy aircraft. The chase was abandoned. It would have taken too long to catch up, with the submarine well away from her patrol area. Miers hoped that two other submarines lurking ahead, HMS *Talisman* and *Rorqual*, would be able to intercept the ship.

The next day was spent dodging aircraft and armed trawlers off Benghazi. On 12 August there was some luck – two merchant ships, escorted by a destroyer, an anti-submarine vessel and a flying boat. *Torbay* fired four torpedoes at long range, scoring a hit on one of the merchant ships. Depth charges were dropped but not close enough to cause problems.

On the evening of 14 August, *Torbay* left the area and headed for Crete and a special mission. On the way the submarine spotted a U-boat on the surface about 5 miles distant and dived. The U-boat did the same. Both submarines popped up to periscope depth trying to find each other before the U-boat disappeared completely. *Torbay* would not claim a second submarine. Two days later she stopped a schooner full of supplies with gunfire and sank her after laying explosive charges.

Miers had been ordered to collect a naval officer, Lieutenant-Commander Francis Pool, who was on Crete as part of a secret mission to liaise with resistance groups and organise escape routes for the many Allied soldiers still on the island. It was arranged that Pool would be waiting on a beach in the south-west, in sight of Paximadia island. On the morning of 18 August, *Torbay* dived near Paximadia and carried out a periscope reconnaissance of the beach, which was deserted. The wind was blowing strongly and the sea was rough. Miers decided to wait until dusk, when it was still light, and send in the folbot with Bremner the SBS commando. That evening *Torbay* surfaced. The sea was still rough, and it would not be easy for Bremner to paddle his way ashore.

'I was hesitating on the wisdom of the enterprise when the correct signal was received from the beach,' said Miers. 'This decided me and the folbot was launched.' According to Chapman, Miers and Bremner, also a Scot, had a heated argument before the commando set off. Miers acknowledged that Bremner undertook the mission 'rather against his better judgement' but 'fully understanding the considerable risk to himself'.

Despite frantic paddling, Bremner headed not towards the beach but out to sea. *Torbay* had to rescue him, hauling the exhausted man and his folbot back on the casing. Chapman recalled, probably tongue in cheek: 'As we watched him paddling frantically, we saw the wind catch him so that he disappeared into the murk travelling in a direction not intended. Of course to us hard-hearted submariners, one soldier here nor there made no difference – they were expendable. But our captain was a Scot. He thought that Scottish soldiers were precious. So we stopped everything and went off to look for him.'

If Bremner thought his mission was over, at least for that night, he had to think again. Miers was not going to give up. The submarine moved closer inshore to a more sheltered spot, launching the folbot a second time. It must have crossed Bremner's mind more than once that all this effort might be for nothing. The Germans could be waiting for him. He paddled for an hour before reaching the beach, but the submarine did not see his arrival in the darkness.

Miers reported: 'In the meantime the lack of any action from the beach after an hour caused me to fear after all that the folbot had met with disaster and I therefore decided to make a short signal to the beach, "Report when boat arrives". This was a most unfortunate decision since it caused Lieutenant-Commander Pool to suspect treachery and leave the beach forthwith. Consequently, when the folbot arrived there was only an Australian sergeant and a New Zealand soldier and a few Greeks present.'

Bremner returned to the submarine with the Australian and New Zealander, and *Torbay* stood out to sea for several hours until dawn recharging her batteries. Miers would have to try again to make contact with Pool.

By the next night the weather had deteriorated and Miers decided that he needed to get the submarine as close to the beach as possible, so close that he would ground *Torbay*. 'This was an unpalatable task in such weather but was accomplished successfully except that the slight pounding on the beach caused the asdic dome to be punctured and the set therefore put out of action,' he said.

It was a bold move because he had no idea if the Germans knew of the submarine's presence after two days of coming and going. Even a small patrol could have caused major problems. But this time Bremner got ashore in his folbot and found Lieutenant-Commander Pool, who said there were 28 troops on the beach hoping to be taken off – and nearly 100 more hiding in surrounding villages.

'Corporal Bremner was in an exhausted condition, the gusty wind making even this short trip both dangerous and difficult and it was therefore decided that the men must swim with the aid of lifebelts and a lifeline,' said Miers. 'The position of the submarine was adjusted to make the journey as short and as sheltered as possible and to ensure that if anyone was caught by the stream he would be swept towards the submarine.'

Kidd went ashore to take charge of the operation and within an hour all the men had been taken on board. It was arranged that Pool's Greek guide would go round the villages to collect as many soldiers as possible so that they could be taken off the beach at dusk the next day. 'I had felt confident that I should be acting in accordance with the wishes of the commander-in-chief if I made every effort to rescue as many as possible trained British troops from the island,' said Miers.

Torbay again went out to sea to charge her batteries – with 12 Greek stragglers. They swam to the submarine independently and climbed aboard. The captain planned to return them to the island the next night.

At 2106 on 20 August, *Torbay* saw the correct signal being flashed from the beach and closed to complete the evacuation. Like the night before, Kidd was sent in the folbot to mastermind the operation. The scene that greeted him was one of chaos. The beach was swarming with hundreds of Greeks, including children, as well as dogs running around barking. There were even farewell parties. News that a British submarine was visiting – for a third night – had spread widely. Remarkably, the only people still in the dark were the thousands of German troops who occupied the island. As a precaution, resistance fighters had set up roadblocks in case any patrols tried to get through, but not one enemy soldier appeared.

'The noise was such as to fill one with the utmost alarm for the success of the operation,' said Miers. 'Many Greeks endeavoured to come off and towards the finish there was a tense, almost threatening attitude amongst the crowd – most of whom were armed with sticks – which caused considerable misgivings to Lieutenant Kidd for the safety of the folbot and the last few men to come off.'

Miers had already encountered trouble with the 12 Greeks who boarded *Torbay* the night before. Most of the men struggled violently when it came to leave the submarine and 'considerable force' had to be used. Others had left the beach and were trying to clamber on board. 'I found it quite horrid having to bat a chap's knuckles with a paddle to make him let go and swim away,' Chapman admitted.[3] One man nearly drowned and was rescued by an able seaman who resuscitated him on the beach. This act of bravery helped to distract some of the crowd when it seemed that control would be lost. The order went out to carefully check every man at the hatch before he entered the submarine. Even so *Torbay* ended up with five 'Greek guides' who were actually stowaways.

Nevertheless, *Torbay* pulled off a remarkable rescue – 62 New Zealanders, 42 Australians, 11 British soldiers, 1 RAF man, 5 Cypriot troops, 3 genuine Greek guides and 1 Yugoslav. The submarine was already cramped with her crew of 61, and the journey to Alexandria was very sticky and unpleasant. Because of the stale air Miers kept his submarine on the surface as much as possible. One of the rescued men was an Australian major, Ray Sandover, who was invited to join Miers on the bridge as *Torbay* entered harbour on 22 August. In his tattered uniform, he felt self-conscious when the captain ordered 'Usual drill, number one'. Expecting some kind of formal ceremony, he was taken aback when he saw crewmen lining up to expose their backsides to the Vichy French ships that had been interned.[4]

In his patrol report, Miers saluted the crew: 'I should like to call attention to the exemplary conduct of the ship's company during this, the hottest patrol that we have undertaken and, in particular, during the last few days when, at a time when fresh food and water were running low and when the general stamina was at its lowest, they were suddenly faced with the influx of more than double their total number, all requiring to be fed and looked after.'

Among the men that Miers singled out for praise were Kidd for his beach operations, Chapman for his 'skilful handling of affairs' on the casing when soldiers were helped aboard often exhausted and in some cases wounded, and Bremner, who risked his life on several occasions and made as many as 30 trips to and from the beach. Bremner was later awarded the Military Medal for his courage, and a number of *Torbay* men, including Miers, Kidd and Verschoyle-Cambell, would receive awards for patrols carried out between August and November 1941.

Raw said Miers had shown 'great courage' in the Crete rescue. He summed up: 'The patrol was carried out in a most determined and efficient manner and valuable results achieved, particularly in the special operation. Lieutenant-Commander Miers is maintaining the high standard which he set on his arrival on this station, and under his leadership *Torbay* has become, and I am certain will remain, an extremely efficient fighting unit.'[5]

But Miers was ticked off for breaking radio silence on two occasions when he was off Benghazi. This may have alerted the enemy to *Torbay*'s presence. A tanker that had been expected to arrive in the port did not show up, and there was considerable air and surface patrol activity.

Many years after the war Miers went on holiday to Crete and was put in touch with a 'few ferocious-looking locals' who took him on a hair-raising drive through the mountains to find the beach where the soldiers had assembled on that August night in 1941. Due to lack of time and 'the wild nature of the terrain' they never found a way down to the beach. Miers had also hoped to visit the nearby monastery of Preveli, whose monks had given shelter to many soldiers.[6] The Germans raided the monastery only five days after *Torbay*'s evacuation, ransacking it and arresting the monks. In 1991 a memorial saluting the courage of the monks was unveiled in the grounds of the monastery.

Bremner never forgot the showdown with Miers over his first attempt to reach the beach – and claimed that the captain had threatened to shoot him. In 1989 he gave this version of events: 'Miers tried to insist that I paddled ashore in a force eight gale. I knew from past experience that I could not survive in such stormy water and I refused to embark in my canoe. After a very heated argument Miers threatened to shoot me for mutiny and he called through the voice pipe for his revolver. After he got his revolver he seemed to calm down and then agreed to my suggestion that we should go below and study the local charts for a more sheltered embarkation, which we found. Over a period of three nights we eventually rescued over 130 allied troops off Crete, in which I played a major role.'[7]

Chapter 7

YOU'RE UNDER ARREST

When Roy Foster woke on 22 March 1941 he anticipated a routine day on the Holy Loch. The young lieutenant was among spare crew on board the submarine depot ship HMS *Titania*. He had been sent on only one submarine patrol before – in HMS *Taku*, which was supposed to make an Atlantic crossing to Halifax. Foster did not gain much experience on that trip. The submarine broke down in a gale in mid-Atlantic and needed a tow to Londonderry. He had only been on board *Titania* for a couple of days when at about 1300 on 22 March he was told to report to Miers, who was hurriedly recruiting. It was the day that *Torbay* had been given orders to join the 'iron ring' in the Bay of Biscay to try to prevent the escape of the battlecruisers *Scharnhorst* and *Gneisenau* from Brest but, of course, half of *Torbay*'s crew were scattered around the country on leave. Miers appointed Foster the submarine's third officer. The new recruit was to be on board by 1600. His first job was to check the state of the torpedoes. 'There was mention of spherical objects being used as neckties if I got it wrong,' said Foster.[1]

After the spell in the Bay of Biscay in appalling weather, 'when we did not see a thing', *Torbay* went on to Gibraltar and then Alexandria. Foster took part in her successful early patrols.

'I do not think I have ever swallowed so much salt water as during this period,' he said. 'I was the clot who had to open the bridge hatch first, scramble through the bridge door to the gun platform and kick open the [ammunition] lockers while the gun crew were training on the target. I am sure that the whistle to open the hatch was blown as soon as the periscope standards broke the surface, just to ensure that a dousing of cold water would wake us up. An incident which is imprinted on my mind was during time alongside *Medway* [depot ship] in Alexandria. We were carrying out water shots on our torpedo tubes to time the AIV [automatic inboard vent] and by graph to record the pressure build-up during firing. We had carried out one or two tests and were about to do another. When ready, I went up on deck to check that there was no boat near the bows, or flotsam around which might get sucked back into the tubes. When I got back into the fore ends, I told the TI [torpedo instructor] to fire. He pulled the firing lever and the recordings were made.

'About one or two minutes later there was an almighty explosion. I rushed on deck and to my horror I saw a huge column of water dead ahead of *Torbay* about half way between *Medway* and the breakwater at Ras el-Tin. I thought, "My god, we have charged the wrong air bottle and pulled the wrong lever and fired a fish [torpedo]". My thoughts were of a sudden end to my career, a firing squad. I went white. When the column subsided, I saw that a small tug had towed a skid with a magnetic coil through the area. There had been an air raid the night before and the skid had exploded a magnetic mine. The explosion brought a large audience to the upper deck of *Medway*. The audience included Crap, who knew what we had been doing. He shouted down, "Foster, you look pale". Contrary to general impressions, he did have a sense of humour.

'Throughout most of the time in Alexandria, the trot [group] of submarines alongside *Medway* had to disperse each evening to minimise the risk of a bomb putting the whole flotilla out of action. We used to leave the depot ship with the duty officer and duty watch about sunset and return alongside at sunrise. To qualify to drive the submarine around the harbour and berth alongside the dockyard or a battleship or cruiser, the junior officers had to be granted a "driving licence". Until this was done, the captain or first lieutenant had to be present and they were then picked up by *Medway*'s boats and in the mornings ferried to the berths. Crap was unusually quiet during these movements.

'After he had satisfied himself, and after consultation with the first lieutenant, myself and Verschoyle-Campbell were given provisional driving licences but told that if there were any dashing alongside or mistakes it would be another case of spherical objects and neckties. For some time after this Crap could be seen on the upper deck of *Medway* in his pyjamas at 0530 seeing how it was being done. With him on deck, I doubt if the wash of the submarine propellers even woke the fishes.'

Foster, like others, had his run-ins with Miers: 'During an attack on a merchant ship off the west coast of Greece one of the torpedoes did a circling routine, probably due to a jammed valve in the gyro. It circled above us about three times like an angry bee. As the torpedo officer I was considered responsible and informed by Crap that I was under arrest. To this day I never quite understood what this entailed, as I stood my watches, did the ciphering, etc. On return to Alexandria, I was informed that I had been released from arrest.

'During one attack when I was at my driving station, which was to operate the "fruit machine" [attack instrument], I received a hard kick up the backside. This was administered by Crap from a kneeling position – Cossack-style – as he was crouched low at the high-power periscope. I had apparently been somewhat tardy in twiddling the knobs with the information of bearing and range and giving him the angle on the bow of the target. I do not know whether this quickened my reflexes for the next periscope look or whether I had moved to the side of the fruit machine out of range of a crouched kick, or alternatively, whether the next periscope look was from the after attack periscope – definitely out of range.

'I still bear the effect of a "crash dive". I was officer of the watch on the surface at night. It was a fairly bright moonlit night, very calm and we were trimmed right down. Crap was also on the bridge and we were over flown by an aircraft, which no one had seen or heard as we were charging. The order "dive" was given and the first lookout pressed the klaxon. The lookouts went down the ladder pretty fast and I followed in quick time, but apparently not quick enough for Crap, who trod on my head.

'My mouth hit a rung of the ladder and when I got down into the control room, I nearly swallowed a front tooth. I took it out of my mouth and wrapped it in a handkerchief. When the flap was over, I put the tooth back into the gum with my thumb and lived on soup for the next four days. I am happy to state that this is my one and only war wound.'

In August 1941 Foster went down with rheumatic fever and spent the next four months in hospital, at a convalescent home and as spare crew. One day he was appointed to the submarine HMS *Osiris*, which was ferrying stores, fuel and torpedoes to besieged Malta. The next day *Torbay* returned from a patrol, going alongside *Medway*.

'The usual crowd, including me, was on the gangway and, on coming aboard *Medway*, Crap asked me how I was and remarked on my healthy suntan,' said Foster. 'I told him I had been appointed to *Osiris*. He said he would see Captain (S) [Raw] about that. About 20 minutes later Commander (S) sent for me and told me that my *Osiris* appointment was cancelled and I should report to Crap. I doubt if Captain (S) did much talking on this matter.'

In 1942 Foster did four patrols in HMS *Turbulent* under another outstanding submarine captain, Commander John 'Tubby' Linton, who was 'as different from Crap Miers as chalk from cheese'. Foster said: 'I never heard Tubby raise his voice and although he was displeased if things did not go right he would let one know in such a quiet way, behind his beard, that everyone resolved not to displease him again.'

On one of the patrols Foster had another experience with a circling 'angry bee' torpedo. 'We were off Benghazi during Rommel's last advance into Egypt in the summer of 1942,' he said. 'At night we sighted a southbound convoy of two merchant ships escorted by two destroyers. Tubby decided to remain on the surface, get ahead of the convoy, dive before first light and carry out a submerged attack before dawn. This was achieved and we were in a good position for firing at both ships when Tubby got a bit agitated about one of the destroyers, which seemed to be steering straight for *Turbulent*. He waited for the last possible moment and then fired a salvo and went deep. The destroyer must have been close as Tubby was sweating and we heard the destroyer pass nearly overhead. There were no depth charges. A feeling of relief came to an abrupt end when the noise of a circling torpedo was heard.

'Then came the sound of three explosions followed by another explosion. The circling torpedo had hit the nearest destroyer. About 45 minutes later the periscope revealed the remaining destroyer stopped and presumably picking up survivors from the two merchant ships and the sunken destroyer. After this episode I reflected that Tony Troup, who was the torpedo officer, was not placed under arrest, as I had been when my rogue torpedo ran amok in *Torbay*. This perhaps showed the difference between Crap and Tubby – but then my torpedo had not sunk a destroyer.'

During his time in *Turbulent* Foster was awarded the Distinguished Service Cross, and received a letter of congratulations from Miers, which was written on board *Torbay* and dated 21 September 1942:

We were all absolutely delighted. I recommended you for it over a year ago and was disappointed that you did not get it – however now you have been mentioned and decorated. Big stuff. Your people will be awfully proud. Please let me know if there is any chance of our gathering to celebrate our awards together in the first ten days of October when I shall be in London.

Have a good leave and do well in your perisher [the tough test for submarine command]. I would in any case like to see you before you start to give you a line on it as I did before you went to Linton. I hope you found that useful – Tubby Linton told me how pleased he was with you and I was very satisfied. You deserved to do well and you have, I think you can say honestly, served two of the hardest taskmasters to please with success. Tubby is a grand fellow and I hope you think so too.

Foster could count himself lucky. In January 1941 he had been one of 13 contemporaries in the Submarine Service. By September 1942 he was one of only three left alive.

He missed *Torbay*'s fifth patrol in September 1941 because of his rheumatic fever. The submarine headed back to the Aegean for this patrol, but it turned out to be a frustrating one, although it began with promise.[2] On the afternoon of 7 September, the day after leaving Alexandria, *Torbay* spotted an enemy submarine on the surface, a comparatively easy target. She turned to attack but because of an error in drill at the torpedo tubes too much time was wasted and the opportunity passed. Miers was still gritting his teeth and decided on a gun attack, surfacing three minutes later, with the enemy, flying the Italian flag, at a range of 1,500 yards. The

4in gun, however, misfired. When the breech was opened, the cartridge separated from the shell, which remained jammed in the gun. For three minutes *Torbay* was a sitting duck, and the Italian submarine turned, apparently to attack – but then dived. The British crew were lucky that the Italians did not have a captain of Miers's calibre.

'The enemy had thus thrown away a splendid chance of a one-sided gun action, while the poor quality of the ammunition had deprived us of an almost certain success,' said Miers.

Raw, in Alexandria, had known that there was a question mark over some of the ammunition being supplied to his submarines. It had come from Malta, but supplies were so low that there was no choice but to hand it out and hope for the best. The cause of the misfire was put down to a defective primer, which must have been damp.

Three days later, in Suda Bay, north-west Crete, *Torbay* found two merchant ships and a torpedo boat leaving. Three torpedoes were fired, all missing, probably because of the broad track. Carefully, the submarine followed the ships, which now had aircraft as added protection. She lost contact, but Miers guessed that they were headed for Candia harbour further along the coast to the east. At dusk the submarine nudged towards the harbour entrance and sent in a torpedo. This hit the stern of one ship, which caught fire and developed a heavy list.

Torbay sneaked away and set course for the Dardanelles, using the Kea and Doro channels. Three days spent hovering at the entrance to the straits proved fruitless, and she was ordered to shift her patrol to the Gulf of Athens. Early on 17 September a small northbound convoy was sighted, but *Torbay* could not get closer than 6,000 yards and an attack was ruled out. The rest of the day was spent avoiding aircraft and a flotilla of minesweepers.

Throughout the next day plenty of targets were seen, and Miers had to put up with more frustration. Two torpedoes were fired at an unescorted merchant ship, both missing. In the last attack of the day there was an alarming experience when the forward hydroplanes – the submarine's 'fins' – jammed as *Torbay* went under the target, a merchant ship escorted by two destroyers. The submarine was out of control and, according to Chapman, in danger of doing a 'salmon leap'. When her trim was finally restored by flooding and then blowing Q tank, the target had escaped.

On 19 September two merchant ships of about 3,000 tons were attacked as they made their way to Piraeus, the port of Athens. Four torpedoes were fired at a range of 4,000 yards and one may have hit. The ships were being escorted by an armed merchant cruiser and two destroyers, which dropped 14 depth charges 'fairly accurately', one of which caused an Aldis lamp to jump out of position and cut the cook's head open.

Two days later *Torbay* sent two torpedoes towards a Romanian merchant ship as she left Piraeus. The range was only 300 yards, but they missed, passing beneath her. The torpedoes were fired from number seven and number eight tubes, which had a five-degree angle downwards, which was not taken into account. *Torbay* was too close. Eleven depth charges were the reply.

The submarine was getting near the end of her patrol, and two further targets eluded her, one a tanker because of bad weather. During this patrol *Torbay* had been forced to deal with 52 aircraft sightings and 22 enemy vessels.

Despite the lack of success, Raw was still impressed: '*Torbay* was very much out of luck this patrol. During the period spent off the Gulf of Athens targets were almost continually in sight but either passed out of range or were sighted too late to be attacked or succeeded in evading the torpedoes. The patrol, however, was carried out with Lieutenant-Commander Miers's usual determination in the face of intense air and surface patrol activity. His pursuit of the convoy from Suda Bay to Candia despite the enemy's air escort and his final determined and successful attack on the ships after they had entered Candia harbour are deserving of the highest praise.'[3]

Cunningham, too, was generous: 'This patrol was conducted with Lieutenant-Commander Miers's characteristic thoroughness and offensive spirit, but *Torbay* was dogged by ill luck and only achieved one certain hit which, by *Torbay*'s standards, was a poor bag.'[4]

Chapter 8

THE SKIPPER'S MAD

Shortly after Stoker Philip Le Gros volunteered for submarines he was sent to the depot ship *Medway*, moored at Alexandria.[1] When he went down to the mess deck to check on accommodation, another sailor, a Cornishman, asked: 'What boat have you got, mate?'

Le Gros replied: *'Torbay.'*

The other sailor grimaced and said: 'You poor sod. The skipper is mad, mad.'

Torbay was alongside *Medway*, and later that day Le Gros decided to have a look at the submarine. He climbed down the conning tower and got as far as the wardroom when a voiced bellowed: 'Who the hell are you?'

He said: 'Stoker Le Gros.' He would recount: 'I didn't even say Sir because I was taken aback. He was unshaven, just in his shirtsleeves, his hair was hanging over his face a bit and he was generally unkempt. He bellowed, "Don't you say Sir?" and I said, "Oh, you took me aback a bit". He said, "I am the captain" and he started beating on his chest like a gorilla, "I am the captain, I am the captain, if you want anything, you come and see me".'

That was Le Gros's introduction to Miers. Despite his surname, which led to him being called Froggy, Le Gros was from New Zealand. He was born in Taumarunui on North Island, one of eight children. His father was a carpenter. After leaving school at 13 he worked as a farm labourer and then got a job helping to build a viaduct, mixing with the riggers, many of whom had been on sailing ships and were employed because they were used to heights. These men talked a lot about their time at sea and so, inspired by these tales, Le Gros joined the navy in 1939, aged 21. He arrived in Alexandria on board the cruiser HMS *Leander* and volunteered for submarines in time for *Torbay*'s third patrol from 28 June to 15 July 1941. He would be with Miers for all the remaining patrols.

Another New Zealander, Bruce Bennett, joined *Torbay* at the same time. Bennett and Le Gros had grown up together in Wairo, milking cows, collecting blackberries and swimming in the local river. Bennett would end up being awarded the Distinguished Service Medal and Le Gros would be Mentioned in Despatches on Miers's recommendations.

The men should have undergone special training, including Davis escape procedures, but that was a luxury in wartime Alexandria. 'We didn't have time, they were that short of men,' said Le Gros. 'When I joined, there were 13 boats in the flotilla. After one patrol of about a month five of them were missing.'

He had to adapt quickly to life on board a submarine: '*Torbay* was closely packed with 60-odd men and you were very close to one another in bunks alongside one another. Even the officers weren't very comfortable.

'You had your own bunk but the sleeping areas were stocked with foodstuffs. You would come aboard and there were all the foodstuffs for when you would go out on patrol stacked everywhere. The escape hatch would be stacked up high and there was always a bit of water in the escape hatch and we used to keep our bread and spuds in there and they used to go mouldy and quite often you would have nice green bread.

'I reckon the cook was an amazing man because besides tending to his other duties he would always put on a fairly good meal. Everything was electrically cooked. The menus were probably made out a month ahead. Food was stacked methodically in a large cool store, about six foot high and four foot by four foot, so that when it came to Tuesday the 15th you had, whether you liked it or not, mutton and dragged it out and cooked it. Sometimes an oven door fell open and a bit of diesel would swirl with the roast, and the cook would say, "That will do for the wardroom".

'It was a topsy-turvey arrangement really. You classed midnight as being midday and then you were having your breakfast sort of business. It was a bit confusing because you ate when you were hungry more or less.

'When you were watch-keeping on the engine platform quite often they would have opened a tin of dried apples and as we went by we would grab a handful of them. We became authors of our own fate because they were dried apples and by the time they got down in our gullets and what not they had swollen up and so we were running around with potbellies.

'The rum was a great standby and I think it caused a lot of trouble in the navy and many a man lost his rank because of rum trouble, but it made you amazingly hungry after you had your tot.'

There was the question of hygiene, or rather the lack of it: 'We reeked of diesel and bilge water and exhaust fumes. When you stop the engines and when you turn them over while they are cooling, the air is sucked in and expelled into the submarine. It always used to smell like very strong garlic to me. I think when the engine was running at top speed and if a bulkhead door slammed shut somewhere there would be only 27 seconds to get an air intake. You had to be very quick with your movements.

'Nobody washed. My wife says I have carried on the habit. You could take a damp face cloth or something and give yourself a wash over, but there was no chance of washing or drying anything. You took several pairs of overalls to sea with you and when one got filthy you cast it aside and went on with the next best overall. The Germans in their U-boats had leather suits, which they could wipe down with some sort of solvent, and that was a good idea.

'Body odour didn't mean a thing to you because so many of us smelt. It took a long while for it to work out of your pores. When we got back to *Medway* there was a great rush for a bath. Oh, heavenly. You felt a new man after a bath.

'You had a locker on the depot ship and you only took a certain amount of gear to sea, which was what they called the steaming kit – several pairs of overalls and clean underwear and a cap and jacket, in case you had to go ashore. Writing materials and your toothpaste, and that was about all. They were very canny – sometimes to not make it obvious that you were going to sea we would go down in twos onto the boat and not be carrying seaman's kit because of prying eyes.'

Such was the need for secrecy that this poem, which may have been penned by Chapman, appeared as a reminder on the submarine's notice board:

When once again we meet with Mother Medway,
Our heads held high and chests puffed with pride,
Whilst dwelling on the historic feats of Torbay
Just listen to the little voice inside.

When on 'Gens' with Bacchus as a chaperon,
And a dainty filly by your side,
She murmurs 'Ave you killed the 'orrid German?'
Just let it slide my son just let it slide.

If strangers buy you beer, be very thankful,
Drink up and have another if you may,
Tell them all about your Aunt in Wigan
But never tell them how we won the day.

Where you've been once you may return in future,
In Alex, Musso's spies abound galore,
And you'd hate to think the depth charge in your breakfast
Was due to something that you'd said on shore.

Le Gros ended up in *Torbay*'s control room. 'When the order came for diving everything was so cut and dried,' he said. 'I used to grab the diving levers and I used to kick the ones I couldn't grab with my hands. I used to kick with my feet to save about two seconds in diving. You had to be quick on the uptake.'

He found Miers a 'real pest' in the control room. In particular, he remembered one incident: 'Somebody woke me to go on watch and I felt hungry and so I grabbed a piece of mouldy green bread. I couldn't find the butter and smothered it in syrup and then proceeded to the control room. The moment I got there Commander Miers apparently gave an order. I couldn't answer him and say, "Yes, sir" or "No, sir" because my mouth was jammed full with this mouldy bread.

'He said, "Did you hear what I said Le Gros, why didn't you answer me?" He knew that I had my mouth full and so he smacked me down for insubordination and said, "Go to the engine room, you are insubordinate".

'Secretly, I suppose, he was grinning like mad. He said to me, "What's the state of Q tank?" That was a silly thing to ask me. I had just come on watch and had no time to talk to my relief. I could only assume it was flooded and said, "I have no idea, sir". Then he said, "You come here on watch and you don't know what the state of Q tank is".

'Q tank is a quick-diving tank which we always flooded on the surface so that it gave you extra diving power when ready. How the hell was I to know? I was eating a crust of bread and so I was insubordinate, which was technically quite correct. I couldn't answer him. I didn't eat mouldy bread any more.'

Le Gros also recalled when Miers had the enemy in his sights: 'I remember the skipper walking up and down the control room deciding which ship to attack, cursing the Germans. "Why shouldn't we make them swim for their lives?" he said. His father was killed in the First World War. He hated the Germans, he had no love at all for them.

'He didn't speak in nice Eton language. He swore like a trooper and he spoke just like you or I, and roared and yelled. He was a terrible man. He was outspoken but he was quite cunning too.'

On his first patrol in *Torbay* Le Gros experienced what it was like to be on the receiving end of a depth charge attack. The submarine had to lie low and the crew had to hope for the best.

'Secretly they kept an eye on you, some blokes particularly when it was a bit tense,' he said. 'They kept an eye on people and probably made a note on how you behaved and that you didn't have anyone going cranky or anything like that. We got depth charged when a destroyer came right over the top and dropped about four charges and then went back over and turned around and you could hear the screws were like a clock ticking, and then you wouldn't hear anything for a while and you would hear this ticking getting louder and they would come back over and drop another one.

'One leading stoker, Mick, his eyes always used to bulge and he would say, "Oh, if they want to kill me for God's sake kill me, don't frighten me to death". There was a Liverpudlian, who said, "I wonder if these German bastards are going to stay for supper".

'Everyone behaved pretty well really under depth charging. I don't think

any one got overexcited. Some would play noughts and crosses and others
a card game. They knocked card games on the nose sometimes when you
were watch diving and silence in the boat because every time someone
would slap a card down it echoed.'

It was on his first patrol that *Torbay* sank the Italian submarine *Jantina*. 'I
was in the control room and Commander Miers said, "Up periscope". It was
just getting half dark. Then "Down periscope" and he said, "Bloody great
U-boat" and he went on like this, "Bloody great U-boat, long straight deck,
flying two flags, get the torpedoes ready straight away and at one-second
intervals fire six torpedoes". The torpedoes only ran 36 seconds, I think,
and the submarine was only three quarters of a mile away. They all hit. She
was a minelayer and she must have had mines in her. Did she blow, blown
to blazes.

'It lifted us up about 30 feet from the water. We started to go deeper to
about 200 feet. We could hear these things hitting the water and we
wondered what the devil it was. It must be mines or something, but it was
pieces of submarine hitting the water.'

On one patrol *Torbay* came close to blowing herself up. Le Gros kept
hearing a rattle towards the stern and told Miers, suggesting that it should
be checked out the next time the submarine surfaced. It was – and then it
emerged that *Torbay* had been towing a mine for at least a week. There were
many minefields in the Mediterranean. The rattle was the wire that had
been attached to the mine. It had snagged on one of the after hydroplanes,
going back backwards and forwards. If *Torbay* had gone astern, the mine
would probably have detonated. Eventually, it broke free.

'How lucky can you get?' said Le Gros. 'Commander Miers used to reckon
that and say, "We don't deserve it". He was a staunch Catholic and would
pray a lot.'

Le Gros was probably praying as *Torbay* pulled off her spectacular rescue
of troops from south-west Crete, when the commando Bremner had so
much difficulty in his folbot. Le Gros swam ashore with a rope so that the
many soldiers unable to swim could guide themselves to the submarine.

'The partisans had helped them a lot and they brought them down to the
beach,' he said. 'When we first contacted them I was sent ashore with a

rope which made fast. Some of them got so excited knowing a submarine was coming they slipped down a cliff and had bits and pieces knocked off them. One night we took off an Australian and a New Zealander, Maurice McHugh, who was a great boxer ["Morrie" McHugh had won the New Zealand amateur heavyweight championship in 1938 and went on to play for the All Blacks]. The next night we came and there was a whole crowd of them who could not swim and we gave them a hand.

'The skipper was up the top taking their official numbers. "Who are you?" he demanded. He interrogated several. The skipper said, "Do you like rum?" Back came the reply, "Too bloody right".

'The submarine was absolutely crammed. We got away from the island and dived. About half an hour later we surfaced. We wanted to run on the surface. And so we took them to Alexandria. When they went up the gangway they were sworn to secrecy. We didn't have our hats on or anything like that, and they ran up the gangway in case of prying eyes. They were lucky to get away. We were due to carry out another rescue but it was thought the Germans might have got wind of what was happening, and we didn't take any more off.'

The folbots used by the commandos were supposed to be a 'top secret', but that had not filtered down to Le Gros's friend from New Zealand, Bruce Bennett. One afternoon in Alexandria, with time on his hands, Bennett decided to take a folbot on a trip round the harbour.

'The next thing he was up before Commander Miers,' said Le Gros. 'And did Miers give him a dressing down.'

Folbots, in more ways than one, would prove a frustration for Miers.

Chapter 9

SPECIAL FORCES

In early October 1941 Miers was given an initial briefing on a bold special forces mission requiring the use of two submarines, but first *Torbay* would have to take part in a reconnaissance operation. The aim of the main mission was to put commandos on a suitable beach on the Libyan coast so that they could attack targets behind German lines and, spectacularly, capture or kill Rommel. That was the plan anyway. The raids were timed to hit the enemy before a general offensive in November.

Torbay left Alexandria on 7 October with two passengers, a special forces intelligence officer, Captain John Haselden, and an Arab guide.[1] Born in Egypt, Haselden had a British father and an Italian mother, and spoke Arabic fluently, as well as French and Italian. With his slightly swarthy appearance and wearing traditional clothes, he could pass himself off as an Arab with ease. He had already shown courage working behind enemy lines, forging links with the 'Libyan taxi service', the Long Range Desert Group. Before the war he had been working in Egypt as an executive of an American cotton company.[2]

Torbay was going to land Haselden with his companion so that he could carry out reconnaissance and make contact with Arabs who supported the British. The spot chosen to put the men ashore was Zaviet el Hamama, 17 miles west of Apollonia. Early on 10 October *Torbay* arrived off the coast, and Miers used a fort on a small hill at Zaviet el Hamama as a landmark. The coast was for the most part rocky and 'uninviting', and there seemed to be only one suitable landing place, a 30 yards stretch of sandy beach, which fortunately was deserted. *Torbay* stayed submerged during the day, creeping to within 1½ miles of the fort just before dusk. She surfaced about three quarters of a mile from shore in darkness. Miers could no longer see the brick red colour of the fort, but conditions were reasonably good, with only a slight swell. He needed to be careful, though, because of the rocks.

It had been intended to land Haselden and his guide in a three-seater folbot, but they had too much baggage – mostly gifts for the Arabs. Two trips were ruled out because of the risk of damaging the folbot on an unseen rock.

Miers reported: 'It was decided after considerable deliberation that the best way to ensure the success of the operation would be for Captain Haselden to swim in first carrying a watertight torch and with it to guide the folbot into safe water. I was loath to expose Captain Haselden to the rigours of a swim at the outset of his expedition but we were both convinced that it was the wisest course and I had a feeling moreover that he would prefer to swim than take his chance in the folbot.'

Torbay moved to within 300 yards of the beach. The 'watertight torch' was a torch sealed in a condom. Haselden swam naked because he did not want to turn up on the beach in his commando outfit if any Germans or Italians happened to be waiting for him. He need not have worried. The beach was still deserted, and 12 minutes after setting off he signalled to *Torbay*. The man in charge of the folbot, Corporal Clive Severn, an SBS commando originally from the Northamptonshire Regiment, then took the Arab guide and the luggage. Severn was back in little over 20 minutes and the folbot was hoisted on to the casing. *Torbay* slipped away to complete a shortened patrol.

'Credit for the success of this operation is due in the first place to Captain Haselden whose swim ashore in the dark onto a shore upon which only a narrow strip of sandy beach was clear of rocks showed a disregard for his personal safety and a complete confidence in the submarine navigation,' said Miers. 'The success of the folbot landing was thus ensured but the handling in a swell and some surf of this craft reflects much credit on Corporal Severn, who was making his debut in this type of work and earned my complete confidence.'

Miers also praised Chapman and several ratings for their work on the casing in getting the men ashore.

Torbay received a message that a convoy was heading for Benghazi and went to a position 120 miles north of the port to intercept the ships, but they were not sighted. Two days later Miers received a report of three cruisers and six destroyers, and shifted position to the south-west. Again, he drew a blank. On 15 October *Torbay* was asked to consider bombarding Apollonia. At dusk the 4in gun damaged an aircraft hangar and a power station. *Torbay* withdrew when two shore batteries opened fire, returning to Alexandria on 18 October.

Raw pointed out: 'Credit is due to all concerned for the expeditious way in which the landing operation was carried out. Although the rest of the patrol was unproductive, through no want of trying on *Torbay*'s part, it was carried out with the sound judgement which I have come to expect of Lieutenant-Commander Miers, whose one ambition is to get at the enemy in any possible way.'[3]

After completing his mission Haselden went to the safety of Cairo . . . by camel.

By this time the reputation of Miers and *Torbay* had spread throughout the Submarine Service. The submarine HMS *Proteus* turned up in Alexandria in the autumn of 1941. On board was Jeremy Nash, the fourth hand, who recalled: 'When we had secured alongside *Medway* our CO, Philip Francis, took his officers up to the cuddy to be introduced to Captain (S) Sammy Raw. Miers was there too, having just returned from a very successful patrol in *Torbay*. He was telling Captain Raw of his exploits and extolling the virtues of his splendid team of officers. We were agog to meet these paragons. When we got down to the wardroom we discovered that the navigator was under arrest in his cabin and the first lieutenant had a black eye.'[4]

A year later *Proteus* returned to Devonport where *Torbay* was finishing a refit. Nash had become first lieutenant and met Miers. Nash said: 'Instead of telling his own number one to show me the ropes Miers himself insisted on taking the time and trouble to show me round the dockyard, and we ended up in the barracks wardroom. "Now, Jeremy, remember this," he said. "If you sit at this table you will only get one pat of butter for breakfast, but if you sit over there – for some reason – you'll get two." In wartime England this was important intelligence, and I always remember that afternoon as an example of his attention to detail and kindness to his juniors.'

Nash would go on to win the Distinguished Service Cross and rise to the rank of commander. He served under Miers towards the end of the war and afterwards.

'I believe that I came to know this complex and unpredictable man pretty well,' he said. 'Though a fairly frequent victim of his furious outbursts I also came to appreciate his endearing characteristics. Not least among these was his tremendous loyalty to those who served under him. We were his people. He could be pretty tough with us if we failed him but, as far as was possible, no one else could touch us and, if we had a problem, he would do his damnedest to help.'

During one of those outbursts Nash was on the receiving end of a punch. 'He could lash out when he was in a temper,' said Nash. 'I was upset at first but I got over it.'

Miers and Philip Francis, the captain of *Proteus*, probably got on well when they met. Francis also showed great determination, a tough and enthusiastic sportsman who particularly enjoyed rugby and boxing. While a 12-year-old pupil at Horton School in Biggleswade, Bedfordshire, he led a revolt against the headmaster, who had refused to grant a holiday to mark the anniversary of the Battle of Waterloo. In the early 1930s Francis was sent to the China Station and later, with three other submarine officers and a naval doctor, sailed home in a 50ft ketch, a journey of 16,000 miles, which took them via Japan and the Panama Canal. In one respect, it was an expensive trip – the Admiralty insisted the men take a year on half pay.

Francis won the Distinguished Service Order and Bar for his Mediterranean patrols in *Proteus*. On the night of 8 February 1942, he experienced the 'tin-opener' attack. The submarine was on the surface when Francis saw what he thought was a U-boat. It was, in fact, the Italian torpedo boat *Sagittario*. Rather than diving and receiving depth charges, which would probably have been fatal, he headed straight for the enemy. A forward hydroplane sliced open part of *Sagittario*'s port side 'like a tin opener'. Each vessel thought it had sunk the other.[5] Francis had one of the best torpedo averages, firing 51 and scoring 20 hits.

Chapter 10

OPERATIONS COPPER AND FLIPPER

The time had come for Operation Copper, the landing of commandos on the Libyan coast behind enemy lines in Cyrenaica so that they could carry out Operation Flipper, with Rommel as one of the targets.[1] The landing involved two submarines, *Torbay* and HMS *Talisman*. On her previous patrol, *Torbay* had successfully landed Captain Haselden and his Arab guide at Zaviet el Hamama. *Talisman* was involved in a similar mission, sending three SBS men and a member of No.11 (Scottish) Commando in folbots to the beach at Ras Hilal further along the coast to check if it was suitable for the main landing. This was the preferred spot because it was sheltered from westerly winds, which were likely to be hazardous for men in folbots and two-man rubber boats. The area around the beach also offered protection for commandos wanting to lie low during the day. The four men were landed without any difficulty, but they failed to return to the beach to be picked up by *Talisman* before daylight the next day. The submarine went back that night and there was still no sign of them. *Talisman* returned to Alexandria, reporting that there had been considerable enemy activity along the coast road on the cliffs above the beach. The group were captured some distance from Ras Hilal in the vicinity of Derna, trying to make their way to the safety of Tobruk. Later it emerged that their two folbots were wrecked in bad weather, and it was suggested that *Talisman* had gone to the wrong beach to collect the men. When the submarine returned without her reconnaissance party, Ras Hilal was ruled out and aerial photographs of the coast were studied again. *Torbay*'s Zaviet el Hamama was chosen. Eleven other beaches were noted for use in emergencies.

Each submarine was set to carry 28 men from 11 Commando, with all their equipment and landing craft. Because of the lack of space it was not possible to take enough folbots. For the same reason five-man dinghies, which would have been ideal, were ruled out. Two-man rubber boats were chosen. *Torbay* and *Talisman* would each take 18 of them, deflated in bags – 14 for the operation and four spare. Sensibly, it was decided to have practice sessions, getting the boats inflated on the casing of the submarines using foot pumps and sending them off with the men. *Torbay* and *Talisman* moved out to buoys in Alexandria harbour at night for the drill. A beach landing using one of *Medway's* launches was also carried out nearby. It was not safe to involve the submarines in this exercise because mines were often dropped in the area. There was just one problem with these exercises – they were held when the weather was reasonably good. A harsh lesson was about to be learned.

On 10 November 1941 *Torbay* and *Talisman* left Alexandria for Zaviet el Hamama. On board *Torbay* were three commando officers, including Lieutenant-Colonel Geoffrey Keyes, who was going to lead the Rommel raid. The officer in overall charge of the commandos, Lieutenant-Colonel Robert Laycock, was in the other submarine, although he had originally intended to be aboard *Torbay*, apparently only switching because another officer reported sick at the last minute. Each submarine also carried four SBS folbot specialists and two of the craft.

The day after leaving port, on diving to 70ft, Miers was told of a serious leak above the port engine. The cause was a corroded hull plate, which was temporarily plugged. This weakness was a major worry. Miers did not know how deep he could go, or what would happen if there was a depth charge attack. One defective hull plate could jeopardise the whole submarine. That night *Torbay* surfaced and the engineer officer, Tono Kidd, and two other crewmen went on the casing. They located the plate but could not repair it from above because there was not enough access. Miers could have returned to Alexandria. He reported: 'The plugging of the hole from inside the hull could not be considered wholly satisfactory especially as the full extent of the corrosion could not be gauged. But, after making a personal inspection of the completed work, I decided that the importance of the operation justified proceeding.'

Miers also decided that it would be foolish to embark on any offensive sea operations. *Talisman* had a problem of her own – a defective cylinder block in the port engine, which had cut her speed. Nevertheless, both submarines arrived at their destination on the morning of 13 November.

Laycock, in *Talisman*, noted: 'Conditions in the submarine were naturally somewhat cramped and surfacing after dusk each evening was a relief. All ranks were greatly interested in what was to us a novel method of approaching our objective and the soldiers were high in their praise of the way in which they were fed and accommodated.'[2]

Torbay carried out a detailed periscope reconnaissance of all the beaches near the landing place. That evening the submarine surfaced. The weather was ideal for a landing 'but owing to over-riding military considerations the opportunity was not accepted'. Keyes explained to Miers that Captain Haselden was travelling overland to Zaviet el Hamama to give the all-clear, but he would not be in position until the following evening. The commandos waited 24 hours – and the weather turned bad.

Miers was the senior submarine officer. It was planned that *Torbay* would land her soldiers first, with *Talisman* standing off as cover. Then *Talisman* would go in. In *Torbay* on 14 November this was the picture that Miers painted, covering the time from 1200 to 1828:

1200 *Served cold dinner to landing party, issued arms and topped up water bottles.*

1230–1530 *Landing party slept. Special hot supper prepared. Tins of food and explosives stacked below gun tower hatch.*

1300 *Entered bay for final periscope reconnaissance.*

1530–1600 *Landing party stowed bedding. Heaving lines stowed in control room.*

1600–1630 *Supper served to landing party. On completion mess traps mustered and stowed away. Fore end cleared of landing party.*

1630–1800 *Both folbots rigged. Rubber boats placed at foot of fore hatch.*

1630–1730 *Landing party issued with ammunition, grenades and packs in control room and engine room.*

1730 *Landing party mustered and inspected by their CO in wardroom, subsequently lining up in the passage abaft fore end in order of disembarkation.*

1800 *Synchronised watches.*

1815–1830 *Submarine in darkness to assist night vision.*

1828 *Surfaced.*

For the commandos the stale air would soon be a thing of the past. They were about to get too much fresh air. The men were tense but they were eager to get ashore. There was a strong westerly swell, and Miers had already decided that it would be too time consuming to retrieve the commandos' boats. Keyes agreed and said they could be hidden ashore.

The fore and gun tower hatches were opened, and the landing party, folbots, rubber boats and equipment were assembled on the casing. The submarine trimmed down by the bow as she made her approach to the beach. Despite a long trek through the desert, the remarkable Haselden was there on time.

'There was a moment none of us will ever forget,' said Lieutenant Tommy Langton of the SBS. 'It was as we were closing the beach in *Torbay*. We were on the forward casing of the submarine, blowing up the dinghies and generally preparing. We could just see the dark coastline ahead. We had been told that Haselden would be there to meet us, but I think no one really believed that he would. He had left Cairo quite three weeks before, and during the interval there had been several changes of plan . . . When the darkness was suddenly stabbed by his torch making the looked for signal, there was a gasp of amazement and relief from everyone – in other circumstances it would undoubtedly have been a spontaneous cheer.'[3]

About half an hour later the first folbot was successfully launched and it headed for the beach, but shortly afterwards a large wave swept over the casing and four rubber boats and a soldier were lost overboard. It took an hour to rescue the soldier and retrieve the boats, with two seamen diving in with lines to secure them. Crewmen working as the casing party struggled to haul in the waterlogged boats. Meanwhile, the men in the folbot arrived back from the beach to find out what was going on. The landing operation should have taken about an hour, and it was more than two hours since Haselden's signal.

Torbay managed to launch seven rubber boats, but she started to drift and the operation was interrupted to regain position. The swell was getting worse and rubber boats were capsizing repeatedly, sometimes losing equipment. It was fortunate that each commando, with all his gear, was wearing two lifejackets.

Once again the folbot came back from the beach to investigate. By this time it was shipping a lot of water, and it was decided to take the folbot back on board the submarine but it smashed against the side, a total loss.

At midnight *Torbay* was still trying to launch the last rubber boat. It capsized three times, spilling its occupants into the sea. The submarine was trimmed right down to make it easier, actually touching the bottom in the shallow water. At 0035 on 15 November, *Torbay* signalled 'Operation completed' to *Talisman*. The operation had started at 1852 on 14 November.

Miers reported: 'It had been accomplished in spite of the weather conditions by the determination, grit and courage of all concerned on the casing, some of whom received a very severe buffeting while handling the boats alongside in the swell, and nearly all were completely exhausted at the finish. No less splendid was the spirit of the soldiers under strange and even frightening conditions. They were quite undaunted by the setbacks and remained quietly determined to "get on with the job".

'The grit of the final pair deserves special mention. They had had several spills during the earlier stages of the operation and were obviously clumsy and unfitted for such difficult conditions. Yet they never lost heart and when I sent a personal message finally to exhort them "to do their very best not to delay (and therefore jeopardise) the operation any further" I received a reply that "they would do their utmost". A few minutes later they were pulling for the shore in splendid style, drenched but in good spirits.'

In *Talisman*, the captain, Lieutenant-Commander Michael Willmott, and Laycock were getting increasingly concerned about the time that *Torbay* was taking to send her commandos ashore. At one point *Talisman* launched one of her folbots with an officer to find out what was going on. This was done with considerable difficulty. In the darkness, the officer failed to find *Torbay* and returned without news. Willmott had a particular problem because he needed to get his submarine out to sea two hours before dawn to recharge the batteries. After a lot of discussion he and Laycock decided to postpone sending their commandos until the following night. Then they received *Torbay*'s message. Quickly, *Talisman* headed for the beach and trimmed down to launch the rubber boats. But as soon as she started doing this – as with *Torbay* – a large wave swept many of the boats off the casing. Most of the commandos held on to a lifeline, but some were washed over the side. Instead of swimming to the boats, these men went back to the submarine. Both of *Talisman*'s folbots were lost.

In desperation the casing party started throwing boats over the side and getting commandos to jump into them. One boat got away in this manner but the rest capsized. By 0400 the moon was well up and *Talisman* was forced to withdraw.[4]

Only Laycock and seven of his men reached the shore. One commando drowned and the remainder were still on board the submarine. Laycock, with a shaky knowledge of Morse code, tried to signal *Talisman*. Another problem became apparent – the raiding party did not have any specialist signallers or sappers.

'I had previously warned Eighth Army that this might prove prejudicial to the success of the operation which was in fact the case,' said Laycock. 'The demolitions were for the most part ineffective for those responsible for carrying them out had only undergone an elementary and inadequate course in the use of explosives, whereas our original establishment [Layforce, which had been partially disbanded] contained a number of highly trained Royal Engineers and Royal Signals personnel.

'Touch with the submarine was extremely difficult to maintain since I was the only person ashore with a knowledge of Morse code and such messages as I sent were made with a torch which had no proper key but a switch which had to be pushed off and on. I do not know how many of my signals were readable.'

When the commandos got ashore they were wet from at least the waist down. It was cold and the wind was strong. Fortunately, it was safe enough to light a fire in the old fort overlooking the beach. Keyes produced a bottle of rum and handed it round. All the rubber boats were hidden in a small cave, and the group from *Torbay* and *Talisman* moved on to a deep wadi about a mile from the shore.

The weather was continuing to deteriorate, and Laycock doubted whether *Talisman* would be able to send the rest of his men the next night. Time and the element of surprise were important, and he decided to rethink the planned attacks of Operation Flipper. Originally, there were four targets: Rommel's headquarters at Beda Littoria, also known as Sidi Rafa; the Italian headquarters at Cyrene; the Italian intelligence centre at Appolonia; and telephone and telegraph communications between Faida and Lamluda. The targets were reduced to two. Keyes, Captain Robin Campbell and 17 other ranks would continue with the raid on Rommel, and Lieutenant Roy Cooke and 6 other ranks, 3 each from *Torbay* and *Talisman*, would try to knock out the communications between Faida and Lamluda. A special group had been carefully trained for this raid, but all the members had failed to land. Haselden said his small party would also carry out sabotage. Laycock decided to remain at the wadi with three men and reserve ammunition and rations.

At 24, Keyes was probably the youngest lieutenant-colonel in the British Army. He had been serving for only four years. After Sandhurst he joined a cavalry regiment, the Royal Scots Greys, going to Palestine in 1938 to help quell the tit-for-tat violence between Arabs and Jews. Keen to see more action and to make a name for himself, he obtained a posting as a liaison officer in the Narvik expeditionary force. The year was 1940, when the commandos were born, and the idea of being one appealed to him greatly. And his father, Admiral of the Fleet Sir Roger Keyes, architect of the Zeebrugge raid in 1918, just happened to be the new Director of Combined Operations, with ultimate responsibility for the commandos. Father and son were thinking along the same lines. The admiral wrote to his son: 'I am so glad you applied for that service – because I was going to apply for you.'

The training in Scotland was tough, and in June 1940 Keyes took part in the Litani river action, when commandos landing from the sea helped an Allied push into Syria, where Vichy French were supporting the Germans. Keyes's courage in fierce fighting led to the award of the Military Cross. Among the many casualties was the commanding officer of 11 Commando, and Keyes found himself in charge. He wrote to his long-time girlfriend Pamela that he was 'not even touched though I had a lot of very nasty frights'. He also confessed that he was not sleeping well because of his new responsibility.[5]

Despite its success in the Litani river action, Layforce, a group of commando units, was reduced in size. GHQ Cairo had found amphibious operations difficult to mount. At this time, the three services were not noted for their cooperation. Keyes knew that 11 Commando needed a mission and he came up with a 'great idea'.

To some, there was only one word to describe the plan to capture or kill Rommel – desperate. However, it appealed to the GOC, Lieutenant-General Sir Alan Cunningham, brother of Admiral Sir Andrew Cunningham, who was interested in using commandos in naval operations.

Shortly before embarking in *Torbay* Keyes received a letter from Pamela. According to his sister Elizabeth, this was the woman he hoped to marry and he was shocked when she informed him of her engagement to another man, someone Keyes knew as a friend. However, Michael Asher, author of *Get Rommel*, doubted that Keyes and Pamela had a serious relationship. Keyes, he suggested, was more interested in his army career. In the submarine, the commando leader wrote a reply, wishing the couple happiness and even insisting on being the best man. He told Pamela that he was on his way 'to do more dirty work' and his chances of getting away with it were 'moderately good'. It is probable that Keyes gave the letter to Miers for safekeeping, with instructions that it should be sent only if he failed to return. Mail was slow and when Pamela eventually received the letter, she was already married.[6]

Miers was impressed with Keyes's enthusiasm and the way he inspired his men. He also noted that a lot of thought had gone into the Rommel operation. 'During the passage the plan was carefully explained to his detachment and in addition he found time to give an interesting lecture on the subject to the crew which was very much enjoyed and appreciated,' said Miers. 'It was a pleasure to have this fine body of men on board.'

The weather had not improved when Keyes and his men set off from the wadi for Rommel's headquarters about 20 miles away on the evening of 15 November.[7] They climbed a steep escarpment and headed inland across wild country, often stumbling over rocks and through thorns in the darkness. After a few miles the group's Arab guides deserted them. Keyes, who remained cheerful and confident, was forced to navigate using a poor map and his compass. Soaked and cold, they only marched at night and hid during daylight.

On the night of 16 November they were close to Rommel's headquarters. They changed their boots for gym shoes and blackened their faces. At one point as they neared the target it was so muddy and dark that the commandos had to go in single file, holding on to the next man's bayonet scabbard. Even so, some men fell.

Zero hour was 2359. The torrential rain did have one benefit. The German sentries at Rommel's six-storey headquarters liked it even less. Only one man appeared to be on guard duty when the commandos sneaked up. What happened next remains open to question. According to Elizabeth Keyes in her biography of Geoffrey Keyes,[8] the single guard, at the entrance to the drive, was killed by the commando leader, who then checked the outside of the building and its grounds. Launching an attack by knocking on the front door might seem bizarre, but that is what happened. Keyes found the back door locked, and all the windows were high up with heavy shutters. He decided to lead the raid, taking Captain Campbell, Sergeant Jack Terry and three other men with him. Three men were detailed to sabotage a power plant and the remainder were spread around the grounds of the building to deal with any reinforcements.

Campbell spoke fluent German and he banged on the front door demanding entry. A soldier opened the door and Keyes, holding a pistol, tried to overpower him, but the man grabbed the gun. A set of doors inside prevented Campbell and Terry from getting to the German quickly and silencing him. Campbell opened fire with his revolver. With the element of surprise gone, Keyes gave the order to use tommy-guns and grenades. Two men started coming down the stone stairs from the first floor and Terry sent a burst of fire in their direction. Two Germans who ran towards the building were shot by commandos in the grounds. Keyes began throwing open the doors of the rooms on the ground floor. There were about ten Germans in one room and he fired several shots before closing the door and waiting for Campbell to toss in a grenade. Keyes opened the door again, the grenade went in, he said 'Well done' and Terry gave a burst with his tommy-gun. But before he could close the door the Germans opened fire and a bullet hit Keyes above the heart and he fell to the floor unconscious. Campbell shut the door and the grenade went off. The room fell silent. Campbell and Terry carried Keyes outside where he died shortly afterwards.

That was the account outlined by Elizabeth Keyes, who relied heavily on the recollections of Campbell. But in his book, *Get Rommel*, Michael Asher has pointed to major discrepancies. He doubted that Keyes killed a sentry at the entrance to the drive and made the startling claim that the commando leader was probably accidentally – and fatally – shot by Campbell during the struggle at the main door.

Campbell himself was badly wounded in the leg when he went round the side of the building to check on the commandos at the back, forgetting they had orders to shoot anyone coming from that direction. He told Terry to leave explosive charges in the house and then to withdraw with the rest of the men and return to the beach. The commandos offered to carry him but he refused, knowing that it would require a superhuman effort over such difficult terrain. Campbell was found propped against a tree and taken prisoner.

In May 1942 the Germans produced an official report on the attack and concluded that 'it is fairly certain that both [British] officers were shot by their own men'. The report was not intended for propaganda. It emerged that the Germans fired only a single shot during the raid.[9]

After the attack, in the rain and darkness, Terry and most of the men stumbled away. They carried on during the day and reached the wadi where Laycock was waiting on the evening of 18 November. Laycock was told that Keyes had been killed, Campbell was wounded and a number of men were missing.

Laycock went to check on the beach and found that 'friendly' Arabs had removed the rubber boats from the cave where they had been hidden and taken them to a better hiding place. However, the Arabs had left without showing the new spot, which was 'most aggravating'. *Torbay* was due to take the men off that night. The weather was still poor but the swell was less than on previous days and Laycock thought there was a 'fairish chance' of evacuation. He returned to the wadi and told the group to head for the beach, leaving three lookouts in case any of the missing men turned up or the enemy appeared.

Back at the beach shortly before darkness fell Laycock spotted *Torbay* through his field glasses, surfaced about a quarter of a mile out to sea. He signalled asking for a folbot to be sent with a line and lifejackets.

'I was perturbed at the request for lifebelts since the soldiers had landed with two each which were to have been hidden at the "dump" with the rubber boats,' said Miers. 'There was also no indication of the number of men on the beach nor the number of lifebelts required.'

A long wait ensued. Miers and Laycock were both wondering what the other man was up to. The commando leader, still relying on an unsuitable torch, had no idea if his messages were being understood. Miers decided to send two SBS men in a rubber boat with lifejackets, food and water and a message that the weather was unsuitable for taking them off in boats but if most of the commandos were on the beach he was willing to take the submarine to within 100 yards of it at dawn so that they could swim out. The rubber boat broke free before the soldiers could get in, but it drifted towards the beach.

Miers reported: 'In order not to alarm the party on shore with the arrival of an empty boat and so as to put a stop to their signalling and clear up the situation I decided to answer with a shaded light and made, "Too rough tonight, have floated in boat with Mae Wests, food and drink. How many of you and what luck, where are your boats and Mae Wests?"

'The signal was well read and each word was acknowledged. The following reply was received, "Twenty-two here, have no boats and Mae Wests. Goodnight". A few minutes later a further signal declared, "Boat with Mae Wests has arrived".

'Upon the results of their operations there was silence, and considering that the receipt of this report, together with any vital information gained might be at least as important as the safe re-embarkation of the force, I asked again "What luck?" The reply was rather garbled but appeared to read as follows, "Goodness only knows. Some killed in camp and missing from HQ".'

In fact, Laycock had signalled: 'Good work. Messed up their HQ but sad casualties. Keyes killed. Campbell, Cooke and six ORs missing.'

Miers believed the men would be in danger if they remained at the beach during the day and signalled his offer to take *Torbay* close to the beach so that they could swim out, otherwise he would try the next night. He got the signal, "Try tomorrow night".

Miers revealed that he was willing to take *Torbay* as close as 50 yards. 'The failure to re-embark was unfortunate but could have been avoided if the officer in charge on the beach had been prepared to let the men abandon their arms and equipment and swim a distance of about 50 yards,' he said.

Laycock had given the 'tempting' offer serious thought, but came to the conclusion that his exhausted men would probably drown in the rough sea. He pinned his hopes on a boat rescue the next night and, after checking the sentries, got some sleep. The men were spread around in caves overlooking the beach. Laycock woke an hour before first light and gave the order for all-round defensive positions. All was quiet until about noon when a few shots were heard from the direction of the wadi. The lookouts had been forced to engage Arab carabiniere stationed at Hania about 8 miles away.

'This did not worry us unduly since we were confident that we should be able to drive them off until darkness allowed us to retire to the beach for evacuation, which now seemed feasible as wind and sea were rapidly abating,' said Laycock. 'I sent two small parties from the main body to outflank the enemy but it soon became evident that they were not on a wide enough front or in sufficient numbers.'

It was about to get worse. Detachments of Germans were spotted moving down the western side of the wadi and more carabiniere appeared. Later a 'considerable' party of Italians was seen on the skyline. 'Fairly accurate fire was brought to bear on us but we were behind good cover and suffered no casualties though it was feared that the party in the wadi had been overrun,' said Laycock.

The enemy were advancing using excellent cover, and by early afternoon it was obvious that the commandos would not be able to hold out until dusk. Laycock ordered his men to split up into parties of not more than three and try to escape. There were three choices. They could head to another beach and hope that *Talisman* would be waiting on the night of 20/21 November to take them off. They could make their way to the area of Slonta where there were friendly Arabs, with the possibility of being picked up by the Long Range Desert Group. Or they could hide in the wadis to the north of the Cyrene escarpment and wait for Allied forces. Laycock made good his escape with Sergeant Terry.

Miers had been right to assume that the commandos would be in danger if they waited another day but, of course, at this stage he was unaware that the men were battling to remain at large. Early in the day *Torbay* began a periscope reconnaissance of all the beaches in the area. Nothing suspicious was sighted. In the submarine, repairs were carried out to the remaining five rubber boats, and improvised paddles were produced to replace the ones lost. The weather had improved, so Miers was reasonably confident of bringing back Laycock's force. *Torbay* surfaced in the evening and closed to the beach.

But there were no signals, although a light was seen in the old fort. Miers decided to send two SBS men, Lieutenant Langton and Corporal Cyril Feeberry, to the beach to investigate. He told Langton to act with extreme caution and to head back to the submarine if he saw anything suspicious. The folbot was launched successfully. Miers waited anxiously for one and a half hours before there was a signal indicating that the men were returning. Five minutes later the folbot was hauled in just as it was about to sink.

Langton had crawled around the beach and on several occasions spotted the glow of a cigarette and heard voices, but he was unable to make out what was being said. Surely, commandos would not have been foolish enough to openly smoke. Langton went back to the folbot, paddling along the length of the beach. As a last resort he flashed the letter T with his torch. Then the folbot capsized in the surf and there was a struggle to save his tommy-gun. In full view of the beach the two men righted the damaged folbot and headed for *Torbay*, minus a paddle and making water fast.

'Everything possible had been done and both folbotists deserve credit for their good work in far from favourable conditions,' said Miers. 'The work on the casing on both this and the proceeding night was again most creditably performed, not, it must be added, without injury and bruises to the personnel concerned.'

Torbay spent the night checking the beaches. At 0626 on 20 November, she dived to carry out a periscope reconnaissance. Later that morning the picture changed dramatically. Soldiers were seen on all the beaches, apparently searching. Aircraft were also patrolling. That evening *Torbay* surfaced and checked the beaches again. By this time Miers was conceding that it looked hopeless, but he did not abandon the search for the commandos until noon on 21 November – nearly two days after Laycock had ordered his men to split up.

One of the enemy planes that had been carrying out reconnaissance was a Ghibli, and Miers noticed that it was using a landing strip on the coast nearby. Always keen to get at the enemy, he decided to carry out an action that probably remains unique – submarine versus a plane on the ground. *Torbay* popped up and opened fire with her 4in gun. Because of the scrub and heavy rain the plane was not an easy target. Miers reported: 'The shooting improved and the necessary hit was eventually obtained – our contribution to the Libyan offensive.' *Torbay* set course for Alexandria, arriving on 24 November.

Although they had returned without the commandos, Miers saw the potential for such operations. Taking and landing such a force did not present any great difficulty – providing the weather was kind. 'The men quite definitely enjoyed their trip and arrived at their destination well fed, well rested and in excellent spirits,' said Miers. 'Many more days could have been spent on board without much detriment to their physical condition.'

The importance of good weather was not lost on Captain Raw. 'The difficulties experienced by both submarines during the operation again bring out how dependent any such landing must be on the weather conditions,' he said. 'That so much was in fact achieved is a great tribute to the courage and determination of all concerned.'

He also praised Miers for continuing with the operation after the discovery of the leak from the corroded hull plate. This was 'typical of the determination and level-headed judgement with which he conducted the whole operation'.[10]

Forty-one days after the landing Laycock and Terry reached the safety of British forces.

'We found little difficulty in avoiding search parties since the cover in the Jebel [a forested region] is excellent and having a good pair of field glasses I could usually spot Germans or Italians at considerable distances,' said Laycock. 'Our greater fear was being stalked by the carabiniere Arabs who moved much more cleverly by tracking us and who got close to us on several occasions during the first few days.

'Later, however, having made friends with the Senussi tribe we adopted the enjoyable policy of moving each night into the very wadis which the enemy were known to have searched during the day.'

Only one other man escaped, John Brittlebank, a Royal Artillery bombardier who had joined the SBS. Keyes was the only death. All the other raiders were captured.

Laycock said he and Terry had tried to reach the beach where *Talisman* was supposed to be waiting but could not get through because of enemy activity. As Chapman later revealed, the use of *Talisman* to take off commandos provoked a major row. When *Talisman* failed to disembark most of her commandos, Miers, the senior submarine officer, ordered her home because *Torbay* could cope with the number expected to return from their mission. It was not worth endangering two submarines. But he did not know that *Talisman*'s captain had made the alternative rescue arrangement with Laycock. And *Talisman* did not tell Miers before leaving for Alexandria.

It is not known if commandos other than Laycock and Terry tried to reach the alternative beach. Chapman said Miers 'went off like a 5 November squib' when he found out.[11]

Less than ten months later *Talisman* vanished. She is believed to have hit a mine in the Sicilian Channel.

There was a second controversy when Haselden, the desert warrior, reported that some of the captured commandos might have marked the beach area where *Torbay* had been waiting on their maps. That would explain why the enemy found Laycock's force so quickly. Keyes had expressly forbidden the marking of maps in any way.

Haselden was awarded the Military Cross for his earlier reconnaissance mission and received a Bar for his actions in Operation Flipper. After meeting up with the commandos he succeeded in disrupting enemy communications and then reaching a patrol of the Long Range Desert Group, which had a fierce encounter with Italian forces. The citation for the Bar noted Haselden's 'outstanding endurance, his cool and calculated bravery, and his unswerving devotion to duty'.

In September 1942 Haselden, then aged 39 and a lieutenant-colonel, was killed in a daring raid on enemy installations in Tobruk, when a group of commandos sneaked in disguised as German guards and British prisoners of war.

Keyes was awarded a posthumous Victoria Cross for Operation Flipper. Militarily, the raids did not achieve much. Of Rommel, there was no sign. The Desert Fox had flown to Rome on 1 November and did not return to Libya until 18 November. During part of the trip he had enjoyed a holiday with his wife and celebrated his fiftieth birthday. At the time of the attack he was in Athens where his plane had been diverted because of engine trouble.[12] Was it really Rommel's headquarters? It had been, but his base was probably many miles away nearer the German front line east of Tobruk. The building at Beda Littoria was the headquarters of his chief quartermaster. British intelligence, through Enigma code breaking, had known that Rommel was not in North Africa, but this information was not passed to Miers, Laycock or Keyes.

Four Germans, including three officers, were killed in the raid. Explosives left in the building failed to go off because detonators were too wet due to the torrential rain, although they had been kept dry during the submarine landing. The building's power plant was partially sabotaged. A communications pylon near Cyrene was blown up. But Operation Flipper turned out to be a propaganda victory. In the dark days of 1941, the attempt to capture or kill Rommel caught the imagination of the British public, and it left the Afrika Korps wondering where the next attack was coming from.

Capturing a German general was not such a desperate idea, as the Special Operations Executive proved in April 1944, when Major Patrick Leigh Fermor and Captain William Stanley Moss, with the help of partisans, seized Major-General Heinrich Kreipe in Crete and spirited him away to Egypt.

Chapter 11

HIGHLY DECORATED

As Jeremy Nash pointed out, Miers could be exceedingly tough with his crew, but he would also support them with equal determination when merit deserved recognition. A good example is Augustus Armishaw. On 3 December 1941 Miers went to the trouble of producing a seven-point report arguing the case for Armishaw to be specially advanced to the rank of petty officer. The report went to Raw and as high as the commander-in-chief, Cunningham.

Armishaw, who had won the Distinguished Service Medal while serving in the Shark class submarine HMS *Sunfish* in the North Sea, was one of the men who suddenly found themselves in *Torbay* when she was ordered to leave Scotland at a few hours' notice in March 1941. He was then an able seaman. It is worth showing how Miers enthusiastically argued his man's case:

His general ability, power of command and good influence were so pronounced that within twenty-four hours of proceeding on patrol he was made temporary acting leading seaman to complete the establishment and was put in charge of a watch at sea.

On arrival at Alexandria approval was obtained for this rating to be retained in lieu of, and paid as, a leading seaman, a state of affairs which persisted until 23 August 1941 when he was rated acting leading seaman on reaching the top of the depot roster.

On 26 August 1941, immediately before proceeding to sea, the second coxswain of the submarine was injured and Acting Leading Seaman Armishaw was selected to fill his place. His performance of these new duties on patrol was so outstanding that on return to harbour it was decided to retain him as second coxswain and approval was obtained for him to be paid as a petty officer . . .

In each of the two subsequent patrols the conduct of Leading Seaman Armishaw has been sufficiently distinguished to earn special mention in the reports and the example of courage and determination that he has set has been magnificent.

For this record of conspicuous leadership and loyal and meritorious service, which has contributed largely to the success of important recent operations, and taking into account his good work in submarines since the outbreak of war, it is submitted that the granting of the higher rate, the duties of which he is already fulfilling with distinction, would be a fitting reward to an outstanding leading seaman.

This rating has requested to pass for petty officer and, although war service in submarines is not wholly conducive to working up for such an examination, I do not doubt his ability to do so. It is unquestionably preferable for the second coxswain of a large submarine to have the status of a petty officer and, as the education, personality and general bearing of Leading Seaman Armishaw have already made him the obvious candidate for second coxswain, it would seem that such an advancement would also be in the best interests of the submarine and of the service.[1]

Cunningham gave his approval. In the *London Gazette* of 7 April 1942, Armishaw was awarded a Bar to his Distinguished Service Medal for his part in landing the commandos who took part in the Rommel raid. His work on the casing of the submarine had been outstanding. For the same operation Miers received a Bar to his Distinguished Service Order, and Kidd and Verschoyle-Campbell were awarded the Distinguished Service Cross. There were also seven awards of the Distinguished Service Medal, and five men, including Chapman, were Mentioned in Despatches.

Six days after Miers wrote his report about Armishaw *Torbay* set off on her eighth patrol.[2] Armishaw was not the only one to get promotion. Miers was now a commander.

The submarine headed for Navarin Bay in the south-western Peloponnese of Greece. On 12 December *Torbay* found a 50-ton schooner loaded with barrels of fuel, which was sunk using the 4in gun. The next day Miers made contact with another submarine, HMS *Porpoise*, as she neared the end of her patrol. *Porpoise* had attacked a merchant ship, *Andrea Gritti*, which was forced to beach at Methoni, and she asked *Torbay* to finish off the victim, mentioning that salvage vessels were on the scene. Miers took a look and decided to let the salvage operation get under way in the hope of inflicting further damage. That evening he received a report of a convoy 60 miles away and went in search of it. Apart from seeing a couple of destroyers, which were out of range, no other ships were spotted and *Torbay* went back to Methoni to deliver the *coup de grâce*. On the way, three sailing ships were spotted and sunk using 31 rounds of 4in ammunition. An anti-submarine boat appeared on the scene and picked up survivors. Despite being armed with a gun, torpedoes and depth charges, it made no attempt to attack *Torbay*, to Miers's surprise.

On board the submarine were two SBS folbot specialists, Captain Robert Wilson and Marine Wally Hughes. On the night of 16/17 December the men paddled away from *Torbay* in their folbot about 3 miles from the entrance to Navarin harbour. They planned to attach limpet mines to a merchant ship and a destroyer that had been spotted earlier. After a 'very cautious approach' using the dark background of Sphacteria island the commandos entered the harbour, which was glassy calm. No targets were immediately visible and it was assumed that the ships were moored close inshore. Wilson and Hughes made a systematic search of the harbour, drawing a blank.

Wilson reported: 'It was decided however, as a last hope, to creep into Navarin to see if there was any small craft worthy of a limpet attack. None was located – instead the folbot was. Voices were heard to be discussing our identity and on being challenged the canoe was turned stern on and no reply was given. About six rounds were fired at very close range but it was assumed that the enemy would think we were Greek fishermen, out of bounds perhaps, hence better not to reply to their fire and thus advertise the fact that we were definitely hostile. No hits were registered and the canoe was very quickly out of sight.'[3]

The men got back to *Torbay*, only to be informed by Miers that the targets had left the harbour as they made their way in. *Torbay*, in fact, had a close encounter with one of the ships, probably the destroyer, which circled the submerged submarine for an hour at a range of 2 miles.

Raw commented: 'The commanding officer, displaying excellent judgement and a fine nerve, kept the submarine end on to the enemy, who was then joined by a second and smaller ship, both making off on a north-westerly course.'[4]

Always keen to engage the enemy, Miers hoped the commandos would return early so that he could give chase. But the men were away for about four hours, having paddled between 10 and 12 miles. Wilson and Hughes were not particularly tired but they were disappointed. Raw thought it was a 'stout-hearted effort deserving of success'.

After learning that the Italian battle fleet was at sea Miers headed west to try to intercept it. He was acting on limited information, and the ships were missed by about 30 miles, although another submarine, HMS *P31*, carried out an attack. Miers returned to the Navarin area and found the destroyer *Vincenzo Gioberti* in the harbour. It was decided to fire a torpedo through a gap between Sphacteria island and rocks. Miers gave the order but was stunned to discover soon afterwards that the torpedo had veered away and was heading back to the submarine at 40 knots. According to Chapman, the captain made a 'blunder of schoolboy howler proportions' by failing to take *Torbay* deep immediately. Miers was 'mesmerised'. Chapman was standing by the sonar operator, who could hear the runaway beast. The torpedo passed over the engine room hatch and made two further circles. *Torbay* had been close to disaster.[5]

It was this incident that led to torpedo officer Roy Foster getting the blame and being placed under arrest by Miers. A gyro failure was really responsible, although the torpedo had passed an inspection less than a month earlier. To make matters worse, a total of three destroyers were seen but chances to attack them were missed. Miers eased some of his frustration by sinking a schooner. A shore battery opened fire and *Torbay* was hunted by an anti-submarine boat, which dropped three depth charges.

On the evening of 22 December it was decided that Wilson and Hughes would pay another visit to Navarin harbour, this time to put limpet mines on the destroyer *Castore*. The commandos took the same route. The silhouette of the warship appeared. 'The water was like glass and highly phosphorescent,' said Wilson. 'Voices were clearly heard aboard ship and it was apparent that the slightest sound from our direction would be heard at even considerable distance.'

They paddled to within 150 yards of the target. Wilson concluded that he would have to swim to the destroyer with the mines. He did not have the luxury of a wet suit, and entered the very cold water, with three limpet mines on a small makeshift raft, which he pushed with his left arm, moving slowly to avoid stirring up too much phosphorescence. He was soon in trouble. The water was too cold. The arm went numb and his teeth started to chatter uncontrollably. When he was about half way to the destroyer he turned back fearing cramp. A fine line had been attached to the raft and Hughes hauled it back. The mines had been primed to go off after two and a half hours – about the time it would take to get back to *Torbay* – and they had to be made safe.

'The operation would, I feel certain, have been successful had I been able to withstand the cold,' said Wilson. 'It is apparent that summer is the ideal time of the year for these operations but I do consider that since cold is the only difficulty every effort should be made to overcome it, so that an operation might be successfully carried out in the near future rather than wait for the warmer conditions in summer.'

Chapman was not sympathetic, observing: 'Wilson was a skinny little man – a plumper operator might have managed.'

Miers gave the matter a little more thought: 'The failure of this operation is a good example of the vital need for every detail of a plan of any sort to be considered at the outset. The weather on the first occasion exceeded the most optimistic expectations and on the second was also very good, while in the preparation and launching arrangements there was not the slightest hitch. Yet the whole plan failed because it had not been appreciated that the human body would not be capable of withstanding the intense cold of the water on a December night in that latitude despite the qualities of daring, initiative and determination that undoubtedly animated both the participants and the stamina that both showed in two exacting operations.'

Miers was still determined to sink a destroyer. Undaunted by the rogue torpedo and the missed chances, he decided to have another go at sending a 'fish' through the gap between Sphacteria island and the rocks. This time the torpedo kept its course and hit *Castore*, blowing a large hole in the bow but not sinking her. *Torbay* was in a minefield and had the 'unnerving and unusual' experience of being counter-attacked by controlled mines, as well as an anti-submarine boat, which dropped five depth charges with 'fair accuracy'. An aircraft also appeared on the scene. But Miers had not finished with Navarin. He had spotted a merchant ship in the harbour and fired another torpedo, which exploded on rocks before reaching the target. Christmas Day was spent at sea, with *Torbay* returning to Alexandria on 27 December.

Raw was sympathetic about the difficulty in sinking Italian destroyers. 'A small, fast, shallow draught ship like the average Italian destroyer is probably the most difficult target a submarine will meet,' he noted. 'This fact was appreciated and accepted when submarines were ordered to attack destroyers in view of their use by the enemy for ferrying stores to Libyan ports.'

Summing up the patrol, he said: 'It is characterised by the determination and unremitting offensive spirit which has always imbued the officers and ship's company of HMS *Torbay*, under the able command of Commander Miers, and comes at the end of a year of highly successful operations against the enemy.'

Another special operation was lined up for *Torbay* when she sailed out for her ninth patrol on 8 January 1942.[6] On board were a group of British soldiers, including two officers, and four Greeks who were to be landed at a beach near Triaklisia in southern Crete, with a large quantity of stores. The submarine arrived off the coast on 10 January, but bad weather prevented a landing for two days. There were two folbots. One reached the beach but was damaged, and the other was wrecked as it tried to cast off from *Torbay*. Miers was not impressed and had plenty to say about folbot 'specialists' and their operations when he returned to Alexandria. The submarine was also carrying an inflatable rubber boat, 10ft long and 5ft wide, which had been nicknamed *Mauretania* after the 31,938-ton Cunard liner. *Mauretania* had originally belonged to the Germans and was seized when the enemy tried to land a group from a U-boat near Alexandria. Miers was further exasperated when he learned that the boat could not be used because it had a leak. The crew then discovered that the only compartment large enough to lay out *Mauretania* to carry out a repair was the control room – with the periscopes raised. Miers took *Torbay* out to sea and the repair was done at 90ft. The next night three crewmen took *Mauretania*, loaded with stores, to the beach, returning with an unwelcome visitor, an Austrian who had deserted from the German army. Miers viewed deserters as 'especially despicable'.

The Austrian, who did not understand English, was questioned by a German-speaking crewman and yielded some intelligence. Miers gave the job of guarding the prisoner to the folboters who were back on board and was annoyed to find later that the Austrian was at one end of the submarine giving German lessons. 'I concluded that my orders had not been interpreted in the way I should have wished, but I was not going to allow the treatment of one enemy private soldier to distract me from the problems of patrol off an enemy base and therefore took no disciplinary action,' he said.

Miers soon had plenty to distract him – once again there were reports that the Italian battle fleet was at sea. *Torbay* was ordered to join other submarines in the Gulf of Taranto. On the afternoon of 22 January, three cruisers and six destroyers were spotted. Because of their speed Miers could not get close, so at a range of about 8,000 yards six torpedoes were fired. Two explosions were heard but they were probably torpedoes colliding.

Torbay returned to Alexandria on 31 January, and Raw commented: 'The patrol was carried out with the customary spirit and determination which characterises all operations undertaken by Commander Miers, whose sole ambition is to get at the enemy on every occasion.'[7]

Miers was still fuming about folbot operations and quickly produced a lengthy report, which went to Raw. He was scathing.[8]

'It has been considered desirable to make this report in view of the number and importance of the operations carried out and the degree of jeopardy in which the submarine is placed during the conduct of them,' he wrote. 'Under such circumstances it is contended that no amount of trouble is too great to ensure that the operation concerned will be carried out with safety and success, and indeed no stone is left unturned in HMS *Torbay* to secure this end, but the same unfortunately cannot be said of the responsible military personnel.'

Miers complained that shortly before the soldiers were due to land at the beach near Trianklisia they had difficulty assembling their folbots. Transverse frames could not be fitted in one folbot because holes in the gunwales were in the wrong place and new ones had to be drilled. Longitudinal frames in the second folbot were too long and three were broken trying to fit them. The senior NCO, a Sergeant Mayland, admitted he had never seen the boats rigged before.

Miers pointed out that it would sensible to try out boats in the sea before an operation. 'These boats had never been in the water,' he said.

It was not an isolated case. Months earlier it had been left to Chapman to come up with a better type of screw for securing the frames of the folbots. 'Both he and I have pointed it out to the OC Folbot Section on several occasions, yet nothing has been done to fit the boats supplied with the modified screws although, on joining, every folbotist has requested the first lieutenant to procure them for his boat before leaving harbour.'

Torbay's engineer officer had also been involved, coming up with ways to strengthen the frames, which could not stand up to winter weather. 'Determined that this lack of administrative interest should not prejudice the success of these operations, I have long ago made it plain that I hold my first lieutenant and engineer officer jointly responsible for ensuring that these modifications are made to all boats before sailing,' said Miers. On the last operation, however, Chapman had been too busy to supervise the preliminary assembly of the folbots.

It also emerged that two of the commandos had never taken part in a folbot operation. Miers commented: 'It is realised that everyone has to make a beginning but I am most averse to war operations being in the nature of experiments and consider that one at least of the folbotists should have had previous experience.'

On the first day of the patrol Sergeant Mayland had complained of a leg ulcer and refused to help with any duties in the submarine, even after one of the petty officers was injured. 'It has never been the practice in *Torbay* for folbotists to spend three weeks on board in idleness,' said Miers. 'The conduct of the second folbotist, Lance Corporal Pomford, was even less satisfactory, for although he is undoubtedly keen he is stupid, impulsive and not therefore the reliable type required for hazardous operations when his judgement has to be trusted.

'These two had literally not the slightest idea how to handle their craft alongside in the swell, both of them insisting on holding on to the fore planes when caught by the swell instead of casting loose. Sergeant Mayland "would not be told" and in consequence his boat was smashed up while his passenger was embarking. Lance Corporal Pomford smashed his in the surf on the beach and to what extent it was his own fault can only be guessed.

'An inexcusable failing was that neither folbotist had any idea of Morse code. Seeing that their lives and ours might be dependent on a knowledge of Morse, it is amazing that they should make no effort, when in harbour, to learn it and I confirmed from them that neither had even considered doing so. This again seems to be a gross reflection on those directly responsible for their training.'

Miers made several training recommendations, adding: 'It is appreciated that the majority of the folbotist personnel are keen and try to be efficient, and the purpose of this report is not to belittle their efforts. But the fact remains that war is a serious business and one is loath to be bound by a system whereby the conduct of vital operations, for which one is entirely responsible and to achieve success in which the submarine crew go to the fullest limits of endurance and courage, are dependent on personnel over whose training or discipline one can exercise no control. The least that one would expect of a folbotist would be that he should examine his own boat before it was embarked and yet even this lies outside the province of the commanding officer.'

He summed up: 'Perhaps the root of the matter really lies in the fact that the submarine crew goes to war in deadly earnest whereas the commando personnel are apt to regard it as a sporting adventure, in which the element of danger is the main attraction.'

Mayland and Pomford never boarded *Torbay* again. And Miers was not involved in any further commando operations.

Had submarines become too valuable for 'adventures' by special forces? Miers may have been responsible for a reappraisal. Submarines continued to be used for certain operations, but surface vessels were the preferred option. In September 1941 Admiral Cunningham had told the Admiralty that submarines were 'worth their weight in gold'. The boats from the 1st Flotilla and the 10th Flotilla, operating from Malta, inflicted heavy losses on enemy shipping, with devastating consequences for supply lines.[9]

Jeremy Nash recalled: 'I do remember that Tony and, I expect, Sammy Raw were pretty fed up that their submarines should be taken off vital anti-shipping patrols for quite a long time in order to take part in a pretty dicey special operation. However, there were many occasions both in the Med and the Far East where minor landings took place pretty economically in submarine time – I took part in one in Greece – where useful results were achieved and where agents could not be got there in any other way.'[10]

Cunningham certainly had his reservations about commando operations. On the failure to hold the small Dodecanese island of Castelorizzo in February 1941, he wrote to the First Sea Lord: 'These commandos we have out here are on a tommy-gun and knuckle-duster basis, and apparently can't defend themselves if seriously attacked.'[11]

Chapter 12

THE VICTORIA CROSS

In February 1942 Miers was about to fulfil the second part of the prophecy made by Alexander Wallace, his tutor at Wellington College. Nine years earlier, he had faced a court martial, and *Torbay*'s tenth patrol would see him win the Victoria Cross. His famous anger helped him to gain Britain's highest award for gallantry. Wallace, of course, had expected him to do one or the other, not both.[1] It has been said that Miers told a wardroom shortly after the outbreak of war that he would get a VC – a boast that was unlikely to have gone down well with fellow officers.[2]

Torbay left Alexandria for her tenth patrol on 20 February, with orders to destroy enemy ships bound for North Africa, Greece or Crete. The order of importance of targets was spelled out: battleships, cruisers, tankers and other merchant ships. Submarines were always regarded as valuable targets. Raw would describe this mission as 'one of the most remarkable patrols that has yet been carried out'.[3]

Torbay arrived in her first patrol area between the Greek islands of Lefkas and Cephalonia on 22 February. The submarine was tossed around by bad weather, with heavy seas, squalls and low visibility. Five days later, in the early hours, the first targets were spotted, a tanker zig-zagging towards *Torbay* with an escorting destroyer. Conditions were still poor, and Miers dived, planning to let the ships pass and then to attack the tanker. When *Torbay* surfaced she was too close to the target and dropped astern. One torpedo was fired as the crew struggled to keep the submarine steady in the swell, but it missed by about 5 yards. The destroyer spotted *Torbay* and Miers gave the order to dive again. He was the last one to drop down from the conning tower but he could not close the hatch. He just had time to reach the control room, slamming the second, lower hatch shut as the conning tower flooded with some five tons of water. The klaxon short-circuited and continued to blare until someone pulled out the right fuse. The destroyer dropped 11 depth charges, several of them exploding close by. It had been a lucky escape.

According to Chapman, Miers blamed the engineer officer, Tono Kidd, and poor maintenance for the problem with the hatch. When the submarine surfaced and water was drained from the conning tower, the real reason emerged. At night on the surface Miers would often be on the bridge so that he could take action quickly. He took a pillow to help him snatch some rest when it was possible. It was the pillow that had jammed the hatch open. Chapman said that Miers offered 'a handsome apology'. In his patrol report, the captain pointed out the difficulty with the hatch and owned up to the mistake with the pillow.[4] Raw, in his report to the commander-in-chief, generously did not mention the pillow that had come close to sinking *Torbay*.[5] It ended up as a family souvenir.

Later on 27 February three small ships were seen. One was sunk by gunfire, and *Torbay* chased a coaster, which found the safety of shore batteries. The submarine was forced to dive because of accurate fire. Over the next few days the weather failed to improve. *Torbay* was depth charged by a destroyer but escaped unscathed.

She was not so fortunate on 3 March, when Miers encountered another destroyer and decided to attack. The weather had improved and the warship was only doing about 12 knots on a steady course. Miers set his torpedoes to run at 6ft, allowing for the shallow draught of Italian destroyers, which were difficult targets, as he knew already.

Raw later delivered a rebuke, commenting: 'This proved a rash venture as the destroyer either saw or gained contact with *Torbay* at short range, for she turned towards her at about 800 yards forcing the submarine deep. The destroyer passed overhead and a pattern [of depth charges] was dropped at that moment. An appalling series of detonations followed, shaking and lifting *Torbay* bodily about 5ft. The decision to attack the destroyer was wrong and unjustifiable and not in any way in accordance with the object laid down in *Torbay*'s orders.'

The submarine shook off her pursuer three and a half hours after sighting her. Miers moved northwards to the area around the island of Paxos. Early on 4 March two merchant ships escorted by a destroyer and a plane were seen and *Torbay* gave chase, eventually losing them in the darkness. Miers set course for the Corfu Channel and just over an hour later a 'magnificent' convoy of four large troopships was spotted, along with three destroyers and two aircraft. But the targets were 11,000 yards away.

'I was already very broad on the bow and the chances of a successful attack were forlorn,' Miers noted. 'However, the convoy was closed at full speed for 55 minutes before it was decided that the range was too great for a shot to be worthwhile even at the rear ship.' The troopships were identified as *Liguria*, 15,400 tons, *Romolo*, 9,800 tons, *Tevere*, 8,400 tons and *Galileo*, 8,000 tons.

Miers was extremely annoyed: 'The disappointing part of it all was that the selected patrol position could not have been bettered to intercept this convoy, the attack upon which was frustrated entirely through the abortive pursuit of the earlier small convoy. Such, however, appear to be the fortunes of war.

'It was nevertheless unthinkable to abandon the offensive on such valuable ships without the utmost endeavour having been made and consideration was therefore immediately given as to the best course to pursue.' Pursue was the right word.

Raw observed: 'Knowing Commander Miers well as I do, it is quite clear to me that he was extremely angry with himself, quite unjustifiably, for not having been in position to torpedo the troopship convoy, especially when he had carefully selected a most excellent patrol point for just such a purpose. Such a situation invariably arouses Commander Miers's "worst instincts" and determines him to retrieve what he considers to be an error.'

Miers faced a double dilemma. The submarine's battery needed charging, and he did not know where the ships were heading. The enemy had several choices. The convoy was going towards the southern end of the Corfu Channel, 30 miles long, with the island on one side and parts of the Greek and Albanian mainland on the other. But it could still turn away and head for the open sea. If the ships entered the channel, would they pass straight through or stop at Corfu Roads, an anchorage off Corfu harbour, say to pick up fuel? Miers reasoned that they would spend the night there. If so, they would have to be attacked before leaving.

'The next problem was how to achieve such a task without unduly hazarding the submarine,' said Miers. 'Had the battery not been well down it might have been possible to have made the approach before dark and escaped on the surface by night. Or, if weather conditions had been favourable, the best method would probably have been to withdraw to the westward until the battery was charged and then approach at high speed shortly before dawn, using the motors in the particularly narrow part of the route.

'But, with a clear sky and the full moon rising only three-quarters of an hour after dusk and not setting until after sunrise, this was plainly out of the question. It was therefore decided to follow the convoy at slow speed submerged during the day and to make the passage of the narrow south channel before moonrise.'

Miers considered finding a secluded spot in the channel several miles from Corfu Roads to charge the battery, but was worried that the ships might slip away to the northern entrance without being seen. *Torbay* would have to find a place opposite the harbour using the mainland as cover. Miers hoped he would be able to pick out targets in the moonlight using the periscope. If he could not, the attack would have to be left until dawn. There was an added worry – the likelihood of surface and air patrols.

Shortly after midnight on 5 March, as the battery was being charged, a patrol vessel approached from the harbour and *Torbay* dived to periscope depth. The moon was right overhead and it was feared that the submarine had been spotted. The vessel, however, carried on southwards and disappeared from view. *Torbay*, remaining submerged, closed towards Corfu Roads. At 0217 a motor launch was seen and it stopped about a mile away. Soon afterwards Miers realised that he would have to make the attack in daylight. Ships could not be picked out because of the dark shadow of Corfu town – except one, a destroyer, which was almost rammed.

'The rest of the night was a fairly harassing experience, endeavouring to remain in position for the attack at dawn and at the same time being continually on the lookout to avoid being rammed by the trawlers and motor launches which were on patrol outside the harbour,' said Miers.

At 0640 he was moving in to attack when, suddenly, he had to turn away to avoid a patrol vessel travelling at speed from the south. This delay meant the attack would have to be made in broad daylight, with the sea glassy calm. Then came a sickening discovery – the convoy was not at the anchorage and had obviously passed through the channel without stopping. There was some consolation, however. Two supply ships of about 8,000 tons and 5,000 tons were moored there, along with a destroyer. The merchant ships were 'perfect targets'.

At 0731 two torpedoes were fired at the smaller ship. Less than two minutes later two further torpedoes were aimed at the other merchant ship. The destroyer was also targeted with two torpedoes but these were set to run too deep and passed under her. As Miers realised the mistake, he heard an explosion – the first ship had been hit. A second explosion claimed the larger ship.

Torbay went deep, turned and headed at speed for the entrance to the south channel, a nerve-racking 20 miles away. At 0800 she came to periscope depth to see small craft searching the area where the torpedoes had been fired. The boats were joined by a destroyer and a plane, and 40 depth charges were dropped, none of them exploding near the submarine. The enemy probably thought the submarine would head for the channel's northern entrance, which was much closer than the southern exit. Miers knew, however, that the northern entrance was much narrower and likely to be mined.

Over the next hour and a half four patrol vessels were picked up coming from the south and going in the direction of the harbour. One passed close down the port side. As *Torbay* neared the southern entrance, a large schooner acting as a boom defence vessel was seen pulling an obstruction across. According to Leading Stoker Philip Le Gros, Miers was in swashbuckling mood, ready to board the schooner and fight it out: 'Commander Miers said, "We will each take a hatchet and guns and we will take their boom defence vessel out of the way and we will get out". He was all prepared to do this. Anyway, we didn't have to.'[6]

The schooner was moving slowly, hampered by a lack of wind, and the submarine slipped through before the channel could be blocked. By noon *Torbay* was back in the open sea, 17 hours after entering the channel, the lion's den. Miers had pulled off an incredible feat.

But *Torbay*'s crew barely had time to breathe a sigh of relief. Forty minutes after their escape another large schooner was sighted, heading for Paxos island, and Miers changed course to head off the boat, ordering a gun engagement. Just before surfacing, a patrolling aircraft was seen and the attack was called off. That evening *Torbay* surfaced and charged her almost exhausted battery.

By the next day even Miers was feeling jaded. He received orders that his patrol was being extended by five days and that he should go immediately to the Gulf of Taranto to intercept a convoy escorted by three cruisers and several destroyers. 'This was not received with quite the customary enthusiasm as most of the officers, including myself, and key ratings were feeling somewhat exhausted as a result of the exertions of the past few days,' he remarked.

The convoy was not found and eventually *Torbay* set course for Alexandria. There was one, last drama. Early on 12 March it was found impossible to shut the door of one of the port torpedo tubes. A check revealed that a torpedo was jammed, sticking out of the tube. Was it armed? Standing on a saddle tank [a main ballast tank attached to the pressure hull] and up to his waist in water, the engineer officer, Kidd, with the help of another crewman, tried to ease the torpedo out using a crowbar. Their struggle came to nothing. It was decided to try to fire the torpedo with a blast of air after diving astern, and this was successful at the second attempt.

Torbay arrived back at her base after a patrol lasting 26 days. Strangely, Miers did not feel elation. He was disappointed. That day, 18 March, he sent a message to Raw: 'A disappointing patrol in which I messed up the attack on the tanker reported by aircraft and was outranged by a convoy of four large troopships. There was also a succession of five most unpleasant episodes and an epidemic of mild influenza to finish off with but tails are well up. One merchant ship of 1,000 tons sunk by gunfire and perhaps two good sized ones by torpedo in Corfu harbour. It is good to be back.'

Raw had not heard the full story of the Corfu raid, and it is not clear if he spoke to Miers immediately, but that day he also sent a surprising message, to the commander-in-chief: 'It is evident that Commander Miers is in need of a rest. Propose that he should be relieved by Lieutenant Rankin, for one or two patrols, before next patrol. Propose also that Commander Miers should be appointed to the Military Staff Course at Haifa commencing 30th March and ending 23rd May, being relieved if necessary to enable him to take *Torbay* home to refit in mid-June.'

On 25 March Raw sent a message to several submarines: 'Prime Minister sends his compliments to officers and ships companies of *Turbulent*, *Torbay*, *Unbeaten*, *Upholder*, *Sokol* [Polish] and *P34* on "admirable success" of recent patrols.'

The captain of the 1st Submarine Flotilla sent his full report on *Torbay*'s tenth patrol to the commander-in-chief on 2 April. While Miers was still out on patrol, Cunningham had learned that he was leaving the Mediterranean. The First Sea Lord, Admiral of the Fleet Sir Dudley Pound, had decided to send him to Washington DC to serve on the Combined Chiefs of Staff committee. It was not an appointment Cunningham wanted but he did not question it, although he left at a time of great difficulty and with deep regret. In his memoirs, he told of Miers's Corfu exploits, noting: 'He finally withdrew after spending 17 hours inside an enemy harbour in the most dangerous and difficult conditions. I am glad to say his bravery was recognised by the award of the Victoria Cross.'[7]

Admiral Sir Henry Pridham Wippell took over as acting commander-in-chief. He, too, was impressed by Miers's bravery. On 12 May he issued an Order of the Day giving a detailed account of *Torbay*'s action in the Corfu Roads, calling it 'one of the most remarkable submarine patrols carried out during this war'. The order ended: 'The outstanding features of this remarkable exploit are firstly the cool judgement and courage displayed by the commanding officer in entering an enemy harbour under most difficult circumstances, having decided that the possibility of successful attack justified the very considerable risk to his ship, and, secondly, the steadfastness and efficiency of his ship's company, without which the operation could not have been attempted.'[8]

In a newspaper interview in 1945, Leslie Philips, who ended the war as a petty officer, winning the Distinguished Service Medal and Bar, gave a rather breathless – and not entirely accurate – account of *Torbay*'s long wait and the attack, or perhaps the reporter's imagination got carried away: 'We rose to the surface in full moonlight to recharge our batteries. Small enemy boats passed to and fro, bringing back Nazi troops from the night's shore leave. We saw people quite clearly silhouetted in the glare of car headlamps and pushbike lights. We watched ships unloading, and heard enemy voices shouting. How the devil they never saw 260 yards [feet!] of submarine lying around is a miracle. Sheer audacity got away with it.

'Early morning we attacked. I was torpedo attack helmsman. We fired four fish in one swinging turn, scoring hits on two large troopships, which went up in vivid sheets of flame. I swung the *Torbay* completely round, and we closed hell for leather towards the fast-shutting boom gates, almost ramming the boom ship. We got through by a split second.

'Hell broke loose. The enemy were blowing up their own harbour, knowing we should be there. Forty depth charges caused titanic upheaval amongst their ships, but we were outside, steaming down the 22-mile long strait. We outmanoeuvred air attacks and anti-sub ships, and dived right under the sub-detector beam at the entrance to the strait.'[9]

Philips, who got a job in a factory at Barking, Essex, after being demobbed, added: 'I've had a wonderful war, loads of action, and a skipper I'd follow anywhere.' He died of cancer about 30 years later. Miers and Chapman went out in a launch from Portsmouth, passing the submarine base HMS *Dolphin*, and scattered his ashes off Spithead.[10]

The *London Gazette* of 7 July announced the award of the Victoria Cross to Miers: 'For valour in command of HM Submarine *Torbay* in a daring and successful raid on shipping in a defended enemy harbour, planned with full knowledge of the great hazards to be expected during seventeen hours in waters closely patrolled by the enemy. On arriving in the harbour he had to charge his batteries lying on the surface in full moonlight, under the guns of the enemy. As he could not see his target he waited several hours and attacked in full daylight in a glassy calm. When he had fired his torpedoes he was heavily counter-attacked and had to withdraw through a long channel with anti-submarine craft all around and continuous air patrols overhead.'

The *London Gazette* listed other awards for the crew of *Torbay*, covering the patrols from December 1941 to March 1942. Kidd received the Distinguished Service Order and Chapman a Bar to his Distinguished Service Cross. Eight men were given the Distinguished Service Medal or Bars and twelve were Mentioned in Despatches.

The award of the Victoria Cross to Miers did not surprise Chapman. In 1984 he commented: 'Commander Miers was given a VC, and the Corfu business was taken as "the occasion". But in truth they had already given him two DSOs, and the VC was really in recognition of his determined pursuit of the enemy over a prolonged period. I recall, in broad daylight, chasing an enemy ship along the north coast of Crete, having to dive to avoid aircraft about every 20 minutes, until I began to worry more about the high pressure air supply than the battery.

'It was no good bellyaching to Commander Miers about the possible difficulties. He came from the same mould as my Lord Hawke at Quiberon Bay. When the sailing master pointed out that he was venturing his fleet on a lee shore in an impending gale, my lord said, quite kindly, "You are right to point out the dangers. Now lay me alongside the enemy".'[11]

How well did Chapman know his naval history? One of the British ships that helped to defeat the French fleet off the coast of France at the Battle of Quiberon Bay in 1759 was called *Torbay*.

Chapter 13

THE LAST PATROL

Captain Sammy Raw's suggestion that Miers should have a rest and go to the military staff course at Haifa would not have gone done well with *Torbay*'s captain. After all the action he had seen, a staff course probably was the last thing he wanted. Miers is certain to have argued that he should stay with his men and *Torbay*, which he knew was due for a refit back in Britain. He won the day. It was agreed that he would take the submarine out on her 11th and final patrol of the commission before returning home.

Raw, not Miers, was the man on the move. During *Torbay*'s 11th patrol Miers's champion was replaced as Captain (S) 1st Submarine Flotilla by Captain Philip Ruck-Keene, known as Ruckers. Raw, who had served in the First World War, was appointed Chief Staff Officer (Operations) to the Flag Officer Submarines in London. He was awarded the CBE for his services in Alexandria. Raw went on to become Flag Officer Submarines in 1950, receiving a knighthood four years later, shortly before his retirement in the rank of vice-admiral. He had been in the navy for 40 years.

Torbay set off from Alexandria on 2 April 1942, with orders to patrol the western approaches of the Gulf of Patras, Navarin, Argostoli, Levkas and the entrance to the Adriatic, including the northern and southern approaches to Corfu, where she had so recently diced with danger.[1] Six days later she had her first contact with the enemy. Air activity had been increasing all day. During the afternoon the sound of a possible target was picked up and the submarine went to periscope depth in the calm sea, but she was spotted because two bombs exploded soon afterwards. *Torbay*, undamaged, went deep and changed course. Surface craft joined the hunt for her, dropping only two depth charges.

The next day, 9 April, the submarine was near Antipaxos island, not far from the southern entrance of the Corfu Channel, when she saw two minesweepers, as well as a trawler and two other vessels inshore, which were probably armed. Despite the numbers and the threat of air attack, Miers decided to attack the minesweepers with gunfire. *Torbay* was brought to the surface and engaged the rear minesweeper. The other target turned and opened fire with a machine gun. But when the rear minesweeper started taking punishment she retreated to shallow water, as did the other vessels. The first target sank. By this time *Torbay* was close inshore and Miers, fearing an air attack, decided to return to deeper water.

In the early hours of the following day *Torbay* was on patrol off the northern approaches to Corfu, but was forced to dive twice to avoid destroyers. On 11 April numerous small craft were seen hugging the Albanian coast and in late afternoon two suitable targets were found, large auxiliary schooners. *Torbay* surfaced and opened fire on one of the schooners with her 4in gun, scoring numerous hits. The vessel was well handled and even tried to ram the submarine, which eliminated the danger by scoring a direct hit on the steering. The schooner, flying the Italian flag and apparently laden with food, eventually sank. The other vessel found the safety of shallow water.

Bigger prey seemed to be on offer when *Torbay* learned that an escorted convoy was heading to Libya from the Adriatic. She moved to intercept it but later received a message ordering her to the Gulf of Taranto, where a three-day search for targets proved fruitless. Only a folbot specialist, a Corporal Booth, was able to relieve the frustration, firing his Bren gun at a barrage balloon, which was billowing in the sea after breaking away from its moorings. He made sure that the balloon could not be used again.

Torbay returned to her original patrol area and early on 18 April she sighted a destroyer rendezvousing with a merchant ship of about 5,000 tons. The sea was rough and, with the merchant ship 3,000 yards away, Miers knew that he needed to find a better position for a torpedo attack. He gave chase. Half an hour later he realised he was losing the race. The target had increased the range to 4,000 yards. With time running out and more in hope than expectation, Miers gave the order to fire two torpedoes. He scored two hits – 'a remarkably fine shot'. *Torbay* went to periscope depth and he saw that the ship had vanished. The destroyer was picking up survivors. There was a brief but ineffective counter attack.

Early the next day, while *Torbay* was on the surface, transmissions from a destroyer were heard. The enemy were sighted ten minutes later and the submarine dived. Soon afterwards the asdic operator reported hearing a second vessel. Miers allowed the destroyer to cross his bows and then surfaced to find two large merchant vessels about two to three miles away. Another chase was on but 'much to Miers's annoyance' they remained out of range and the pursuit had to be abandoned.

Miers liked gun actions at close quarters, and *Torbay* had an impressive record dispatching enemy vessels in this way. But the strategy was risky. One hit with a 4in shell on a boat or ship was unlikely to be fatal. A submarine, however, might find herself stranded on the surface after a similar blow, unable to dive. On the morning of 21 April, Miers decided to carry out his most audacious gun action yet, one that could have cost him his submarine. He had spotted a petrol carrier off the north coast of Crete, but this vessel was more than a match for *Torbay* – there was an anti-aircraft gun in the bow, a 4in or 4.7in weapon amidships and a smaller weapon aft. The guns were manned and the German naval flag was flying. This was likely to prove a 'tough customer', and Miers knew that it would be too hazardous to carry out an attack if he did not have the element of surprise. Because the petrol carrier probably had a shallow draught, the use of torpedoes was ruled out.

Torbay broke the surface and Leslie Philips, the sailor who gave the dramatic account of the Corfu attack, was quickly in position at the submarine's 4in gun, acting as gunlayer. Corporal Booth was on the bridge with his Bren gun. The action did not start well. The 4in gun misfired as the enemy changed course and *Torbay* tried to close the range. Then Philips scored a direct hit, blowing the main gun over the side. Booth opened up with the Bren gun, spraying bullets at the bow and aft gun positions. His 'splendid' shooting prevented the men at the bow from opening fire, and the gun crew aft jumped into the sea. According to Chapman, this sight drew 'roars of applause' from the bridge and the 4in gun platform.

Miers changed his mind about using torpedoes and gave the order to fire two. They missed. The 4in gun used 23 rounds, most of them hits. The petrol caught fire and the vessel was soon blazing. The crew abandoned the petrol carrier, which was a total loss. *Torbay* turned away as a coastal battery opened fire, the first shell passing overhead.

Miers praised Philips for his shooting. The sailor had helped to account for 21 enemy vessels in the course of a year. There was also praise for Chapman, who had been in charge of the gun, giving ranges. It was 'the first shoot of his life'. Philips joked after the attack that he had not paid too much attention to Chapman's instructions.

Miers knew he had been lucky. He had shouted to Philips from the bridge: 'If you don't get that gun [the large one amidships] it will get us.' Philips recalled: 'It was an anxious time. I blew the 4.7in gun overboard, and the next rounds set the ship ablaze. The whole thing lasted six minutes. The enemy hunted us for 24 hours.'[2]

Chapman admitted that he had reservations about launching the attack, but he knew it was wiser to keep quiet. Miers was determined to 'go out with a bang', though it is surprising that his superstitious nature did not restrain him. Several submarines were lost on their final patrol, including David Wanklyn's HMS *Upholder*. Booth, whose use of the Bren gun had been critical, reported that the attack was 'not a good idea'.

Miers had carried out a successful attack, but he still needed to escape. Leaving the scene, he dived to avoid a plane, surfacing to periscope depth about two hours later to find two German anti-submarine boats nearby, listening out for *Torbay* in a calm sea. This was a 'somewhat disconcerting' discovery. The submarine had two problems – her battery was low after the earlier fruitless chase of two merchant ships and so, too, was the air supply. For several hours *Torbay* was unable to elude her hunters. Chapman said Miers told him: 'We are in the most desperate danger, you know.' The second in command would reflect: 'Miers had never said that sort of thing before, not even in Corfu Roads. It came to me that Miers was oppressed by the thought that he had taken the pitcher to the well once too often.'[3]

Miers and Chapman discussed the options if they were forced to come to the surface and found the enemy still there. *Torbay* would fight it out with the 4in gun and Booth's Bren gun. 'Admittedly the chances of hitting small, fast targets in the dark with the 4in were remote, but at least we should be able to riddle their upper works with the Bren,' Chapman noted. That evening, at 1950, Miers took another cautious look at periscope depth and was relieved to find that the anti-submarine boats had gone. *Torbay* slipped away from the area.

Raw's replacement, Ruck-Keene, reported: 'The patrol was carried out in the best *Torbay* tradition, all three attacks being well planned and brilliantly executed. It will be remembered that *Torbay* arrived on the station just over a year ago with an almost scratch crew owing to the last minute drafting changes and an immediate operation in the Atlantic. The commanding officer had no executive officer over the age of 21, but in spite of this *Torbay* went from success to success under the bold and determined leadership of Commander A.C.C. Miers DSO, RN. Her record reflects the greatest credit on the commanding officer and the ship's company.'[4]

It was time to go home. Early in May *Torbay* left Alexandria with Miers in command for the last time. There were cheers from crews of submarines and ships as she sailed away. Ruck-Keene had given a brief farewell speech. More submarines than usual were in harbour because the 10th Submarine Flotilla had been forced to leave its base at Malta, which was being pounded daily by the Luftwaffe. Miers was asked to drop off supplies for the island, but he opposed the idea. The approaches to Malta were heavily mined, and he did not believe it was worth taking such a risk with *Torbay*. The submarine HMS *Olympus* had just been lost to a mine after leaving Malta with nearly 100 men on board, including crewmen from other boats who were returning to Britain. Most of the sailors got off *Olympus* before she went down, but only nine survived the 7-mile swim in the cold sea back to the island. One man who reached the shore stood up only to drop dead.

The problem with mines was not restricted to Malta, as Miers knew well. Philip Le Gros, the New Zealander, recalled: 'At that time not many submarines got through the Strait of Sicily because of the minefields and we had to be very, very careful. During the time we went through the minefields we were all given something to do to take our minds off it. They decided they would put a new piston in one of the engines and we had to clean the piston up and get it all ready. I remember Commander Miers saying to the first lieutenant, "If you were laying a minefield you wouldn't lay it where it was covered with [shore] guns, would you? That would be duplicating resources. If we can go close to shore, don't go too shallow, they obviously won't expect us to go there". We got through all right. Previous to us there was poor old *Tetrarch*. She was going to England and then eventually to the States and she got lost in a minefield.'

Torbay stopped off at Gibraltar where there were the twin distractions of drink and women. 'Blokes who were normally quite sane would often do stupid things when they got ashore,' said Le Gros. 'We didn't have a lot of money but as submariners we had more than the sailors on the upper-deck ships, which was two bob a day. Compared to the others we were barons and they didn't like it. Sometimes we would go ashore and we would find ourselves in a fight with sailors from the surface ships. Quite often they would run out of money and they got really fed up. They were worse than someone being locked up. In Gibraltar there was a bust-up with the marines from [the battleships] *Nelson* and *Rodney*, but sailors from *Nelson* came to our assistance fortunately.'[5]

After leaving Gibraltar the crew of *Torbay* had the bizarre experience of flying the Nazi flag. The submarine was on the surface when she came across a Portuguese schooner named *Leopoldina*. Miers did not want to advertise that British submarines were using the route and gave the order to run up the flag. The three-masted schooner of about 600 tons responded by dipping her ensign. 'I kept the Nazi flag flying in order to encourage an unfriendly spirit between our main enemy and a neutral power,' said Miers, who obviously enjoyed the joke.

Shortly after midnight on 5 June he found a fleet of a dozen trawlers and ordered the nearest vessel to stop. The 4in gun was trained on the trawler and the Aldis lamp illuminated Spanish colours. 'Upon which I wished her captain goodnight in Spanish through a megaphone,' said Miers.[6]

The rest of the journey through the Bay of Biscay to the English Channel and then on to Portsmouth was uneventful. Flying the Jolly Roger showing all her victories, *Torbay* passed a cheering crowd along the shore from Southsea to Portsmouth and berthed at Fort Blockhouse, Gosport, where

Miers had done his submarine training 13 years earlier. Perhaps Le Gros paid the ultimate tribute: 'Whatever he had wrong with him, he always got us home.'

Torbay had to go to Devonport for her refit. Lieutenant-Commander Robert 'Rumble' Clutterbuck was appointed her new captain. Miers met Clutterbuck in London and took him for lunch at his club.

'He said he'd fix my transport when I went to Devonport to relieve him in a few days' time,' said Clutterbuck. 'I found a first-class sleeper booked and slept in state while high-ranking officers vainly bribed the attendant in the corridor. When the train came in to Devonport, who should be there, standing great-coated on the platform but the great man himself, though it was six or seven in the morning. He had two stewards to handle my baggage and a service car waiting. No queuing for taxis for me. Crap was very proud of *Torbay* and was determined that I should be too. He took me round all the senior officers in the port in the next few days and each night we had the most hectic round of parties. There was not much time for work. I could take it for granted, of course, that the submarine was OK and that the officers were looking after everything.

'It all ended up when Crap was escorted by his ship's company to the midnight train, while maudlin songs were sung until it pulled out. It was some outfit to take over, and you may be sure that I was proud of it and especially grateful to Crap for his welcome. I know he hated to leave *Torbay* and wanted to do the next commission but he was determined to give me a good start.'[7]

Indeed, Miers was desperate to remain a submarine captain but, approaching his 36th birthday, he knew that the chances were slim. The powers-that-be decided 'very wisely that he was over the hill' as far as submarines were concerned. There was also a strong belief at this time that 'they don't come back a second time'. *Torbay*'s crew during the refit was virtually unchanged but when they learned that the boat was going back to the Mediterranean for her second commission many of the men applied to leave.

One man who stayed was Le Gros, who found Clutterbuck very different from Miers. 'He was a very quiet man, very nicely spoken and he used to say please and thank you. When he went past in the gangway, he always said, "Do you mind if I pass, thank you very much." Whenever there was a depth-charge attack he never got ruffled and he would say to the men with asdic, "I must have a reading on the leading destroyer, it is most disconcerting sitting here like this."

'He must have thought I was going a bit balmy because I used to wear a fez in the engine rooms.'

Chapter 14

NEVER MIND PALACE PROTOCOL

Nearly two months after returning to home waters Miers and his officers found themselves with an important engagement. They were to go to Buckingham Palace to receive their decorations. For Miers it was the Victoria Cross. But he was not happy after learning that his non-commissioned crewmen were due to receive their own awards – the Distinguished Service Medal or Bar – at a lesser ceremony much later. Miers, who had already received his Distinguished Service Order and Bar, was determined to put his sailors first, even if it meant turning palace protocol on its head. The whole point of decorations was to reward good service and raise morale – all the men should attend the same public ceremony, he argued. Told there was no precedent, he asked if King George VI had been consulted.

The naval authorities and the courtiers tried to browbeat Miers into giving way, but he held firm. The King was consulted, and he approved the idea.[1] So, on 28 July 1942, Miers, 3 of his officers and 24 of his sailors went to the palace to receive their awards, one after the other.

Miers had two tickets for guests and, being unmarried, offered them to his brother's wife Honor and their eldest son, Douglas, 9. By this time Ronald Miers was a lieutenant-colonel in command of the 5th Battalion the Queen's Own Cameron Highlanders and on his way to do battle in Egypt. Miers, Honor and Douglas took a taxi to the palace, and Douglas's 5-year-old brother David and a family friend went in another taxi to join a large crowd at the palace railings. Honor and Douglas were shown to their front-row seats in the long gallery where the ceremony was being held, and shortly afterwards a palace official approached, bent down and whispered that the King would like to meet Honor when the investiture ended. 'Imagine it!' she wrote in a long letter about the occasion to her husband the following day.[2] But she was anxious that the King and his officials should be fully aware that she was the wife of Ronald, not Anthony, or Tony as the family always knew him.

The first presentation was made to another Victoria Cross winner, Captain Eric Wilson of the East Surrey Regiment, who had been badly wounded defending his post in Somaliland against enemy attacks that lasted for five days. Such was the intensity of the fighting that the citation originally said he had been killed in action.

Miers appeared before the King 'looking magnificent and most bulldogish'. Honor wrote to her husband: 'Then Tony came and sat behind us and pushed the Victoria Cross into my hand and I nearly cried to have that honour. He was so sweet, and I did long for you to have been there. You would have been proud of Doug. He sat like a ramrod and never moved an inch.'

Miers was followed by his officers, Chapman (Distinguished Service Cross and Bar), Kidd (Distinguished Service Order and DSC) and Verschoyle-Campbell (DSC and Bar), and the rest of the crew. The King spoke to every man. *Torbay* became one of the most decorated boats in the Submarine Service. Miers was generous in recommending awards. It was suggested that one man received the Distinguished Service Medal to cheer him up because his wife and children had been bombed out of their home in an air raid.

After the long investiture Miers, Honor and Douglas went to another room to meet the King, who 'looked so young and seemed far more nervous than any of us'. Douglas gave such an impressive bow that it appeared as if 'he had lived at court all his life'.

Miers's battle with officialdom had paid off. The King told him that it had been a splendid idea to have *Torbay*'s crew all together, and he would try to do it again when a similar situation arose. Honor need not have worried about any misunderstanding over her husband. The King, Colonel of the Camerons, said he had met Ronald at Aldershot recently and knew he was commanding the 5th Battalion. He turned to Douglas, who was wearing a kilt, and asked him what he wanted to be. In a loud, clear voice – his mother had told him not to mumble – he replied: 'A Cameron Highlander, I hope, sir.'

Miers, Honor and Douglas emerged from the palace to find the courtyard bathed in sunshine. They were spotted by David, who ran past a policeman at the main gate to join them, shouting: 'Hello, Uncle Tony! Well done, Uncle Tony!'

Honor wrote: 'The crowd roared with delight. There were hundreds of cameras and there were awfully good photographs of Tony and the boys in the evening papers. As we crushed through the crowd, all the lady reporters were asking Tony if he was married and he said, "Yes, I have been married for 13 years and my wife is the White Ensign". There were roars of approval from the crowd and shouts of "Is she a good wife?" And Tony said, "Absolutely." Amid shouts of laughter and "God bless you, sirs" we got into a taxi.'

They headed to the Connaught Rooms, off Kingsway, where Miers had arranged a lunch for every member of his crew, with families and friends. Admiral Sir Max Horton, Flag Officer Submarines, who would shortly take over as Commander-in-Chief, Western Approaches, masterminding the war against U-boats, made a short speech before saying he had to dash back to work. Captain Sammy Raw, who had recently relinquished command of the 1st Submarine Flotilla at Alexandria, was also there. Miers sat with the backdrop of *Torbay*'s Jolly Roger, a proud man.

One of the guests was the Mayor of Paignton, which had adopted *Torbay* because the resort of that name was under the local council's control. Honor was sitting next to the mayor and during the course of the meal she pointed out that her brother-in-law had arranged the celebration and would have to pay for it out of his own pocket. Perhaps the civic authorities could show their gratitude to the men who had displayed so much courage? As the drinks flowed, the mayor stood up and announced that Paignton would pick up the bill.

Young Douglas did fulfil his wish to join the Queen's Own Cameron Highlanders, following in the footsteps of his great-grandfather, grandfather and father. He joined the regiment as a second lieutenant in 1953 and continued his army career when the Camerons and the Seaforth Highlanders were amalgamated in 1961 to form the Queen's Own Highlanders, rising to the rank of colonel. His brother David was also commissioned into the Camerons – to do his National Service – but he pursued a diplomatic career and had the challenging task of being the ambassador to Lebanon for two years from 1983 at the height of the Beirut troubles. He was knighted in 1985.

Anthony Miers may have been a naval officer, but in 1942 his fighting spirit was well known to the Camerons. That year the regiment's magazine saluted his Victoria Cross, saying it was 'a cause for great satisfaction and pleasure to innumerable Camerons, as this very gallant sailor is intimately connected with the regiment' through his father and brother. The magazine recalled that Miers had spent part of his leave with the 1st Battalion on exercises in Yorkshire in 1938, and 'whilst taking part in night operations led a platoon of Camerons during a dawn attack with such dash and energy that the surprised "enemy" from an English unit were routed from their last strong point'.[3]

The day after receiving his Victoria Cross at the palace Miers was again in fighting mood, but this time the press were the enemy. Journalists were obviously keen to promote their latest hero. The *Daily Mirror*, for example, told of 'the daring submarine ace who fights with a prayer book at his elbow'. But Miers did not like the publicity.[4]

The Ministry of Information had arranged a press conference in London for him. Miers, who was normally obsessed with keeping appointments on time, turned up half an hour late, failed to apologise – to the surprise of his audience – and launched an immediate attack: 'Although I am sure no naval officer enjoys publicity, yet I feel certain that most of us in submarines fully understand the importance of the press and the good effect on recruiting and public morale that well conducted propaganda undoubtedly has.

'But in spite of this there are many of us who do everything we can to avoid giving an interview or having anything whatever to do with the gentlemen of the press. As recently as yesterday I myself was extremely discourteous to a group of press photographers who had gate-crashed my private lunch party with my men, and I ordered them to leave at once.

'The reason for this is that we do not feel the press plays fair with us, and are so afraid of the appalling bunkum – I use the word deliberately – that may appear in the papers afterwards except in an organised interview such as this. For instance, I have seen reports in the papers of talks with commanding officers of submarines whose words, modestly and even reluctantly dragged out of them, have been converted into a paragraph of boasting and self-praise.'

Miers gave an example of a 'cock and bull' story published by a daily paper a few days earlier. A submarine was lying doomed on the ocean floor but miraculously rose to the surface after someone accidentally kicked an instrument as the crew were singing the hymn *Abide With Me*. 'Such a ridiculous and impossible story is, to say the least of it, utterly distasteful to the men of the Submarine Service,' he said.

But journalists had committed a worse crime. They had described Miers, a proud Scot, as . . . Irish. He was supposed to have a home in Waterford. Miers fumed: 'Neither I nor my father, who was killed in command of a Highland regiment in the last war, has ever, to the best of my knowledge, set foot in Ireland. This sort of inaccurate statement antagonises me.' When it was pointed out that the Admiralty had supplied the information that he came from Waterford, he remained silent. In fact, it was his sister's husband who was the Waterford man.

Journalists who had been 'frankly delighted to have the opportunity of meeting him' were not so keen towards the end of the press conference: 'It was significant of the astonishment with which this attack on newspapers was received that after Commander Miers had gone on to give some glimpses of life in the *Torbay* no one was interested enough to ask him for any more. Most of them thought it a pity that so gallant an officer should go out of his way to indulge in such hasty strictures.'

Miers had obviously touched a nerve because the report continued: 'All responsible journalists sympathise with his protest against garbled interviews alleged. But is it not reasonable that people who boast aggressively about never having anything to do with the press may be helping to bring about the very inaccuracies they deplore by the pride they apparently take in refusing all information? Or that such an attitude of disdainful aloofness is in marked contrast with that of the commander's superiors when they are dealing with the press?

'As to his ordering press photographers away from his party, one might observe that this horror of being photographed was certainly not in evidence at Buckingham Palace, when he said, "I will never forget the great honour His Majesty paid us in allowing us to be photographed together in the quadrangle".' (5)

Perhaps Miers had a point about accuracy. Throughout the lengthy report of the press conference he was referred to as 'Meirs'. Or maybe that was down to the Admiralty again.

The following month, August, saw Miers with a lot of paperwork to get through after a spell in hospital – he was suffering badly from varicose veins. On his 'termination of appointment' as *Torbay*'s captain, he had to write confidential reports on his officers. With marks out of ten, he scored his first lieutenant, Chapman, as follows: professional ability, seven; personal qualities, nine; intellectual ability, eight; and administrative ability, seven. Chapman scored only six for leadership, although he was recommended for submarine command.

Miers wrote of him: 'An extremely shrewd and capable young officer with excellent judgement and a first-class brain. His personal qualities are of the very highest order and it would be hard to find a more trustworthy, loyal or reliable officer. During 15 months of arduous operations he has shown an ability to adapt himself to the many moods of his commanding officer and has been infinitely patient in the face of criticism and reproof even when it was undeserved; conversely he has shown strength of purpose and never hesitated to put forward his view or to insist on having his own way when it seemed necessary to do so. His sound advice and sincere friendship have been of inestimable value to me in times of stress and I find it hard to confine my praise to reasonable proportions when I look back upon the brilliantly successful way in which he overcame difficulties with which such a young officer can seldom have been faced.'[6]

Chapman, it will be remembered, was catapulted into the key position of first lieutenant soon after *Torbay*, manned by a scratch crew, sailed from Scotland for war. He left behind a young wife seriously ill in hospital with diphtheria. Miers admitted he was 'a somewhat intolerant commanding officer, 14 years his senior, who had no submarine war experience'.

He continued: 'Lieutenant Chapman undoubtedly made many mistakes but his courage and determination never deserted him and within a month of arriving at Alexandria his unceasing labours for the welfare of his men and the discipline of the ship had brought their reward and there was not to be found a more spirited or contented ship's company.'

Miers, of course, could be brutally honest. Chapman, slight of build, lacked an outstanding personality, did not have a natural gift for leadership and showed no proficiency at games, other than boxing. But he was 'highly critical of inefficiency in others'. That was a huge plus.

Like Miers, Chapman was leaving *Torbay* for good, and he was suffering health problems brought on by the demands of life in the submarine. Chapman had a mouth full of rotten teeth, and only the 'immensely strong' Verschoyle-Campbell was 'in good nick'. Chapman went to the depot ship HMS *Forth* on the Holy Loch as a 'spare officer'. He successfully completed 'perisher', the submarine command course, and in 1943 took HMS *Upstart* to Malta and later La Maddalena, Sardinia, winning the DSO for nine patrols. In 1952 he reverted to general service and seven years later went to naval intelligence where he spent the last ten years of his career, retiring as a commander. He was given the OBE in 1963 for his intelligence work.[7]

In September 1993, shortly before his death at the age of 73, Chapman gave an interview in which he spoke about Miers and *Torbay*. 'Miers was very demanding,' he said. 'He wanted your best and if he thought you were not giving of your best he would let you know all about it, but at the same time loyalty to his people was absolute. He would deal with his people and nobody else would be allowed to touch them. Now loyalty going that way inspires loyalty going the other way.

'There were many furious rows but friendship lasted until death us temporarily parted. He couldn't bear inefficiency. He didn't mind people making mistakes because we all do that. What he couldn't stand was sloppiness.'

Asked if there were many 'sloppy people' among *Torbay*'s crew, he replied: 'I think they were soon cured of the habit.'

There was a long pause after he was questioned about the attitude towards the enemy. 'I don't think there was a personal hatred,' he said. 'We just deplored Hitler and all his works, and if they were part of his works then they were due to be clobbered. I was perhaps more anti-Hitler than many. I didn't have any German at that time. I only had Latin, French and Greek, but in case I was captured I got a German-speaking friend to teach me how to say, "Herr Hitler is a devil".'

Chapman spoke of being depth charged: 'I suppose we had over 200 [depth charges] scattered around over various patrols. One particular time during the tenth patrol was very nastily close indeed. It did us a lot of damage.

'Lights go out, needles jump. There is, of course, a horrible noise, swishing of water that's being impelled by the explosion, swishing against the hull, and if you're on your feet and the boat seems all right then it's over until the next dose comes a few minutes later.'

With typical understatement, he added: 'It's a bit like putting your head under the bed clothes. There's not a lot you can do.'

On escaping from submarine hunters: 'Well, I followed much the same pattern that I had learned from Miers. I would stay fairly shallow so I could get up quickly to see what was happening on the surface and I didn't use high speed except in the immediate aftermath of a depth-charge attack. As soon as the first charge went off, without any word from me, the boys from the motor room would go full speed or half speed for about half a minute, just giving us a little nudge in the right direction. With the reverberations of the depth charges and the wake of the attacking ship or ships, short bursts of speed like that were most unlikely to be noticed.'[8]

Chapman was not asked about Miers's physical outbursts, but in private correspondence he did refer to two members of the crew being hit, Ronald Drake, a teenage midshipman, and Kidd the engineer officer. He wrote: 'Midshipman Drake did at least one patrol in *Torbay*. On the way home, to Alexandria, he was on watch alone on the surface at night (quite illegal for a midshipman but I did the same many years later). He heard an aircraft, assumed it must be one of ours, pulled a recognition flare and stayed on the surface. Then he made the mistake of telling the captain what he had done. So he got a black eye. I recall Tono Kidd, near the panel, saying, "Do not hit me, sir". This was more than once.

'I would wish this sort of thing to be erased in the mists of time. *Torbay* had jobs to do and did them rather better than might be expected. Let that be Tony Miers's requiem, and not the internal squabbles.'[9]

Drake must have done something to impress Miers because he was Mentioned in Despatches.

Chapman himself ended up with a black eye in *Torbay* on at least one occasion. Despite thumping Kidd, Miers had a lot of admiration for him, too, or at least that is what he conveyed in his confidential report about the 26-year-old engineer officer: 'From the day that this officer joined HMS *Torbay*, his first submarine, at short notice at Gibraltar in April 1941, his quick grasp of submarine essentials, his capable brain and his sound judgement have been most impressive. It was soon evident that in him the submarine branch has been fortunate to acquire a born engineer who will make a great name for himself and prove his worth later on when called upon to take a hand in the improvement of design in new construction hull and machinery.

'This personal opinion has been confirmed by a succession of flotilla engineer officers and senior engineers of the 1st Submarine Flotilla, all of whom have had nothing but praise for Lieutenant Kidd. The contentment and excellent organisation of his department, no less than the expert care and attention which he has lavished on the machinery of the submarine, have proved his sterling worth, but the qualities of this officer by no means end there.'

Miers pointed out that he was a splendid seaman who could handle a boat under sail as well as any executive officer, and singled out the part he had played when *Torbay* rescued the large number of Allied soldiers from Crete.

He scored Kidd as follows: professional ability, eight; personal qualities, seven; intellectual ability, eight; administrative ability, eight; and leadership, eight. Overall, he was marked higher than Chapman.[10]

In April 1943 Kidd went to a new T class submarine, HMS *Tantalus*, under the command of Hugh Mackenzie, who had been with Miers in

Rainbow on the China Station before the war. *Tantalus* saw action in the Far East and survived the war.

If Miers had a favourite it must have been Verschoyle-Campbell, who was only 20 when he joined *Torbay* in March 1941. By August 1942 he had replaced Chapman as first lieutenant. He was the highest scoring officer: professional ability, nine; personal qualities, seven; intellectual ability, nine; administrative ability, eight; and leadership, eight.

Miers wrote of him: 'I think it probable that Lieutenant Verschoyle-Campbell is the most outstanding officer of his age in the service, and I am confident that he would fill any post with distinction. He is fortunate in possessing intellectual and technical gifts of a very high order and combines these with a strong dynamic personality, exceptionally good power of command and a charm of manner which is the heritage of the Irishman.

'He is extremely high spirited and knows his own capabilities, so I have kept a tight rein on him for his own good lest, through lack of modesty, he might jeopardise a career which is full of promise.

'He has been successively navigating officer, armament officer and first lieutenant of HMS *Torbay*, and in all my submarine experience I have never known an abler nor more gifted young officer. He is a stern disciplinarian and does not suffer fools gladly but has been a patient and successful teacher.

'He has greatly distinguished himself in charge of boarding and demolition parties, has been absolutely fearless in the face of danger and shown himself a real leader of men in action and moreover I have come to rely as much on his judgement as on my own.'

Miers noted that his young officer had been married for nearly two years, which 'has had a most beneficial effect on his character'. There was just one problem with Lieutenant Verschoyle-Campbell – 'he does not play games well'.[11]

Nevertheless Miers recommended him for accelerated promotion. After passing the 'perisher' course in 1943 Verschoyle-Campbell was given command of HMS *Sealion*, one of the youngest Royal Navy officers to captain a submarine. Towards the end of that year he took the new S class boat HMS *Stonehenge* to Ceylon. On 25 February 1944 Stonehenge sailed from Trincomalee on her third Far East patrol, covering the northern part of the Malacca Strait. She was never seen again and is believed to have hit a mine, with the loss of her entire crew, including a certain Sub-Lieutenant Drake, who had received a black eye in *Torbay*. He was only 20.

Another officer Miers passed judgement on was 22-year-old Sub-Lieutenant Antony Melville-Ross, who only went on the last two patrols of *Torbay's* first commission, originally as fourth hand. He remained with the submarine when Clutterbuck took command, eventually becoming first lieutenant. Miers wrote: 'An able officer with a high sense of duty, sound technical knowledge and plenty of common sense. Not very clever and somewhat slow in the uptake but once he understands a thing he remembers it. Extremely loyal and hard working, very keen on his job, he has a fine physique, stout heart and, for a young officer, a very calm and well-ordered mind.'[12]

Melville-Ross got the lowest score, collecting only five for intellectual ability, but he went on to command several submarines, including two former U-boats. In 1944 he won the Distinguished Service Cross. After the war he was involved in intelligence work, but in 1952 he was forced to leave the navy because of ill health. The lieutenant-commander had a bad case of the 'twitches', a legacy of his life in submarines. He got a job with BP and was involved in oil exploration in North America and South America. Like many travellers, he bought thrillers at airports. He came to the conclusion that he could write better books, basing them on his own experiences but changing names and places to circumvent the Official Secrets Act. He found an audience for a trilogy of spy thrillers (*Blindfold, Two Faces Of Nemesis* and *Tightrope*) and submarine adventures. Melville-Ross was even compared to Ian Fleming, but he found it difficult to promote himself. The 'twitches' made him too nervous to give television interviews or to speak in public. To earn money during his transition from oil company employee to author he made use of the 'fine physique' that Miers had noted, working as a male model to push sales of clothes and whisky. He died in 1993, a few months before Chapman, aged 72.[13]

In August 1942 Miers wrote a report about another member of his crew, but it took on a completely different dimension. For some time he had been troubled by the case of Acting Leading Stoker Leslie Jones.

On the evening of 20 May 1941, after her first patrol, *Torbay* was in dry dock at Alexandria so that an extensive programme of work could be carried out over 48 hours. The duty officer – probably Verschoyle-Campbell – left the submarine and went to an adjoining vessel, leaving the wine cupboard in the wardroom open. Jones, who had been at the bottom of the dock working hard in the heat, passed through the wardroom and 'succumbed to the temptation'. He took several bottles and shared them with his mess mates.

Miers, of course, exploded when he discovered what had happened. No doubt he remembered the disappearance of his special cake in Chatham dockyard. He wrote in his report: 'I was absolutely determined to make an example of this case in order that there should be no doubt in the minds of the crew that . . . strict discipline was to be maintained.'

Miers went to Captain Sammy Raw, who told him to calm down. In Raw's view, Miers was exaggerating the seriousness of the offence. *Torbay*'s captain would have none of it, and insisted that Raw support his move to punish Jones severely. The Captain (S) of the 1st Submarine Flotilla reluctantly issued a warrant, depriving Jones of two good conduct badges, with a consequent loss of pay. In those dark days of 1941, when Britain was facing possible defeat, the case of the thirsty stoker even went to Admiral Cunningham, who approved the warrant.

Miers had been under 'great stress' with his scratch crew, and was experiencing 'the very gravest misgivings as to the outcome of our pending operational patrols'. But in time he knew he had been unfair. The aim of the report he was writing more than a year after the event was to change Jones's character assessment for 1941 from 'good' to 'very good' and to restore his good conduct badges and lost pay.

Miers admitted: 'I have realised for many months since that time that Stoker Jones had never intended to steal and had acted upon the foolish impulse to have a drink when he was tired and hot (we had not even any white uniform on board and were wearing blues in the Mediterranean summer), and I very much regret that I allowed my anger and obstinacy to get the better of my good judgement on this occasion.

'The conduct of Stoker Jones since that date has been so outstanding that "very good" is an understatement. His efficiency has been so exceptional that he has been the most trusted stoker in the submarine and has been invariably called upon to perform the duties of any leading stoker who might happen to be sick at any time.

'His "part of ship" (the after compartment) has exceeded in cleanliness any that I have seen in peace time and he has not only committed no misdemeanour of any sort, but has shown the utmost loyalty to myself and the other officers, and has been a magnificent influence among his mess mates throughout the commission.

'There is no doubt in my mind that it is the sterling character of this man, and not in any way the effect of the punishment awarded, that has brought about this state of affairs, and I am sure that if I had known him then as I do now, I would not have pressed for so heavy a penalty to be imposed.'

Jones had been awarded the Distinguished Service Medal, and when *Torbay* returned to Britain he went on a course for leading stokers in Devonport at the earliest opportunity, despite being owed leave, 'in order that he might be sure of rejoining before the completion of the submarine's refit'.[14]

With some irony, Miers said he was sure that Raw would support his appeal, which 'is put forward solely in the interests of the service that justice may be done to an outstanding individual'.

This time the matter went as high as their lordships at the Admiralty. Miers won a partial victory. They decided that Jones's character assessment could be rated 'very good' – but he only got one of his good conduct badges back.

Jones was the only sailor to be punished formally. Miers personally dealt with the other wine drinkers, and the duty officer was 'severely reprimanded by myself for his carelessness and folly'. One can only speculate as to how the angry captain meted out those punishments.

Chapter 15

THE LARGEST SHIP IN THE WORLD

The Admiralty could almost guarantee to throw up surprises, and Miers's next task was unexpected. After the confines of *Torbay*, waging war in the Mediterranean, he found himself on board the largest ship in the world, the 83,673-ton *Queen Elizabeth*, doing an 'office job'. There was one similarity. Despite her size, living conditions in the Cunard liner could be as cramped as his submarine. The *Queen Elizabeth* and her sister ship, the *Queen Mary*, were dashing back and forth across the Atlantic as troopships, often carrying 15,000 men on each voyage, against their normal complement of around 2,280 passengers. Miers was in charge of a naval draft of 2,015 officers and men, sailing from Scotland to Canada, and the trip appears to have caused him more frustration than the missed opportunities when he was hunting the enemy. On the shortcomings he encountered during the voyage in December 1942, he produced probably his longest report, which was addressed to the head of the Admiralty delegation in Washington.[1] He made 38 detailed points, some of which were unintentionally funny, along with recommendations 'for the improvement of conditions in future voyages'.

The first problem when he embarked on 1 December was his cabin, which he found with difficulty. It was supposed to double as his office, but it did not have a desk, table or drawers, not even a chair. 'There was absolutely no possibility whatever of using such a place as the naval headquarters,' he complained.

He had joined the ship the evening before his draft was due to arrive but he could not get any information about the accommodation. The only person he found from the sea transport section, which was supposed to be organising everything, was a lieutenant in the Royal Naval Reserve – which would not have impressed him from the outset. This unfortunate man was 'undertaking his duties for the first time and was quite unable to help me'.

The following morning, after considerable difficulty, Miers managed to get an office, with a safe and telephone, and a cabin, which he decided to share with his assistant, a lieutenant who never turned up. To add to his annoyance he discovered that there had been a conference involving representatives of the army and the air force to arrange offices and accommodation for their drafts, but the officer in charge of the sea transport section, a Captain Fulford, another man of the Royal Naval Reserve, had not bothered to invite him. Miers was soon involved in a row with Fulford: 'He did everything possible to frustrate me, and even went so far as to suggest that I should resign my appointment if I could not carry out my duties without an office.' It was the Royal Air Force that came to the rescue of the submarine hero. A wing commander and the liner's staff captain helped Miers to sort things out.

But he was less than impressed when he found that civilians had managed to snap up the best cabins. He singled out Paul Gore-Booth, second secretary at the British Embassy in Washington, who was travelling with his wife in the equivalent rank of rear-admiral. Gore-Booth, only 32, had secured a better cabin than a vice-admiral and a genuine rear-admiral who were obliged to share accommodation. Miers subsequently discovered that the diplomat was only entitled to the equivalent and relatively humble rank of lieutenant-commander. Absurdly, 14 other civilians were also travelling as 'rear-admirals'. But perhaps Gore-Booth was right to have illusions of grandeur. He was later knighted and given a peerage.

Confusion reigned when the naval draft came on board. Miers's small staff of petty officers and ratings was soon tied up running the mess hall. 'This left me single-handed to organise the working parties for the kitchens, officers' baggage, clearing up decks etc and to arrange for nearly 400 gunnery ratings to man the ship's armament before sailing,' he pointed out.

'Hundreds of the men and many of the officers were making their first sea passage, were quite unknown to me and to one another, and were

ABOVE LEFT: *The Cameron Highlander. Miers's father, Captain Douglas Miers, who was killed in action in 1914, six weeks after the outbreak of the First World War.*

ABOVE RIGHT: *Best friend. Miers's brother, Colonel Ronald Miers, who was awarded the Distinguished Service Order after leading the 5th Camerons at El Alamein in 1942.*

BELOW: *The brothers. Anthony Miers, right, with the older Ronald leaving the officers' quarters at Edinburgh Castle in 1914 shortly before their father went to war.*

ABOVE: *First submarine. Miers was posted to M2, which was originally armed with a 12in gun from an old battleship. Critics pointed out that the gun could have done more damage to the submarine than to an enemy target.*
(Royal Navy Submarine Museum)

BELOW: *Submersible aircraft carrier. If the idea of putting a 12in gun on a submarine seemed bizarre, M2 underwent an even stranger transformation in 1927. The gun was replaced by a watertight hangar to accommodate a two-seater biplane with folding wings and floats. In 1932 M2 sank with the loss of her entire crew after the hangar doors were opened too soon as she rose to the surface.*
(Royal Navy Submarine Museum)

ABOVE: *China Station. Miers joined the submarine Rainbow as first lieutenant in Hong Kong in 1933.* (Royal Navy Submarine Museum)

BELOW: *Armed. Rainbow crewmen loading a torpedo at Wei-hai-wei.* (Royal Navy Submarine Museum)

ABOVE: *Smart turnout. Members of Rainbow's crew on board the depot ship Medway. Miers is in the middle row, second from left.*
(Royal Navy Submarine Museum)

BELOW: *First command. When Miers became captain of L54 in 1936, he made sure it was more of the same – the efficiency of the submarine and sport.*
(Royal Navy Submarine Museum)

ABOVE: *Torbay. The submarine that would make Miers's name. On taking command in 1940, he was pleased to find that she had the pennant number 79 – a poignant reminder of his father's regiment, the old 79th Highlanders.* (Royal Navy Submarine Museum)

BELOW: *Nerve centre. The control room of a T class submarine – Tribune.* (Royal Navy Submarine Museum)

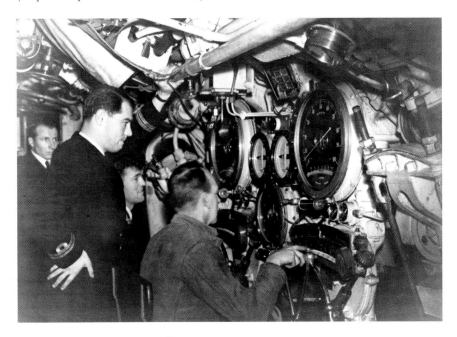

ABOVE: *Another victory. Beneath Torbay's 4in gun crewmen paint further success on their Jolly Roger. The bars and stars represent attacks on enemy shipping, including the destruction of the Italian submarine Jantina in 1941. The ram symbolises the ramming of a vessel.* (Royal Navy Submarine Museum)

Italian supply ship sunk by gunfire from H. M.S. TORBAY in March, 1942 outside Corfu.

ABOVE: *Target. An Italian supply ship being destroyed by Torbay's gunfire off Corfu in March 1942.* (Royal Navy Submarine Museum)

BELOW: *Mother ship. Medway with the 1st Submarine Flotilla at Alexandria in 1942.* (Royal Navy Submarine Museum)

ABOVE LEFT: *Admiral Sir Andrew Cunningham, Commander-in-Chief Mediterranean, in 1940.* (Imperial War Museum)

ABOVE RIGHT: *Admiral Sir Max Horton, Flag Officer Submarines 1940–2.* (Imperial War Museum)

BELOW LEFT: *Captain 'Sammy' Raw, who commanded the 1st Submarine Flotilla at Alexandria 1940–2.* (Royal Navy Submarine Museum)

BELOW RIGHT: *Lieutenant-Colonel Geoffrey Keyes, who led the raid that aimed to capture or kill Rommel in 1941.* (Imperial War Museum)

ABOVE: *I'm proud of you. On the casing of Torbay at Alexandria in May 1942 Admiral Sir Henry Pridham Wippell, who took over from Admiral Cunningham as Commander-in-Chief Mediterranean, says farewell to the crew before they head home after the submarine's first commission.*
(Royal Navy Submarine Museum)

BELOW: *My officers. Miers presents his lieutenants to Admiral Pridham Wippell.*
(Royal Navy Submarine Museum)

ABOVE: *Mission accomplished. Torbay leaving Alexandria for home in May 1942 after her first commission. She still needed to avoid air and sea attacks – and mines.* (Royal Navy Submarine Museum)

BELOW: *Heroes all. Miers with his lieutenants, left to right, Chapman, Kidd and Verschoyle-Campbell, at their Buckingham Palace investiture in July 1942. Verschoyle-Campbell was in command of the submarine Stonehenge when she vanished off the west coast of Malaya with all hands in 1944. He was 23.* (Royal Navy Submarine Museum)

Above: *Honoured. A smiling Miers leaves Buckingham Palace after the investiture with his nephews Douglas and David, who would both go on to join the Cameron Highlanders. In his left hand Miers holds the case containing his Victoria Cross.*

ABOVE: *Wedding day. Miers with his teenage bride Pat in Perth, Western Australia, in January 1945.*

ABOVE: *Victory. Sailors and marines wave souvenir swords and flags as they celebrate the Japanese surrender of Hong Kong in August 1945.* (Imperial War Museum)

BELOW: *Royal visitors. Miers, Captain of the 1st Submarine Flotilla in Malta, 1950–2, welcomes Princess Elizabeth and Princess Margaret on board the depot ship Forth.*

ABOVE: *Flag officer. The highly decorated rear-admiral.*

ABOVE: *Proud father. Miers at a ceremony in Portsmouth in August 1979 when his son John, a lieutenant-commander, was presented with the Queen's Commendation for Brave Conduct by Admiral Sir James Eberle.*
(The News Portsmouth)

BELOW: *Frail. Miers at the launch of the nuclear submarine Torbay at Barrow-in-Furness on 8 March 1985. He died on 30 June.*

'Of course, there's no suggestion he ate them.'

ABOVE: *Launched. The nuclear Torbay, the fifth vessel to bear the name, slides down the slipway.*

INSET: *A cartoonist's view of Ludovic Kennedy's war criminal allegation.*
(The Spectator, 11 February 1989)

spread out all over the largest ship in the world. They arrived on board independently, immediately set off to locate their quarters, get their dinners and were then anxious to look around the ship.

'The only way to contact officers for the many duties required of them was to send chits to their cabins in the early morning, as once they had left their cabins it was a matter of extreme difficulty to trace them since there was no table plan in the salon and many officers were found to be of altogether different rank than that shown on the nominal list.

'There was no broadcasting system available and no space in the ship reserved or large enough to fall in such a large draft, and moreover, the meal hours in sessions occupied a large portion of normal working hours. The only practical method of passing orders and information was found to be verbally in the mess hall at breakfast.

'Even when detailed, many men genuinely lost their way in such a large ship. Others probably used this as an excuse, and a large number were seasick.'

When the ship was under way, more problems emerged: 'Great difficulty was experienced in the prevention of smoking between decks and the proper maintenance of the blackout. I was asked to assume responsibility for this latter requirement and it took over 30 officers all their time to achieve the requisite degree of efficiency. Cases occurred of civilians of high standing being loath to allow their portholes to be shut, of others, including ship's officers, opening their portholes before it was light and of senior military officers resenting being prevented from smoking and striking matches on the upper deck after dark. There appeared to be little realisation of the suicidal nature of such actions which was especially perturbing to me as a submarine officer.'

Miers had a point. Hitler had offered the equivalent of $250,000 to any U-boat commander who could sink the *Queen Elizabeth* or the *Queen Mary*.[2] Only the previous month, the Germans were claiming that *U-704* had torpedoed the *Queen Elizabeth*. But the grey-painted liners, the Grey Ghosts, used their speed – around 28 knots – to escape danger throughout the war.

It was just as well. The Royal Navy was responsible for boat drill on the voyage, and Miers quickly came to the conclusion that the arrangements were inadequate for such a large number of men. If the ship, sailing without escorts, had been torpedoed and sunk, a high death toll would have been inevitable. 'This is presumably realised and acceptable,' he said. With 15,000 men on board, there were only enough lifeboats and life rafts for an estimated 8,000, a gamble of staggering proportions.

However, Miers had a more immediate problem – form filling. His office was required to supply plenty of completed forms, mostly lists of the men on board, despite the commander's belief that a lot of the work appeared to be unnecessary. Shortly before sailing Miers managed to get hold of an Empire typewriter, no mean feat, but then he saw the catch – there was no ribbon. He put in an urgent request for a 1in ribbon to the naval base at Greenock – and received a half-inch ribbon in return. He was left to beg the use of typewriters from the RAF and the American army, which also had a draft on the ship. 'I cannot feel that it is in keeping with the dignity of the Royal Navy that the officer commanding a large and important draft should be thus forced to beg typewriters from other services,' he observed. At least he did not have to spend much time on the forms, recruiting a small team of navy writers and a lieutenant who replaced his missing assistant.

He faced a 'further example of unnecessary work' involving sailors from the naval unit at Calshot air station near Southampton. These men boarded the ship with little gear and they had not been paid for three weeks. They were not impressed when a large group of Italian prisoners of war were given a special advance so that they could buy their daily ration of cigarettes. Miers made sure that each Calshot man received 10s, opening a contingency account and preparing emergency paylists.

If Miers thought things would get easier when the ship docked at Halifax on 9 December, he was mistaken. He was told that the prisoners of war would be the first to disembark, and this would take about three hours from 1700. It took much longer. All Royal Navy officers were due to leave next, but they were kept waiting until 0015. Most of them, including Vice-Admiral Reginald Holt, spent four hours in a queue 'as no one would admit the delay was not a temporary one'. They faced a further hour's wait for a train, which did not leave until 0600.

There was also a problem with baggage: 'Lack of information as to the order of disembarkation had made it impossible to make any previous provision for the baggage to be unloaded in the right order, and it therefore came out in roughly the reverse order to that in which it had been embarked.

'There was an appalling scene of confusion on the jetty where nearly 800 officers and men, to say nothing of the other services, were searching for their gear from among thousands of identical bags and hammocks, with many of them not yet unloaded – and this in a temperature of about zero degrees.'

Baggage had been carefully labelled 'cabin', 'wanted on voyage' or 'not wanted on voyage'. It all ended up being dumped in the holds.

Twenty-one troop trains had been ordered but it was discovered that there were not enough tracks for them. Some men got so fed up waiting that they went back on the ship and missed their trains. 'The maintenance of order and good discipline under such deplorable conditions taxed the powers of leadership of the officers concerned to the utmost,' Miers admitted. He was not pleased when railway officials insisted that he check a large number of tickets, which turned out to be a complete waste of time.

During the voyage he had been entrusted with a large quantity of sports gear, including 50 pairs of gym shoes. For probably the only time in his life Miers could not work up any enthusiasm for games, nor could anyone else: 'This was an added embarrassment as they all had to be carefully checked and rechecked and returned at the end of the voyage, during which there had been no demand for any of the gear. For such a short passage it is considered that the expense and trouble involved is not justified in time of war, especially when the ship is so overcrowded as to make playing of games impractical.'

As the sailors were finally leaving in trains from Halifax in the early hours of that cold December day, the ship's armament officer went over to Miers and complained that various items of warm clothing were missing. It was too late to do anything about it. 'I considered that he was entirely to blame in this matter since the ratings detailed for gunnery duties had been placed under his orders and he had issued the gear to them. They should not have been discharged from these duties until their warm clothing had been collected from them.'

Concluding his report, Miers wrote: 'It is fully realised that in time of war, when so many men are being moved so rapidly across the ocean, a number of inconveniences will be caused and should be accepted by the personnel concerned; but discussion with officers who have been placed in charge of similar drafts has shown me that the conditions experienced on this occasion are not exceptional, and I have therefore considered it to be my duty to represent the whole circumstances fully, together with suggestions for improvement.'

Miers crossed from Canada to the United States, making his way to the British Embassy in Washington, where he launched into his report. In January 1943 he wrote to his sister-in-law Honor, mentioning the voyage: 'The crossing was the world's worst possible performance and I was absolutely worn out with exertion. Nothing whatever was organised and I had a fearful time. Hence on arrival I not only was not in good fettle for my job but had to make out a long and very rude report about the whole affair which took me until Christmas Eve.'[3]

There were compensations. Miers had lunch with the ambassador, Lord Halifax, who had been the Foreign Secretary at the outbreak of war, and his wife. He found them charming. On Christmas Eve there was dinner with Sir Ronald Campbell, who held the office of Envoy Extraordinary and Minister Plenipotentiary to Washington. Miers had known of Sir Ronald when he occupied a similar post in Belgrade and 'one of our submarines had such excitement in trying to rescue him from Yugoslavia'.

Even grander entertainment awaited Miers on Christmas Day. He was taken to the White House and met President Franklin D. Roosevelt and his wife Eleanor. He had a 'most enjoyable time' playing with their grandchildren and opening presents. Miers received gifts – a box of chocolates, a box of cigarettes and a pair of gloves. 'It was entirely a family affair and I was taken by an officer who knows them well and they knew nothing about me,' he said. Miers stayed for dinner and watched a film in the president's private cinema, leaving after midnight.

After the Christmas holiday he made brief visits to New York, Philadelphia and the submarine headquarters at New London, Connecticut, but he was 'not in good form and felt very ill'. Miers was due to take up a post as the Royal Navy's submarine liaison officer at Pearl Harbor, headquarters of the US Pacific fleet, under the command of the formidable Admiral Chester W. Nimitz, and headed west, reaching San Francisco. His health was not improving: 'I felt a permanent nausea and could eat nothing. When I arrived I saw a very good Scots doctor who refused to allow me to go on and put me to bed with jaundice. I went all yellow and felt frightfully weak. He said I had got run down with overwork and picked up the germ as a result. I had no energy to write and didn't want to see anyone or do anything. However, I seem to have recovered in absolute record time and in ten days I was convalescing and going about. He then made me spend a week there and I got extraordinarily fit as a result of the wonderful weather and sunshine. I played good men's doubles at tennis three days running at the end – for the first time since leaving staff college. Also, everyone was extremely kind to me.'[4]

Miers was convalescing in Beverly Hills. There were parties every night and, although married to the White Ensign, he 'lost his heart' to three girls in six days, which he admitted was very complicated. The first two girls had 'loads and loads and loads' of money, but the third was poor – and she won the day. He was impressed that she offered to drive him from Beverly Hills to Los Angeles in her gas-guzzling car, when petrol was rationed to four gallons a month.

The war was forgotten temporarily: 'California is the most wonderful place you can imagine. The weather is absolutely prefect, which is why the films are all made there as it would cost thousands to have large casts hanging about for the rain to stop. I saw several studios, Walt Disney, Metro Goldwyn Mayer, Fox and Columbia. It was remarkable to see the vast acreage that they take up. You drive about and see London streets, Paris streets, Dartmoor, eastern towns, villages, even the Houses of Parliament – all ready when required.

'Los Angeles is the biggest or second biggest city in space in the world and literally covers miles and miles. They have practically no buses and everyone has a car – except me!'[5]

Food rationing was one sign of war. Meat could only be obtained in the best restaurants. Like Britain, sugar, butter, eggs, tea and coffee were available in small quantities. Service in hotels was a problem because so many people were taking better-paid jobs in factories helping the war effort.

Miers observed: 'I am told that in the middle of the country there is not the same spirit, but certainly all the people I have met – a great many – have absolutely no idea of isolation and are very angry that they have had to fight two wars so close together, and are very determined to get together and see there is no third. There is a great feeling of admiration for all that is going on in Britain, and as I say they could not possibly be kinder to me.

'A lot of things are surprising. The film star Errol Flynn is being tried for rape here and it is just like a musical comedy or farce [the actor, known to have a voracious sexual appetite, was cleared of raping two teenage girls]. On the other hand there have been two major strikes since I have been here in which the federal authorities and the strikers could not see eye to eye, and in each case the president has ended it by ordering the men to return to work – as commander-in-chief of the armed forces – and they have at once obeyed. Most remarkable.'

Miers got off lightly with American reporters, unlike their more tenacious British counterparts. They immediately agreed to his silence. 'I have merely said I am not allowed to say anything and the press have been magnificent – they accepted it at once.'

He had started his letter to Honor enquiring about his brother Ronald's adventures in the Middle East. Ron or Ronnie, as he was known, had also distinguished himself. The *London Gazette* of 31 December 1942 listed an award of the Distinguished Service Order for his command of the 5th Camerons at the Battle of El Alamein. 'I do hope he is continuing to do great things and to enjoy good health and strength,' said Miers. 'They really have done magnificently.'

The 5th Camerons took considerable casualties in North Africa – 564, about 70 per cent. After battling against the Afrika Korps, Lieutenant-Colonel Miers was appointed to the Middle East Training Centre. The regimental history paid this tribute to him: 'Colonel Ronnie had commanded the battalion for eighteen months, during which he had completed the training so ably begun by Colonel Cattanach in the early days, mobilised the battalion and brought it overseas, and finally fought it with outstanding success from El Alamein to Tunisia. He will be remembered by all members of the battalion who served with him as an outstanding personality to whom the 5th Camerons rightly meant everything. His leadership in battle was as forceful as his battle-planning was clear and efficient, which both contributed in no small way to the high state of morale existing throughout the battalion during his period of command. He set the battalion a high standard of administration as well as fighting efficiency, both of which were to be maintained by his successors until the end of the war.'[6]

The importance of efficiency was not lost on both brothers.

Chapter 16

NOT AGGRESSIVE ENOUGH

For nearly eight months Miers kept himself busy as the submarine liaison officer at Pearl Harbor, getting to know the US Pacific fleet and sending reports to his superiors. It was more 'office work', but he found entertainment. Miers enjoyed challenging the American officers to wrestling matches, apparently beating them all until he came across one Ben Jarvis, executive officer of the submarine USS *Sailfish*. Jarvis just happened to be a talented wrestler and footballer.

Miers, of course, was itching to get back to submarines and see action. By September 1943 he had persuaded the Americans to let him go on one of their submarine patrols. The boat chosen was the USS *Cabrilla* (SS-288), a 1,526-ton Balao class submarine named after a fish found in the Mediterranean and the waters off California. *Cabrilla* had been built at the Portsmouth navy yard in Kittery, Maine, and launched on Christmas Eve 1942 as Miers was being entertained at the British Embassy in Washington. She was commissioned in June 1943 under the command of Lieutenant-Commander Douglas Hammond – whom Miers would later virtually accuse of cowardice.

Cabrilla arrived at Pearl Harbor on 30 August and sailed on her first war patrol on 12 September. The voyage, in the western Pacific, would last 56 days, considerably longer than a *Torbay* patrol. For the first time, Miers was going to war against the Japanese, not the Germans and Italians.

Early on 16 September *Cabrilla* arrived at Midway submarine base and topped up with more than 13,000 gallons of fuel. With the ability to sail nearly 10,000 miles without refuelling, she headed for her patrol area later that day. Miers was surprised to discover that the executive officer was the only officer who took any interest in navigation. *Cabrilla*'s position would be put on the chart only once every 24 hours, unless in sight of land, which Miers found very unsatisfactory, though 'there is no need to suppose that this is typical of all US submarines'. There were frequent drills, and in the afternoon those officers not on watch would play poker in the wardroom.

The Americans were in the fortunate position of being able to break Japanese naval codes, and on 21 September *Cabrilla* was ordered to increase speed to intercept a force of four ships, including two aircraft carriers, sailing to Japan from the island of Truk (now known as Chuuk), an important enemy base in the south-west Pacific. The intelligence report received by the submarine gave four possible locations for the force, with dates and times, and *Cabrilla* reached one of them at 0700 on 24 September. Twenty-seven minutes later Miers, who was taking turns at the periscope with the captain and the executive officer, spotted the mast of a destroyer or light cruiser. The ship was heading straight for them. Battle stations were ordered. The carriers were soon in sight.

Miers must have been electrified. These were dream targets. And the weather was perfect for a submarine attack, rough enough to hide the boat from any patrolling aircraft and to cover torpedo tracks, but unlikely to affect the running of the fish. Each carrier was around 17,500 tons. In line ahead, they were not even taking the basic precaution of zig-zagging. There was just the one destroyer escort, with no air patrol.

'Such a gift from the gods, hard though it is to believe when judged by our standards, is fairly typical of the Japanese who send these carriers heavily escorted and loaded with aircraft for Truk and leave them to make the return passage empty and with only a token escort for the major part of the journey across the open sea,' Miers noted.[1]

There was only one drawback. The force was travelling at speed, about 20 knots, and Hammond manoeuvred the submarine too late to attack the leading carrier. He was saved by his executive officer, Lieutenant-Commander Charles Henderson, who insisted on firing at the second carrier using a 60-degree track while the gyro angle was reasonably small. At 0801 six torpedoes were sent at eight-second intervals when the second carrier was about 900 yards away. At 0803 a very loud explosion was heard. Miers knew it was a torpedo hit, but Hammond believed his submarine was being bombed and took her down 400ft, rigging for depth charging. Ten minutes later three depth-charge explosions were heard, followed by two similar patterns, but they were far away. According to Miers, they were 'easily the least noisy that I have ever experienced – we had evidently got clean away with our attack'. At 0900, as the submarine continued to creep away, 'pinging' from the destroyer was picked up.

'From a plot of bearings of the pinging it was evident that a north and south patrol was being maintained in the vicinity of the attack and when this was continued for more than two hours after the attack had taken place it seemed almost certain that the carrier must be lying damaged and that the destroyer was patrolling around her,' said Miers. 'It is not normal for Japanese escorts to search for more than about an hour and in this particular case, if the attack had failed, it would be ludicrous for the only escort to have been left behind in the open sea with no chance of regaining her station and thereby leaving such important ships completely unguarded. It was not, however, until after the pinging had ceased that anything other than evasive action was contemplated by the CO.'

At 1037 Hammond, experiencing his first combat mission, ordered the reloading of the bow tubes, ignoring a suggestion from Henderson, who had been on five successful patrols, that they should see what was happening on the surface. It took 32 minutes to carry out the reloading and then the after tubes were checked. One torpedo got stuck half way out of its tube, and this problem took some time to sort out because of 'the lack of leadership of the young officer in charge and an inexperienced torpedo rating'. Finally, at 1315, Hammond went to periscope depth, took a look round – and decided to open the submarine for ventilation.

Miers was getting increasingly frustrated: 'His lack of aggressive spirit cannot be better emphasised than by the fact that it was not until nine minutes later, at 1324, that the executive officer, who had relieved the CO at the periscope, sighted the carrier stopped and down by the stern in plain view about 6 miles to the north-east with the destroyer circling round her. My impatience can be imagined when no change of course was ordered for a further 20 minutes in order to ensure the submarine being thoroughly ventilated and the crew recuperated.'

At 1345 Hammond changed course to approach the carrier at dead slow speed, but about half an hour later a seaplane was spotted and *Cabrilla* dived again. It was not until 1535 – eight hours after first sighting the enemy – that Hammond returned to periscope depth. Twenty minutes later, despite all the time wasting, the American captain was still being offered the chance to pull off a spectacular success – the first carrier had returned to the scene and was taking the crippled vessel in tow. 'Great activity' could be seen on deck in both ships. But the seaplane was spotted again and *Cabrilla* dived.

At 1647 the submarine returned to periscope depth, but the carriers had disappeared over the horizon, helped by the cover of rain clouds. *Cabrilla* went on a course the enemy was thought to have taken, abandoning the hunt at 2215 – after nearly 15 frustrating hours. Miers was still fuming: 'At no time since firing had the slightest risk been taken despite the immense importance of the target. Even now, when it was virtually certain that the two aircraft carriers were undertaking the 550-mile journey to Tokyo at slow speed, it was thought best to leave their destruction to one submarine known to be off Tokyo, who might have no torpedoes left or be frustrated by an eventual increase of screen, even if she succeeded in making contact (which she did not).

'Conduct such as this could not be justified by inexperience since the executive officer, while displaying perfect loyalty, was plainly in favour of more energetic action, and I myself had done what I could within the limits of having to be most careful not to injure the reputation of the CO in the eyes of his crew. I tried to realise this was not typical of the average US submarine CO. But the fact is that the enemy had considered it a practical venture to order one valuable carrier back almost unprotected to rescue a second one already badly damaged in an area where a US submarine was known to be at hand. Obviously such an insult could only be the result of previous experience justifying such a procedure, and it is to be hoped that in future similar circumstances submarines will reap the benefit of any further rash enterprises that episodes such as this may encourage the enemy to undertake.'

There was more friction when Miers prepared a report on the day's activities for naval headquarters at Pearl Harbor. It obviously pointed to the shortcomings of the attack because Hammond objected to its contents. A 'vague and ambiguous' report was sent instead. A baffled Pearl Harbor asked for clarification and radio silence had to be broken unnecessarily. Hammond's report stated that a second attack was prevented by 'escort and air activity'. As Miers would point out, this amounted to one very inefficient destroyer and a seaplane spotted twice.

Even the crew had grown weary at the lack of action. There was excitement when the torpedoes were fired at the second carrier. After *Cabrilla* dived, silent running was ordered, making conditions almost unbearably hot. But morale was high. Miers toured various compartments and men asked 'How many hits?' and 'Did we sink her?' Later, however, 'no one appeared in the least interested' in the fate of the enemy. Those off duty were concentrating on games of cribbage and draughts.

When Miers produced reports of *Torbay*'s patrols, they were full of detail. He was not afraid to show emotion, his frustration when he missed chances to get at the enemy. He pushed *Torbay* to the limit, sometimes beyond, and he gave his men credit when they deserved it. Hammond was the opposite. His report for *Cabrilla*'s first patrol was matter of fact and, despite running to 32 pages, he did not name anyone, not even Miers, the man who had spotted his dream targets.[2] It is worth giving Hammond's version of the moment when one of his torpedoes almost certainly hit the Japanese carrier, but he mistook the explosion for an attack on his submarine: '0803 Sound picked up fast screws close aboard on the port beam and almost simultaneously a very loud explosion, which shook the boat a' bit, was heard. Interpreted this to be a second escort, which had been suspected but not sighted, starting a depth-charge attack, or bomb dropped by aircraft, and immediately ordered deep submergence and rigged for depth charge. As it turned out, this was probably a mistake, which prevented firing the stern tubes since only one explosion was heard at this time. It was later decided that this explosion could have been on board the carrier.'

The captain's recording of the destroyer's counter attack is misleading – '0813 received three depth charges', '0852 received two depth charges' and '0900 received four depth charges'. His submarine, according to Miers, was nowhere near the area of the explosions.

Caution stares out from Hammond's patrol report:

1324 *Sighted carrier . . . well down by the stern and apparently stopped. Destroyer was searching between us and carrier.*

1330 *Commenced approach. Sighted seaplane circling in vicinity of damaged carrier.*

1400 *Sighted seaplane at estimated range of 2,000 yards angle on bow zero. Went deep for bombing, or to avoid being sighted if not already located.*

1420–1425 *On way back to periscope depth, sound picked up loud screws . . . Depth control was poor as periscope depth was reached . . . Screws drew rapidly across bow and suddenly stopped . . . Believed plane had coached destroyer on again, went deep and commenced evading.*

1500 *Decided destroyer was not in contact or that he had no more depth charges and started back to periscope depth.*

1535 *Reached periscope depth and sighted both carriers . . . one destroyer patrolling between us and carriers. Thought the second one would be well on the way to Tokyo by this time. The damaged carrier was close astern of the other one – either in tow or at slow speed under own power. Due to distance of possible aid, had assumed up until this time that there was plenty of time to finish the damaged one off since he had not moved appreciably in seven hours, and had considered the problem to be a matter of reaching firing range without being detected. Estimated enemy speed 5 knots. Went to normal approach course.*

1606 *Lost sight of carriers in rain squall. When last seen one or more planes were still circling.*

There was some excitement the following day, 25 September. *Cabrilla* was on the surface at 0924 heading for her patrol area when a plane was picked up on radar at 8 miles. The submarine crash-dived and a depth charge exploded three minutes later, well off target, as were three or four depth charges dropped about half an hour later.

At 1210 smoke was seen and shortly afterwards an attack was started on the larger of two vessels. Then it was realised that they were submarine hunters, with an air patrol. *Cabrilla* went deep and rigged for depth charging and silent running. At one point one of the vessels was nearly overhead. The cat-and-mouse game lasted all afternoon.

Miers noted: 'Even taking into account the sighting by aircraft earlier in the day it was remarkable that these two hunting vessels should have appeared on the scene within three hours and have selected the exact piece of water in which we were diving to carry out an intensive search over 120 miles from the nearest land. They too would probably have been most surprised had they known how close to us they passed.'

There was more criticism of Hammond: 'The crew were closed up at battle stations for five hours in the most unpleasant conditions with no ventilation and one felt that most of it could have been avoided by an early burst of speed as the enemy's speed was very low and the initiative would have been retained in the event of a target being sighted.'

By 1 October *Cabrilla* was on patrol off the east coast of Luzon in the Philippines and under the orders of an American rear-admiral based in Fremantle, Western Australia, Ralph Christie, commander of Task Force Seventy-One. The submarine saw little for nearly two weeks except sailing boats and heavy rain.

The monotony was relieved shortly before dawn on 13 October, while on patrol west of Negros island. An intelligence report gave details of an important target, a Japanese convoy of four transports carrying 5,000 soldiers. The southbound ships were expected to enter the Sulu Sea at noon and pass through the Sulu Strait at dawn on the 15th. There were approximate positions for the convoy at noon on the 13th, 14th and 15th. No aircraft had been sighted for some time, and Miers reasoned that *Cabrilla* could travel at speed on the surface to cover all the possibilities for sighting the enemy. Hammond disagreed, deciding to go submerged at slow speed for the possible noon position on the 14th. This position was reached, and a submerged patrol was carried out along the enemy's predicted route, rather than across it. Nothing was sighted, and Hammond decided to return to his patrol area 'where there seemed little prospect of any target'. Miers suggested that by going at speed for six hours the submarine could reach the Sulu Strait by daylight. The enemy was unlikely to pass through the channel in the dark. But Hammond was having none of it.

'The dread of his fuel falling below ten per cent deters this CO from using speed however worthy the occasion even though the engineer officer gave an assurance that we had ample for the task,' Miers reported. 'All the calculations were based on proceeding to Fremantle direct as the CO was determined to avoid putting into Exmouth Gulf (where a tanker is maintained expressly to refuel submarines that run short) as he had been told that there was no pilot available and that the buoys were out of position. I later visited this place. It had an entrance of three to four miles across and a straight run in to the tanker with deep water all the way.'

Hammond's patrol report covering 13, 14 and 15 October is exceedingly brief, referring only to a 'possible shipping route'.

A few days later *Cabrilla* was ordered to carry out a special mission – picking up a Filipino flying ace, Jesus Villamoor, who was a major in the US Army, and three other officers in the vicinity of Doog Point on the west coast of Negros. Villamoor had been dropped off by another submarine in January to carry out intelligence work for General Douglas MacArthur. *Cabrilla*'s mission should have taken a day but ended up lasting three days because of Hammond's caution. Miers, who had been involved in special missions with *Torbay*, was not impressed.

The plan was for *Cabrilla* to lie off the coast and wait for signals. A white sheet would be displayed onshore if it was safe for the operation to go ahead and then the four officers would leave in a sailing boat flying white sheets in the bow and stern and rendezvous with the submarine. For a reason not apparently obvious the signals were changed to a white disc onshore, a white disc in the bow of the boat and a white sheet in the stern. When *Cabrilla* finally made contact with the group two discs were seen on the beach and two sheets in the boat, but the only person who worried about the mix-up was Hammond.

On the morning of 18 October the submarine approached Doog Point, submerged, and made a preliminary reconnaissance, but nothing was seen all day. Hammond made it clear he would only surface when it was dark, even though the signals were for daytime use.

'I was fearful some patrol would intervene and capture the party with a number of incriminating documents while we, with characteristic apathy, were waiting for dusk,' Miers reported. 'Having seen no sign of aircraft since our arrival in these waters, it really did seem practicable to make a quick surface, embark the passengers and dive again, all of which would take only a matter of minutes and probably be the least troublesome course.'

On the afternoon of 19 October two discs were spotted on shore. Villamoor and the others, of course, could not see *Cabrilla* because she remained submerged, but they still set off in their sailing boat. Doog Point had been chosen because there was deep water to within a few hundred yards of the beach. Hammond, however, refused to go nearer than 4 miles. The group sailed a mile offshore and waited, getting increasingly despondent, until 0400 before heading back. *Cabrilla* had surfaced at dusk but crewmen could not pick out the boat against the land. The submarine dived about 20 miles to seaward so that Hammond could be 'fully rested' before repeating the operation on the 20th. That afternoon the discs were seen onshore again and the boat was at last sighted, flying white sheets. Reluctantly, Hammond moved to within 2½ miles of the shore, and the rendezvous was made at dusk. Sailors armed with machine guns – calling themselves *Cabrilla*'s Commandos and 'keen as mustard for some action' – helped Villamoor, another US Army officer and two captains in the Philippine Army on board. About a dozen Filipinos were crewing the sailing boat and some of them helped to carry the officers' gear.

'I was particularly impressed at the genuine enthusiasm with which these people greeted American officers and sailors alike,' said Miers. 'There was no mistaking their delight as they rushed about pressing souvenirs of Japanese money or cigarettes into our hands before the boat cast off.'

Some supplies were handed over to the Filipinos, but not arms, ammunition, quinine or flour, which they urgently needed. Hammond was anxious to get away in minutes. At the last moment a tommy-gun was given and a package containing quinine was thrown into the sailing boat.

Miers observed: 'So much could have been achieved in half an hour, and after having been a witness to this little scene and subsequently hearing of the loyalty of these hard-pressed people to their American allies, I feel that everything possible should be done to maintain their cause and that when submarines carry out these missions they should either be loaded with a good quantity of stores or informed by signals of the most needed articles if they can be spared onboard.'

Before leaving the Philippines *Cabrilla* was given the option of spending a couple of days off Davao, Mindanao, where 'good pickings were promised'.

Miers would remain disappointed: 'This seemed a splendid chance to retrieve our fortunes, but the CO, still ignoring the existence of Exmouth Gulf, declared that the state of fuel did not permit it, and set course to pass about 60 miles east of the place. This decision cost us an attack on one large tanker for certain and possibly other ships.'

In his patrol report, Hammond stated: 'Fuel and time factors will not permit return via Davao . . .'

On the way to Fremantle a small tanker was picked up on radar. Rain was falling heavily and the target could only be seen during flashes of lightning. Hammond made a long-range attack, firing a total of six torpedoes, which all missed. 'Decided not to expend any more torpedoes and gave it up as a bad job,' he recorded.

Cabrilla arrived at Fremantle on 7 November with plenty of fuel – 14,000 gallons, against Hammond's minimum of 9,000 gallons, or ten per cent – and could have been there two days earlier but for bad weather and dives to avoid aircraft. The submarine had travelled 10,481 miles, spending 34 days submerged. She still had 12 torpedoes.

Hammond's daily entries for his patrol report were often exceedingly brief. For example, the entry for 21 October:

Underway on surface en route to Surigao Strait.
0444 *Submerged.*

1755 *Surfaced.*

2328 *Commenced transit of Surigao Strait.*

He had only this to say about his crew, who had endured a great deal of monotony: 'The performance of duty under combat conditions of all officers and men was in keeping with the highest traditions of the naval service. At the beginning of the patrol a large percentage of the crew was new to submarines as well as going to sea under any conditions. The efficiency of the crew began to improve noticeably shortly after the attack and depth charging while en route to the area and continued to improve throughout the patrol. The state of training at the end of the patrol is considered to be very good.'

The patrol report went to the commander of Submarine Squadron Sixteen, Captain John Haines, who thought Hammond should have taken a greater risk in going for the kill in the attack on the carriers, which were such important targets.[3] Rear-Admiral Christie, the commander of Task Force Seventy-One, charitably came to the conclusion that the scarcity of targets in the Philippines was partially due to Hammond's unfamiliarity with the area.[4]

If Hammond was not keen to name names, Miers felt no such restraint – starting with *Cabrilla*'s captain, a 34-year-old bachelor. Before the war Hammond had volunteered for the naval air service but was discharged during the course as unsuitable and later went to submarines.

'Unlike most submarine officers he was neither interested nor very proficient in the subject of engineering,' Miers noted, with some irony, 'and had very little knowledge of gunnery or torpedoes. He had specialised in staff duties. He was a capable administrator, had plenty of power of command, and in his dealings with officers and men was firm but just and reasonable. He was at all times polite to me, but was too self-centred to be interested in my comfort and too self-satisfied to pay any attention to advice and suggestions. In many respects he is a competent officer but is lazy, utterly lacking in aggressive spirit and imbued with the idea of "safety first" and in my opinion quite unfitted to command a submarine in time of war.'

Miers was exasperated when he discovered after this 'very unsatisfactory' patrol that Hammond had been promoted from lieutenant-commander to commander.

On 12 December – without Miers – Hammond took *Cabrilla* out on her second patrol in the South China Sea. In 52 days he laid a minefield and sank a 2,700-ton ship. It was to be his last trip in *Cabrilla*. Christie relieved him, echoing Miers: 'I had to take his command from him – a swell officer but not aggressive enough.'

Despite his failings, Hammond received letters of commendation from Pearl Harbor. He went to Washington to take up a post in the anti-submarine warfare section, but later that year he was given a reprieve – command of a famous submarine, USS *Guardfish* (SS-217), which had taken a heavy toll on Japanese shipping. In November 1944 he left Pearl Harbor in *Guardfish* and headed once again for the Philippines, where targets eluded him. On 23 January 1945 *Guardfish* was returning to Guam when radar picked up what he believed was a Japanese I class submarine on the surface. Hammond sent two messages reporting the contact, one of them to Vice-Admiral Charles Lockwood, in command of all US submarines in the Pacific, who stressed that friendly ships might be in the area and that Hammond needed to be sure he had an enemy vessel in his sights. Hammond observed his target several times and, convinced it was a Japanese submarine, fired four torpedoes . . . sinking the US salvage vessel *Extractor*, with the loss of six lives. Twenty minutes after the sinking *Guardfish* surfaced and headed towards the wreckage. 'Upon drawing close to the first life raft, realised the full extent of our mistake,' said Hammond later. 'The survivors were American.'

It was Lockwood who had given Hammond his second chance. *Extractor* was the only American vessel to be sunk by a US submarine during the war. Blame for the tragedy was shared by Hammond and *Extractor*'s captain, who had not asked for a garbled message to be sent again. The message had told him to return to Guam, taking his vessel out of the danger zone.[5]

Surprisingly, Hammond remained in command of *Guardfish*, going on two further patrols. The submarine's only success was a Japanese fishing boat sunk by gunfire.

Hammond left the navy in 1953 on health grounds in the rank of captain, and took up cattle farming at Magnolia, Arkansas. Deteriorating health forced him to move into a nursing home in 1971, and he died 12 years later, aged 74, leaving a widow and two daughters.[6]

There was a bizarre footnote to Miers's patrol in *Cabrilla*. Because of the damage inflicted on the Japanese carrier it was deemed a successful mission, and *Cabrilla*'s crew, including Miers, were awarded the US Navy's submarine combat insignia. Miers 'took an active part in this patrol and his performance as officer of the deck was outstanding as illustrated by his first sighting of the enemy carrier which resulted in a later successful attack and damage'.

The matter was referred to the Admiralty, which came to the conclusion: 'It is not quite clear what exactly the combat insignia award is . . .' But the Admiralty had no objection.

However, shortly before D-Day and the invasion to decide the fate of Europe, a Treasury official who chaired a committee on awards decided to intervene, opening a special file. Sir Robert Knox asked the US Embassy in London to supply a full explanation of the award.

Sir Robert duly received a lengthy report about the submarine combat insignia. Thirteen days after D-Day, after considering this weighty issue, he signalled his disapproval: 'It seems clear that this distinction is granted on a regular scale, very much in the same way as the clusters to the [US] Air Medal and clusters to the [US] Distinguished Flying Cross. We should regard it as of the automatic type, therefore, and would greatly prefer that it should not be accepted.'[7]

Miers was probably not that impressed with the award anyway. Although Admiral Nimitz himself was acknowledging his 'outstanding' co-operation and assistance, it was a brief, standard message of commendation . . . and Miers was told that he would have to buy the insignia from the nearest military PX store.

A better offer came in 1946 when he was awarded one of the more prestigious medals of the United States, the Legion of Merit, which he was allowed to accept . . . free of charge.

Chapter 17

UNDER FIRE AGAIN

Fremantle, a short distance from Perth, had been used as a US submarine base since March 1943. After the attack on Pearl Harbor the Japanese hounded American boats of the Asiatic fleet from Manila in the Philippines and then Soerabaja in Java. Darwin was considered as a base but high tides were a problem and the approaches could be mined easily. Fremantle soon flourished and was popular with crews. It also became an important base for British and Dutch submarines. During the war some 170 Allied boats made a total of 416 war patrols from Fremantle. When Miers arrived, Rear-Admiral Ralph Christie had recently taken over from Rear-Admiral Charles Lockwood, who went on to control all US submarines in the Pacific.

Within a couple of days Miers was happily running around on a tennis court. He went to a tennis party with Christie, playing four sets, all of them going to 'five-all'. Miers was due ten days' leave and planned to visit Melbourne and Sydney, but first he wanted to do some work.

'I intend to keep an eye on myself, however, and see that I don't overdo it,' he said. 'Everyone here has been as kind as at Pearl and I have had a very warm welcome, not only from the submarine people but also from many people in Perth. I attended the ex-naval men's association reunion and had to respond to a toast, which I think went very well. If our submariners come here they will get really well looked after and won't want to go home.'[1]

Before getting down to the serious business of his report covering *Cabrilla*'s patrol and the scathing attack on her captain, Miers wrote a long letter to Claud Barry, the Rear-Admiral (S) at Northways, London, headquarters of the Submarine Service.[2] 'I was very disappointed at the lack of offensive spirit shown and can honestly say that I was easily the most aggressive officer on board (although the oldest),' wrote Miers, who dated the letter 11 November 1943 – his 37th birthday. He pointed out that he had had the 'good fortune' to spot the only 'respectable' target of the patrol, the task force of two aircraft carriers. Also mentioned were the night attack on the small tanker that had been picked up by radar and the special mission to collect four officers.

Then it emerged what Miers was leading up to. He was still desperate for another submarine command: 'My physical and mental condition remained excellent throughout, despite living in a tiny four-berth cabin (intended for CPOs) with three junior officers and no privacy whatsoever, and nowhere to sit except at the wardroom table. I feel, in fact, fully capable of resuming command of a submarine (preferably of *Torbay* if Clutterbuck requires a spell) as soon as I am relieved.'

Miers must have known his chances were slim because of his age, but he reasoned there was no harm in trying. He also asked Rear-Admiral Barry to take up another cause – get his pay fully restored. When Miers arrived in Fremantle after working 'really hard' in *Cabrilla* for two months, he was upset to find a signal from their lordships at the Admiralty informing him that he would only get 3s 9d a day for the patrol 'putting me on the basis of a general service navigator going out for the day to swing compasses, or a gunnery officer judging a shoot'.

Jumping from sterling to dollars, he also complained that his monthly pay was being cut from 240 dollars to 120 dollars after income tax. 'Expenses are high all the time and though one can't officially mention these things I had to sit in the mess [*Cabrilla*'s wardroom] all day and couldn't possibly avoid playing poker with the officers except by being most unfriendly (they all played) and that cost me £25 in the two months,' he continued. 'Now I am taking the whole crew in two large buses for a drive in the bush and lunch and beer at the other end – officers in two separate cars. I am delighted to do this for the sake of good relations, but not to give a submarine CO submarine pay when he goes in a foreign submarine on the longest possible war patrol seems to me to be a really shabby trick.

'I felt so depressed and disgusted that I nearly succumbed to everyone's exhortations to make a strong complaint by return signal but, under my peculiar circumstances, it would have been put down to swollen-headedness and I am far too keen on the service to want to give offence like that. But, apart from the monetary consideration, I feel it is such a discouraging way to be treated when one always has spent every penny of one's money on trying to promote good relations and making both ends meet . . .

'I hope you will realise how disgusted one feels when one volunteers to risk one's life (and feels very frightened!) to do one's job, to be denied such a small sum . . .

'I do not believe the First Sea Lord would approve of such treatment and would like the matter to be brought to his notice except that he has so much else to worry about. Still, I hope you will be relieving me soon and bringing me back to a normal life where a shilling equals a shilling instead of about three pence.'

Miers, of course, did not get another submarine command, and there is no indication that he sorted out his pay before moving on to the next post. He was almost certainly right in thinking that their lordships would not be particularly sympathetic to the difficulties of financing poker-playing sessions.

A few days after penning his letter to Barry about 40 officers and men of *Cabrilla* took up Miers's invitation to drive into the bush. After a few stops for refreshment they ended up at the Mundaring Weir Hotel, not far from Perth. Miers need not have worried about the cost. Australia's Naval Comforts Fund paid the bill. 'I subsequently made a donation of £10 to this fund and was told that they were all looking forward with keen anticipation to the arrival of British ships in Western Australia and had £5,000 saved up for their entertainment,' he said.

During November 1943 he visited various bases, giving talks and attending functions in Perth, Darwin and Adelaide. There was even a trip to the races. On 27 November he flew to Colombo, Ceylon, and saw the Commander-in-Chief, Eastern Fleet, Admiral Sir James Somerville, returning to Australia on 10 December. There were personal visits as well as formal engagements. After Christmas he spent a couple of days in Adelaide with the parents of Lieutenant Ian McIntosh, who was on his way to becoming a distinguished submariner. McIntosh's mother Islay had seen a newspaper article about the VC hero and sent him an invitation. She had not seen her son for six years since his departure from Australia, aged 18, to join the Royal Navy. McIntosh made his name in the submarines HMS *Thrasher* and HMS *Sceptre*, but his greatest feat was helping to sail a lifeboat more than 1,500 miles to land. He had been on the troopship *Britannia* heading for the eastern Mediterranean when she was attacked and sunk by the German commerce raider *Thor* about 600 miles off Freetown, Sierra Leone, on 25 March 1941. McIntosh found himself in lifeboat number seven – designed to carry 56 – with 81 others. The hull was riddled with shrapnel holes and McIntosh, held by his legs and hanging over the side, plugged them with pieces of blanket and tin. McIntosh and *Britannia*'s third officer, Bill McVicar, tried to sail for the African coast but found it impossible because of the north-east trade wind and headed off in the opposite direction, hoping to reach Brazil, with supplies of 16 gallons of water, 48 tins of condensed milk and 2 tins of biscuits. After 23 days of incredible hardship 38 survivors waded ashore near Sao Luis, Brazil. McIntosh and McVicar – 'we seemed more like twin brothers' – received the MBE. McIntosh's father and the headmaster of Geelong Grammar had tried to deter him from joining the Royal Navy 'because we did not think that he was the type required'. At Dartmouth, McIntosh graduated in first place and rose to vice-admiral, receiving a knighthood. Miers also saw his grandmother 'and afforded them pleasure which was at least as great as their hospitality afforded me'.

A few days later, in Melbourne, Miers saw the parents of a lieutenant who was serving in the submarine HMS *Shakespeare*. 'This was another visit which I felt very glad to have made especially as their only other child has been killed in the RAAF,' he said. Miers also met the mother of Lieutenant Alastair Mars, a submarine ace in the making, and told her that he had been awarded the DSC, 'which was news to her'.

At Northways on 12 January 1944, Rear-Admiral Barry was busy writing to Miers about a plan to send 12 specially adapted X-craft to the Pacific for operations against the Japanese.[3] Following the success of the midget submarine attack on the German battleship *Tirpitz* in a Norwegian fjord, the Admiralty was keen to expand the role of X-craft. The Americans, however, were not so enthusiastic, even though they could have operational control of the British-manned craft, which would be towed to the scene of attacks by Royal Navy or US submarines.

In a letter marked 'most secret', Barry said: 'This offer was politely turned down on the grounds that they did not wish to divert American submarines from their all-important patrols in order to tow X-craft – to my mind a peculiar decision as there was absolutely no catch in our offer and we were quite prepared to tow them ourselves.

'However, it is not my intention, and I believe Admiralty are behind me, to be deterred by this, and the construction of these special X-craft will go forward. When ready, they will I hope be sent to the East with *Bonaventure* [Royal Navy depot ship] as part of our eastern submarine force, and will operate against the Japanese, towed by British submarines.

'You must not know any of this inner and so secret history in any conversations you may have with senior US officers on this matter, but I am sure you will agree with me that a little propaganda on your part with regard to the remarkable capabilities of the X-craft would help generally against the time when they arrive in the East . . .'

Barry thanked Miers for his 'many enthrallingly interesting and excellent reports', ending: 'I much appreciate all the good work you are doing and I can assure you that the information you send is of the utmost interest and use to us.'

Later that day Barry sent another letter to Miers, but his mood had changed completely.[4] He was angry. The admiral had just seen a letter from Miers enthusing about the superiority of American submarines. 'I am most favourably impressed with these modern US submarines and believe them to be a long way ahead of ours for all forms of patrol except in very shallow water,' said Miers. 'I feel really strongly that we should produce something very similar for ocean warfare.'

Barry was 'brutal' in his response: 'This document in effect extolled the US submarines – and I agree with great reason – but pointed out how infinitely superior they were to ours in practically every way with regard to the war in the Pacific; really advocating that we scrapped all our present designs and embarked on an entirely new programme as our present ones were so entirely unsatisfactory and not up to their job.

'I fully realise that you did this with the best possible motives, but had you paused to think a little more I doubt if you would have broadcast your views in the manner you have. To me, certainly, always be frank to the point of brutalness; but not always to others, especially on this occasion when your allegations might well lessen the confidence of all concerned in British submarines at a time when we are about to embark on the submarine campaign in the East.

'Your criticism is, of course, entirely destructive . . . it would be quite impossible to embark on a complete redesign and new programme at this stage of the war, as it would merely lead to a practical cessation of building at all.

'Further, you must remember that you have been some time away from here and are not always altogether up to date with your information . . . With this letter you will receive details of the new A class, in which you will see that at least most of your criticism has been met. As you well know, our problem generally is very different from that of the United States who have the comparatively easy task of designing a one-ocean submarine, which is far from the case with us; and I feel very happy that in all circumstances we have done the best with our very complex problem, and with far more limited building and manning facilities than have your friends.

'I have spoken to you on this matter with the utmost frankness – indeed brutally – and having done this we will consider the matter entirely closed, as I know so well that you sent your letter to all these fellows with the best possible motives. It was merely a case of your judgement being somewhat out on this occasion . . . Please leave everything as it stands, and do not do anything such as writing to all the fellows concerned correcting your letter. It is much better left alone, as in most cases they are fully aware of all the facts and can see your case in its right perspective.'

Miers made sure that his letter had a wide circulation. He sent it to Rear-Admiral Herbert Pott at the British Embassy in Washington, with copies to Barry, the Commander-in-Chief, Eastern Fleet, the First Naval Member, Australian Commonwealth Naval Board – and, apparently, all Captains (S).

In 1943 orders had been placed for 46 A class submarines. They were indeed designed specifically for the Pacific theatre, but the first two boats, HMS *Amphion* and HMS *Astute*, were still on trials in Scottish waters when Japan surrendered.

On 25 January 1944 Miers finally sent off his full report on *Cabrilla*'s patrol to Pott at the embassy. Normally the report would have been typed by an American sailor, but it was so sensitive that Miers made other arrangements. He explained: 'After due consideration it seemed only proper, if this report is to be of any value, that it should contain the facts and honest opinions and in order that no criticism of mine as a liaison officer should affect the relations between this submarine commanding officer and his superiors, I am on this occasion not forwarding the report through US channels.'

Three days later, at the invitation of the Americans, Miers set off on another adventure, flying to Guadalcanal in the Solomon Islands, which had seen ferocious fighting between US forces and Japanese troops who preferred to die rather than surrender. Lying in the shallow waters off the north-east coast were a large number of enemy ships that had been destroyed. After landing at Henderson Field Miers was taken on a quick tour, meeting senior American officers. 'I was surprised at the vast scale on which the island is being developed and doubt whether half the stuff will ever be used,' he observed.

On the morning of 29 January a PT [Patrol Torpedo] boat travelling at more than 45 knots took him to the island of Tulagi to inspect the fleet anchorage and repair facilities in Purvis Bay. He went on board two submarines, USS *Blackfish* and USS *Guardfish*, as they were being refuelled, and spent the night at the post office in Tulagi, which had been taken over as officers' quarters. 'There were many bullet holes in the walls testifying to the struggle for its recapture by the US Marines but it made very reasonable accommodation,' said Miers.

The next day he flew in a Liberator bomber, specially converted for the use of Rear-Admiral Aubrey Fitch, to Milne Bay. But he was feeling low. The heat and humidity had given him a heat rash and skin infection. The condition was difficult to clear up because of continual sweating, and he was confined to his room for a week. He spent the time writing another report before deciding to abandon the medical treatment to see if 'a breath of fresh air would not be more beneficial'.

Miers went in the submarine USS *Darter* to Finschhafen, where there was a PT boat base. Within hours of arriving he was getting plenty of fresh air, speeding along in PT 336, which had just been fitted with rocket launchers, a weapon in the early stages of development.

On 10 February he went in another PT boat to Saidor, the most advanced Allied position in New Guinea. 'I went ashore and attempted to visit the military headquarters but as the temporary bridge across the river had been destroyed by floods on the preceding day these could only be reached by swimming, which I felt disinclined to undertake,' he reported. 'I was, however, driven round the various encampments and was surprised at the scale on which such a small place had already been developed.'

A destroyer bombardment before the recent American landing caused considerable damage, but already a large number of tractors and trucks were in use and a battalion of army engineers had set up a camp which boasted electric lighting, refrigerators and a distilling plant. The Americans were holding their positions, waiting for the arrival of Australian troops who were advancing up the Huon peninsula. 'It was gratifying to hear on all sides from the US troops of their unstinted admiration for this Australian division who are bearing the brunt of the fight in this unsalubrious climate,' said Miers.

That evening after a swim and supper he went out on a PT boat patrol hoping to destroy Japanese barges taking reinforcements and supplies to Madang. PT boats had inflicted heavy casualties on barges. Submarines were also possible targets. For four hours from midnight Miers's boat cruised off the coast searching for targets, but there was no sign of the enemy. A floating log inflicted the only damage – to one of the propellers.

Miers observed: 'The lookout kept was of poor quality and it is not surprising that their boats are so little menace to submarines which are known to make many night supply trips to the New Guinea and New Britain coast. The crew of this PT boat had been shot up from the beach on several occasions and were distinctly jittery and in need of a rest but the officers – two ensigns – lacked nothing in courage and determination.'

The boat returned to base and soon afterwards Miers was given the opportunity to go out on another patrol that afternoon. Naturally, he jumped at it. Three PT boats were aiming to attack Japanese destroyers evacuating troops from Rein Bay on the north coast of New Britain. Miers was in the leading boat, PT 328, with a lieutenant of the Royal Australian Navy Volunteer Reserve who was acting as a pilot because he had gained considerable knowledge of the waters before the war. The lieutenant was highly regarded by the Americans, who were baffled that the Royal Australian Navy had not paid him since joining them four months earlier.

That night the search for enemy destroyers proved fruitless. 'There were a few nasty minutes when our boat was inside Rein Bay investigating an object on the beach at 0200,' said Miers, who acted as a lookout. 'The other boats, which had been ordered to remain outside, were taken under fire by an enemy 3in battery on the point which we had passed close to. All three boats returned the fire, which was soon silenced, and we had to creep out by a different channel in range of the battery but unable to speed up for fear of grounding on a reef. It was perhaps unwise of our boat to disclose its presence by opening fire – which was done by the after 40mm gunner without orders – but it was exhilarating while it lasted, until stopped by the CO.'

Later that month Miers met General MacArthur and Vice-Admiral Thomas Kinkaid, commander of the US Seventh Fleet, 'and found them both very favourable to the projected reinforcements of British submarines. The general asked me a number of questions concerning the relative merits of the British and US submarines and both assured me of a very warm welcome if I should return to the south-west Pacific area with the advent of British submarines'.[5]

Early in March Miers returned to Australia and a few days later he went to Pearl Harbor, where he arrived 'very thankful' to settle down in one place. He had travelled 22,000 miles by air and nearly 11,000 miles by submarine since leaving.

He would not be at Pearl Harbor for long. His last duty there, on 13 May 1944, was to present the DSC to an American officer who had distinguished himself in the submarine USS *Shad* during 'a magnificent and gallant attack' on a blockade runner, escorted by destroyers, in the Bay of Biscay.

Lieutenant-Commander Richard Lakin, who had served in HMS *Ursula* and HMS *Safari*, winning the DSO and DSC and Bar, was appointed to replace Miers as the British submarine liaison officer.

When US submarines had gone to war against Japan two major problems emerged.[6] The first problem concerned many of the older skippers who had been trained in peacetime. They were too cautious when it came to launching attacks – as Miers had found with *Cabrilla*'s captain. In the 18 months following the raid on Pearl Harbor, dozens of them were relieved because of their lack of aggression. They were replaced by younger men willing to take calculated risks.

The second problem concerned American torpedoes. Torpedoes would run too deep, deviate from their course or simply fail to explode when they hit the target. On one patrol the submarine USS *Sawfish* sighted 18 ships in or near the Sea of Japan and launched seven attacks, failing to inflict any damage. It was enough to drive a brave and experienced submarine captain 'berserk'. Two submarines were even sunk by their own circling torpedoes. Miers helped to solve the problem, and in this respect he left an important legacy.

The American torpedo had been developed in peacetime but, surprisingly, it had never been properly tested on targets. Complaints from skippers that they had fired duds were not well received by the 'experts', who took a long time to come round to the idea that there might be something wrong. Eventually, after testing, it was decided there was a problem with torpedoes running too deep and settings needed to be changed. But skippers continued to fail to sink or damage enemy ships.

The torpedo had two 'exploders', a magnetic exploder, which was designed to go off beneath a ship – supposedly its most vulnerable area – and a contact exploder, which would detonate on hitting the side of a vessel. More research revealed that there was fault with the magnetic exploder. The British and Germans had also experienced problems with magnetic exploders and the solution was to deactivate them. Later the Americans realised that there was even a fault with their contact exploder. It was not until September 1943 that the fiasco ended, with all the faults corrected. If US submarines had been able to fire reliable torpedoes from the outset, the war in the Pacific might have been considerably shortened.

Sir David Miers commented: 'The story of the torpedo scandal is now well known, but my uncle's role is not. My first knowledge of this story came from Uncle Tony himself. When he arrived at Pearl Harbor he found there was a general feeling of dissatisfaction at the failure of the US submariners to sink more Japanese ships. The COs complained that their torpedoes were defective. But this excuse was not generally accepted.

'It was widely believed that the US submariners lacked the gumption to get close enough to their targets and were reluctant to press home their attacks. Uncle Tony respected the US submariners as individuals and did not believe them to be faint-hearted – whatever he may subsequently have thought about the captain of *Cabrilla*. He listened carefully to what he could learn about their torpedoes and became convinced that they were right in regarding them as defective. Importantly, as an independent observer, and above all as a submariner with a matchless personal record of aggression and success, he was in a unique position to argue their case with Nimitz and his staff and to deploy the technical arguments which had convinced them, and him, that they were right. Gradually the submariners won the battle and secured recognition that they were not cowards. For his persuasive advocacy on their behalf the US submariners were deeply grateful, and Uncle Tony made many friends amongst them.'[7]

Chapter 18

BIGAMY!

After some 18 months as a liaison officer Miers was set to take a more direct role in the war against Japan. He became Commander (S) of the 8th Submarine Flotilla, which was made up mostly of S class boats, with HMS *Maidstone* as the depot ship. He joined the flotilla at Trincomalee, Ceylon. It was under the command of Captain Lancelot Shadwell, who would be 'almost totally eclipsed' by his second in command, whose word was 'law'.[1]

David Blamey would always remember his first encounter with Miers. Blamey, a sub-lieutenant in the Royal Naval Volunteer Reserve, had switched from MTBs, the British equivalent of PT boats, to submarines. He was trained 'on the beach' at Trincomalee by Jeremy Nash and Phil May, who were spare COs at the time. A few weeks later he was made torpedo officer of HMS *Sturdy*.

'One day I had to bring *Sturdy* alongside *Maidstone*,' he said. 'It's one thing bringing an MTB alongside, quite another a submarine – much more difficult. Our coxswain warned me that Commander (S) was on the upper deck looking very threatening. We came alongside absolutely perfectly. When I went up the gangway Crap was there to greet me with the words "All right, sub, you win. Come down for a gin". I needed it.'[2]

The return of a submarine from patrol was usually an excuse for a good party in the wardroom. 'There was a great shortage of beer out in "Trinco", but Crap always ensured that there was a good ration for any returning submariners,' said Donald Douglas, fourth hand of HMS *Stratagem*. 'I think he used to keep a good supply in his cabin.'

Returning to *Maidstone* one night after a week's leave, Douglas heard 'one hell of a noise' coming from the wardroom. 'On looking through the large windows the sight that met my eyes was astonishing – an enormous mound of bodies, many completely unclothed, all fighting and yelling,' he recalled. 'All of a sudden bodies started leaving the massive pile and rushing for the wardroom door. The first to arrive out on deck dashed to the ship's side and dived overboard.

'I realised that the wardroom had been enjoying – with a capital E – a mess night and that most people were ten sheets to the wind. I was spellbound watching this mêlée when I saw that the body at the base of the pile was Crap Miers himself, the president of the mess. Old Crap was a great bull of a man, liked by one and all, and loved a scrap.

'Then I suddenly realised that the ship had sentries, armed with rifles, stationed on the upper deck with orders to shoot anybody seen swimming at night near the ship. I rushed round the upper deck yelling to sentries not to shoot as several officers had gone for a swim. Luckily no one was shot but there were many red faces – and thick heads – the next day.'[3]

Douglas was lucky to be there. The previous year he had been posted to HMS *Untamed*, but he was recalled almost immediately to give way to an officer with seniority. The next day the submarine sailed from Campbeltown, Mull of Kintyre, on an exercise and failed to return to the surface after diving, with the loss of her entire crew.

Another young officer who served in the Far East was Tony Troup. At 22, the lieutenant was in command of the submarine HMS *Strongbow*, and he encountered the 'physical' Miers after accepting a dinner invitation. 'We were in the bar having drinks before dinner and he was beaming on about submarines and radar,' Troup recalled. 'I had hardly said a sentence. Suddenly I went flying. He had punched me below the throat. I don't know why he did it. Perhaps it was because I was too young and he was the almighty Crap. He was a bloody shit and carried on being one.'

Troup – later Vice-Admiral Sir Tony Troup – had served in *Turbulent* with the Victoria Cross winner Commander John 'Tubby' Linton, whose submarine vanished off the coast of north-east Sardinia in March 1943. Years later it emerged that *Turbulent* had struck a mine.

Troup, who won the DSC and Bar, escaped depth-charge attacks lasting

14 hours by Japanese escorts off the west coast of Malaya in January 1945, but *Strongbow* was so badly damaged that she had to be scrapped.

With some irony, he found himself at another dinner engagement with Miers in the early 1970s. By this time Troup was Flag Officer Submarines and was hosting a celebration for former submariners. Miers was seated next to him. 'He turned to me and said, "I can't understand why that chap Tubby Linton was awarded the Victoria Cross". He went on about Tubby. I was taken aback and thought like saying, "I can't understand why you got the VC". I had been Tubby Linton's first lieutenant and I loved the man. He was the complete opposite of Crap Miers. I never understood Crap.'4

In the summer of 1944 the 8th Submarine Flotilla transferred to Fremantle, which was still a key US submarine base under the command of Rear-Admiral Ralph Christie. The 8th Flotilla came under his operational control.

With pressure easing in the European theatre, Britain had felt the time was right to build up its naval forces in the Pacific and avenge the humiliation of Malaya and Singapore, which saw the devastating loss of the battleship HMS *Prince of Wales* and the battlecruiser HMS *Repulse*. By this time the Americans had the Japanese on the run and their submarines, now equipped with torpedoes that actually worked, were inflicting heavy losses on enemy shipping. The United States, of course, had its own humiliation to avenge – Pearl Harbor. The Royal Navy joined the fight against a common foe. However, British submarines did not have the range of US ocean-going boats and could not reach areas where targets were more plentiful. Instead, they were deployed in operations in the shallow coastal waters used by the Japanese in the Java Sea and off the east and west coasts of Malaya, which were more suitable.

Fremantle, with its friendly inhabitants, inviting climate and beaches, continued to be a popular posting with submarine crews. Many American skippers asked to end patrols there. A war was still going on, but time could be found to enjoy the social life. And Miers was about to find a love to rival the White Ensign. During his first visit to Perth the previous year, 1943, he had been invited to a dance. Admiral Christie also went. Turning to Miers, he asked: 'Who would you like to dance with?' The commander surveyed the scene and replied: 'I'll have that one.'

That one was Patricia Millar, attractive, slim and 18 years old. Always known to family and friends as Pat, she was a university student. Miers made an impression on the young woman, though not the one he might have been anticipating. 'I thought he was very old and very fat,' she said. 'He was 20 years older than me.'

Pat's mother, Gwen, a widow, also met Miers and invited him to their home for dinner. 'He came with a large suitcase which he flung on the floor and opened, saying, "There are lots of things that I need mending",' said Pat. 'So I said, "Well, you can shut it up because I can't sew".'

After dinner Miers provided the entertainment. 'He loved acting and did some funny play with another guest – the *Death Of Nelson*, I think,' said Pat. 'He said that if he had never been in the navy then he would have loved to have been a barrister, so he could do his acting. He could talk. He would have been a very good barrister.

'He stayed so long that he missed all the buses and had to stay the night. I found him rather overwhelming, and I didn't think I would really see him again. But he had a hell of a personality.'

Miers was so keen on acting that he had appeared at the Fortune Theatre, Drury Lane, in December 1938 as a member of the Strolling Players, a well-known amateur group. *Distinguished Gathering* by James Parish enjoyed a week-long charity run. The programme listed him as 'Detective Inspector Rutherford . . . Lt Commander A Capel Miers'. Perhaps some of his outbursts owed more to theatre than genuine anger.

Pat's father, David, had his roots in Perth, Scotland, and her mother was from Perth, Western Australia. When war broke out, her parents were living in Penang, north-west Malaya, where her father was manager of the Chartered Bank of India, Australia and China [now the Standard Chartered Bank]. Pat and her brother, also called David, lived with grandparents in Australia so that they could go to school in Perth. Every year in the school holidays they spent a month with their parents in Penang, where Pat had been born. During the Japanese attack on Singapore Gwen flew to Australia on the last plane out. Her husband, who moved from Penang to Singapore in 1941, was ordered to escape because his opposite number in Hong Kong had been tortured to death by the Japanese. He left in a ship, which was sunk. With other survivors, he ended up on an island off Sumatra. David Millar suffered from kidney failure and needed plenty of water, but he would give up his share to help others. Rescuers eventually took him to Colombo, where he died. He was 50.

Miers was quick to propose marriage to Pat, who turned him down. Then he 'disappeared' for a while. 'He was quite cunning – he never rang up or did anything,' she said. 'I used to go out with lots of others, but after a bit I wondered what he was doing, so I rang him up and, rather cunningly, he came back. By which time I thought I had missed him a bit.

'He was very interesting and had tremendous charm. The newspapers had announced the arrival of this Victoria Cross hero, but he didn't talk about his wartime things at all. In fact, he was modest and disarmingly self-critical, as I think he remained throughout his life.'

Later she discovered more about his character: 'He was very tough and had a very fiery temper, but the next minute he would say, "Come and have a whisky". He never harboured grudges. He wasn't a bully.

'And he was the most romantic person. He wrote these incredible love letters. He was very sentimental. If you were to tell him a sad story, he would cry. He cried at films, he was really soppy. At dinner parties I would see him sitting next to some woman who was looking a bit astonished, and he would be telling her a sad story about somebody and the tears would be going down his face.'[5]

The revelation about Miers's sensitive side would have come as a surprise to many of his men, especially those who had incurred his wrath.

Romantically, his tactics had been right. The couple met again when he returned to Australia with the 8th Submarine Flotilla. By this time Pat had become a driver in the Australian Wrens. Miers proposed again and was accepted. The news that Miers planned to marry Pat surprised his fellow officers, and there were cries of 'Bigamy!' Commander Jeremy Nash explained: 'We were all brought up to believe that Tony Miers was a confirmed bachelor. He was married to the White Ensign. So we were all quite surprised to find him falling in love and getting engaged. We decided to crack on, and a nightdress was made out of a White Ensign.'[6]

Pat said: 'Tony didn't know anything about it. They gave me the nightie and asked me to wear it on my wedding night, so he would have both his wives with him. I've still got the nightie . . . rather moth-eaten.' The couple married at Perth Cathedral in January 1945. Because Miers was a Roman Catholic, Pat converted to Catholicism.

The previous month Rear-Admiral James Fife had replaced Ralph Christie as the submarine chief in Fremantle. But with the Japanese in retreat, American submarines and the 8th Flotilla would soon be moving to a new base at Subic Bay in the Philippines. One evening in May 1945, at Subic Bay, a large group of sailors were watching Bing Crosby in *Pennies From Heaven* on the well-deck of *Maidstone* when the film was stopped and it was announced that Germany had surrendered.

'There was a loud cheer from the lads, but then we were told that we could not splice the mainbrace until the next day,' said Albert Gillespie, who had served in the submarine HMS *Tantalus*. 'All real interest in the film was lost. The wardroom was crowded with officers splicing their own mainbrace. After they had a few, they came out into the open, creating a hell of a commotion and firing flares. Needless to say we objected by shouting abuse at them. I remember Commander Miers jumping on top of the ship's launch and throwing out a challenge to a very large Scouser. Even with Commander Miers's reputation, I don't think he would have been so cocky facing this man in civvy street.'[7]

Commander Arthur Hezlet and his submarine HMS *Trenchant* were still based at Fremantle, with the depot ship HMS *Adamant*, but he was asked to stop off in Subic Bay at the end of a patrol in July because Admiral Fife wished to congratulate him in person. *Trenchant* had sunk the Japanese cruiser *Ashigara* in the Banka Strait off Sumatra in a remarkable attack, and Hezlet – a future Flag Officer Submarines who ended his naval career as Vice-Admiral Sir Arthur Hezlet – was 'overjoyed'. But disappointment awaited him in Subic Bay.

He recalled: 'It has been the custom in the Royal Navy for centuries for a ship which has been in a successful action to be cheered when she re-enters harbour. I had certainly expected this to happen, but we were received alongside *Maidstone* in silence. Of course I did not comment and no explanation was furnished. I do not know to this day why this happened, but of one thing I can be sure. The decision would not have been made without Tony Miers's approval. Perhaps he thought that we should wait until we got to Fremantle to be cheered by our own depot ship, *Adamant*.'

Miers did, however, arrange for Hezlet to get his hair cut.[8]

The following month, August, the Japanese surrendered, except for the enemy in Hong Kong. Many British warships in the Far East gathered in Subic Bay to sail to Hong Kong. S class boats were among the first into the colony's harbour.

Sub-Lieutenant Antony Rowe, who later made a name in publishing, was in the second submarine, HMS *Sleuth*, and he wrote later: 'When we got to the great harbour we sailed between junks straight into the inner basin where delighted Chinese caught our ropes and tied us up alongside, watched by Japanese soldiers with rifles ready. Minutes later we saw boatloads of marines going in from the big ships astern and heard gunfire. We were told that after a short, sharp action the whole dockyard area had been regained for His Majesty.

'There was then an interlude of a week or two. The Japanese commanding officer would not surrender and Admiral Harcourt [Rear-Admiral Cecil Harcourt], commanding the British fleet, and other senior officers, including my hero, Commander Crap Miers, shuttled between the dockyard and Kowloon day after day trying to persuade him to do so peacefully.'

Most of the Japanese soldiers were holed up in Victoria barracks on the hill above the dockyard. For a reason not entirely clear, it was decided that a group of submarine sailors would take over the barracks. They were being led by a lieutenant-commander, who agreed – after a 'probably liquid' lunch – that 21-year-old Rowe could join the group.

'We assembled by the great dockyard gates at 0830 the next morning,' Rowe recalled. 'In three ranks were 21 submarine sailors in white tops and bell bottoms, who just remembered from their training days which end of a rifle was which and how to slope it, and ahead of them three officers in white shirts, shorts and stockings with .45 service revolvers. The barracks were occupied by about 4,000 Japanese soldiers.'

They were the only British servicemen to leave the dockyard since the fleet's arrival a couple of weeks earlier, and they were 'amazed' when

Japanese soldiers lining the streets presented arms as 'we shambled by'.

Within sight of the barracks the group split into three. 'I don't think that the apparent lunacy of 24 of us trying to surround 4,000 Japanese soldiers struck me until later,' said Rowe, who struggled through bushes with seven of the men. 'The barracks was a large building with many windows and a flat roof. Out of every window poked a gun with a man behind it. On the roof was a flagpole wearing an outsize Japanese flag. More significantly, behind the parapet of the roof were quantities of rifles, machine guns and men, all aiming at me.'

Suddenly, the Rising Sun was lowered and the Union Flag was raised. Another sub-lieutenant had gone to the back of the building, climbed through a first-floor window and made his way to the roof 'where all the soldiers were looking away from him, pulled out a large Union Jack which he conveniently had with him, and replaced the Rising Sun with it – as soon as he did that, the surrender was achieved'.

Half an hour later Rowe and his men were sent to guard a nearby villa, which had been occupied by a high-ranking Japanese officer. It was nearly midday, the heat was intense and all the men were thirsty. Rowe began searching the home and found a case of Orange Curacao.

'At that moment Admiral Harcourt and Commander Crap Miers arrived in a jeep looking very happy,' he said. 'They looked even happier when they saw what I had found and drove off with it.'[9]

Chapter 19

THE MEN WHO NEVER RETURNED

Maidstone sailed from Hong Kong after the Japanese gave up their arms. The depot ship, badly in need of a refit, was returning to Fremantle. On the way to Australia, she stopped at Macassar on the Indonesian island of Sulawesi to pick up nearly 500 sailors recently freed as prisoners of war. These men had survived the destruction of the cruiser HMS *Exeter* and the destroyers HMS *Encounter*, HMS *Electra* and HMS *Stronghold* in the battles of the Java Sea in 1942, and the brutality of the Japanese, but only just.

'I'll never forget the sorry sight of these men boarding *Maidstone*,' said Albert Gillespie, who had been in the submarine *Tantalus*. 'Most of them were crying like babies. Their condition was pitiful, with beriberi and bodies full of ulcers. I remember seeing one poor lad with his testicles the size of rugby balls. We rigged the men out as best as we could with the spare gear we had.

'When we arrived at Fremantle, the dockside was crowded with old friends to welcome us back. We stayed for a month. Our ex-PoWs were sent to rehabilitation centres to recuperate and, believe me, we didn't know them when they returned – they had put on so much weight.'

Miers was already with his wife in Perth, having been flown from Hong Kong on medical grounds. Like him, a significant number of British sailors had married Australian girls. Now it was time for many of the men to go home. 'The most moving experience I ever had was when we left Fremantle for the last time,' said Gillespie. 'There must have been literally hundreds of people to bid us goodbye, and everybody started to sing *Now Is The Hour* as we started to pull away from the jetty. I had a lump in my throat the size of a cannonball. We had a good reputation in Western Australia, and I was proud to be part of it.'[1]

Maidstone arrived back in Portsmouth in December 1945. Many submariners would not, of course, be going home. In the Submarine Service between 1939 and 1945, 3,508 were killed or taken prisoner, out of a total of 9,310, a staggering casualty rate of 38 per cent. Only Bomber Command of the Royal Air Force had a worse rate. Winston Churchill had been quick to acknowledge the sacrifices of submariners. In 1941 the Prime Minister told the House of Commons: 'There is no branch of His Majesty's forces which in this war has suffered the same proportion of fatal loss as our Submarine Service. It is the most dangerous of all services.' Overall, the Royal Navy had 58,979 killed or taken prisoner. With 776,000 serving in 1945, this worked out at a casualty rate of 7.6 per cent.

Sixty-five submarine commanding officers were killed. During the war the Royal Navy had 206 submarines at sea, losing 74 – 36 per cent. The greatest number of losses was in the Mediterranean – 41 boats, a sobering 49 per cent. Mines were responsible for many of the losses. By comparison, the United States used 311 submarines in the Pacific, losing 52 – 16 per cent.

Only three British submarines were sunk in the Pacific theatre, but the Royal Navy came late to the war there and was forced to operate in the shadow of the Americans. When Japan went to war, Britain did not have any operational submarines in the Far East. Two boats were sent from the Mediterranean but they arrived as Singapore fell. It was not until Italy's surrender in 1943 that Britain could afford to release submarines. By March 1944 the number of boats had risen to nearly 20. But targets were scarce. For much of the time hunting was restricted to the Malacca Strait.[2]

Torbay was one of the newcomers in March 1945, but her glory days were over. Operating from Trincomalee under the command of Lieutenant-Commander Pat Norman, she sank a coaster and two sailing vessels during patrols. In May the submarine suffered engine failure as she headed for a special mission and was forced to return to base.

Many years after the war a question mark was placed against the 'scores' of submarine aces, especially with regard to merchant shipping. Vice-Admiral Sir Arthur Hezlet, who carried out an analysis, explained: 'The post-war totals are often less than those claimed during the war, and this may lead to protests. Over-claiming was not usually done on purpose and is very understandable. Hits were generally heard rather than seen and it was rare for a submarine – because of the need to avoid counter attacks – to be able to watch what happened after an attack. All that can be said is that the figures, unlike those for attacks on heavy warships or U-boats, are not so reliable. The tonnage sunk is the best indication of the damage done to the enemy, and is obviously a better yardstick than to count the number of ships sunk. It is not, however, an indication of the skill of the submarine commander. It is, in fact, easier to hit a large ship with a torpedo than a small ship.'[3]

As an example, Commander John 'Tubby' Linton was credited with sinking 90,000 tons of enemy shipping. Hezlet revised this to 42,270 tons, plus the destruction of ten small vessels.

There seemed to be some confusion over how to calculate and present the tonnage of ships sunk and those that were only damaged.

Miers was said to have sunk or damaged some 70,000 tons of enemy shipping. In 1989 Vice-Admiral Sir Ian McGeoch, Flag Officer Submarines from 1965 to 1967, suggested that Miers had exaggerated his claims. McGeoch said that from March 1941 to April 1942 *Torbay* sank a submarine and six supply ships totalling 11,481 tons, plus seven sailing ships, and damaged four supply ships totalling 17,385 tons.[4] However, Hezlet, Flag Officer Submarines from 1959 to 1961, calculated that Miers had sunk seven ships of 27,670 tons, as well as ten small vessels. He excluded the ones that were damaged. It appeared that not even the men at the top could agree.

Beyond dispute was the fact that Lieutenant-Commander David Wanklyn of *Upholder* fame had the highest total. He was said to have sunk or damaged 120,000 tons of enemy shipping. Hezlet reckoned he sank ten ships of 89,059 tons and damaged five others. Wanklyn's feat was remarkable because his early patrols were fruitless and he came close to being replaced.

In 1986 Lieutenant-Commander Richard Raikes, who commanded the submarines HMS *Seawolf* and HMS *Tuna* during the war, was asked to give his opinion of 'the characters I served with or under'.[5] Miers, Wanklyn and Linton, all winners of the Victoria Cross, are of particular interest.

Of Miers, Raikes said: 'A VC and two DSOs are proof that he was a most successful wartime CO. His undoubted courage and his single-minded offensive spirit was perhaps the keynote of his very strong character. He was completely confident in his own ability and opinions and never considered that he could possibly be wrong. He was commendably loyal and supportive of his subordinates.'

Of Wanklyn: 'He was in many ways the opposite of Miers. He was very quiet and totally modest. A VC and three DSOs were proof that he, too, was a most successful CO. His officers and men worshipped him. He was a great thinker, confident in his own ability. After a rather shaky start with a few misses, he inspired total confidence. His loss was a serious blow to morale among his contemporaries.'

Of Linton: 'A solid and totally dependable character who inspired complete confidence. I served with him in *Warspite* [battleship] when I was a midshipman and he a lieutenant. He made a considerable impression on me at that time but our paths never crossed in submarines. Like all the best COs he was quiet and modest. He was tremendous fun at a party and always the unconscious leader in everything.'

Raikes, who was awarded the DSO, made a name for himself when *Tuna* dropped off the 'cockleshell heroes' for their audacious commando raid on Bordeaux harbour in 1942. The attack, using canoes, was turned into a 1955 film, *Cockleshell Heroes*, with Christopher Lee playing the submarine captain.

Sir David Miers agreed that his uncle was 'not a quiet person' like some of the other successful submarine commanders. 'He was an extrovert and he believed in expressing his views with clarity and vigour,' Sir David noted. 'Uncle Tony was not in favour of tearing up the rules. But he was never distressed to find himself in opposition to conventional wisdom, provided he was sure he was right. By inclination he was intensely competitive.

'In the 1920s the Submarine Service was still very young, and according to Uncle Tony was looked on rather condescendingly by the rest of the navy. Its necessarily confined quarters, its sweaty pullovers, its tolerance of BO and its limited opportunities for gunnery made it an unappealing choice for those sailors for whom spotless decks, gleaming brass and well-pressed uniforms were the hallmarks of an efficient ship.

'Uncle Tony, as a submariner confident in his own achievements and in those of his service, was not afraid of, perhaps even enjoyed, being in cultural conflict with more traditional sailors. This did not mean that he had any less pride than they did in the traditions and achievements of the navy. It just meant that he didn't have to subscribe to all their conventional attitudes. Some colleagues, but not the Cunninghams or the Nelsons, thought him brash for this.'[6]

Chapter 20

PEACE AND WAR

Miers did not return to Britain in his depot ship *Maidstone*. Instead he stayed on in Perth for a few months. He had been suffering from another bad skin rash but he was told not to hurry back anyway because a decision still needed to be made about his next post. Like the other services in 1946, the navy was busy shedding men who were not needed in peacetime. Eventually Miers boarded the Orient Line's *Orion* for the homeward journey. With him were his wife Pat and a daughter, Angela, who had been born at Christmas 1945.

Orion was still being used as a troopship. The liner, designed to carry 1,250 passengers, was packed with about 5,000 servicemen, among whom a near-mutiny broke out. She became 'the hell ship *Orion*'. Miers was not in charge 'but he sorted things out'.[1]

Pat had been to Britain before, but she was about to exchange the pleasant climate of Perth for one of the country's worst winters. Home would be Portsmouth. Miers had been given command of HMS *Vernon II*, which comprised the old battleships HMS *Ramillies* and HMS *Malaya*.[2] These ships were being used for accommodation and training by the torpedo school HMS *Vernon* at Gunwharf, which had been badly bombed during the war.

Pat faced a major test – meeting Miers's formidable mother, who was now living in a flat in Queen's Gate Place, Kensington, London. In those days it was common for women to go to the cinema to have a chat, an arrangement that must have been annoying for members of the audience who wanted to see and hear the film. Pat duly received an invitation. Barely 21 and with the responsibility of a daughter a few months old, she sat in the cinema 'absolutely terrified'. But she realised she had passed the test when Mrs Miers eventually turned to her, saying: 'You were very lucky to marry my son. You could have married an Australian.'[3]

Miers was still at *Vernon II* in January 1947 when he was promoted captain. There was more good news in June when a son, John, was born. In February 1948 Miers was given an appointment completely different from anything he had done before. He was sent to Cheshire to take command of HMS *Blackcap*, the Royal Naval Air Station Stretton. The airfield had been planned originally as an RAF fighter base to counter German bombing raids on Liverpool and Manchester. It was still under construction in 1941 when the threat receded, and it was agreed that the Admiralty would take it over in exchange for facilities at Machrihanish in Scotland. RNAS Stretton was commissioned on 1 June 1942 and would survive for 16 years. After the war few frontline squadrons used the base. One of its main functions was to store aircraft that were in reserve, including Mosquitoes, Ansons, Tiger Moths and Sea Furies. These planes were dotted around the airfield, often cocooned in a skin of rubber latex to protect them from the weather. At times there were so many surplus aircraft that a large number ended up being destroyed for scrap long before their useful life was over.

One night an RAF Spitfire was forced to land. The pilot, a squadron leader, was furious that he had been waved down by air mechanics because the control tower was closed. Walking away from his plane, he demanded: 'Who's in charge of this bloody place?' Told it was Captain Anthony Miers VC and DSO and Bar, he carried on walking 'suitably chastened'.

Miers had arrived with his fearsome reputation, and no one was in any doubt about who was in charge. He gave orders that his car required a salute if the pennant was flying 'whether I am in it or not'.

One morning he turned up for a flight to find that his plane was not ready. 'Where the hell is my aircraft?' he demanded. 'I ordered it for 0900.' Told that work was being carried out for safety reasons, he replied: 'Damn my safety.'

But, as always, he cared about the men under his command. Air mechanic George Rose had been badly injured when an engine fell on him, and Miers made sure that he received the best treatment possible. Rose would have 'no word said against him'.[4]

Miers had also arrived at RNAS Stretton with his usual enthusiasm. The submariner took flying lessons and obtained a pilot's licence. He remained at *Blackcap* for two years before moving to more familiar territory, as Captain of the 1st Submarine Flotilla in Malta, with HMS *Forth* as the depot ship.

Two of the visitors he welcomed on board *Forth* were Princess Elizabeth and Princess Margaret. The future queen spent several long spells on the island when Prince Philip was based there as first lieutenant of the destroyer HMS *Chieftain* and then in command of the frigate HMS *Magpie*. Miers was determined that Forth, though only a depot ship, would compete with the cruiser and destroyer squadrons, particularly in sport. One result was victory in the fleet regatta.

Miers acquired a Maltese steward called Cini. Years later, after leaving the navy, Cini went with his large family to live in Australia where he had the distinction of winning the lottery not once but twice, becoming extremely rich. On a visit to Sydney Miers looked up his old steward – who insisted on pressing his coat.[5]

In 1952 Miers was appointed Captain of the Royal Naval College, Greenwich, which provided a number of courses for officers. One of the men on the Royal Naval Staff Course was Commander Terry Lewin, who went on to become Admiral of the Fleet Lord Lewin of Greenwich and was Chief of Defence Staff during the Falklands conflict. At this time Miers was 'well known as one of the most outspoken officers in the service'. At the end of the course, which lasted nearly six months, he gave Lewin a glowing report, with one exception: 'An outstanding officer who has found the staff course almost too easy . . . no praise is too high for him . . . if he fails at all it is in public speaking . . .' The failure at public speaking was 'corrected later'.[6]

There were also courses for the most junior officers. Acting Sub-Lieutenant Julian Oswald, a 21-year-old Scot, was at Greenwich for two terms. Thirty-five years later he was appointed First Sea Lord. He retired as Admiral of the Fleet Sir Julian Oswald. Miers made a great impression on him after he arrived at the naval college as a 'slightly grown-up schoolboy'.

He said: 'We were supposed to be having our minds broadened and very obvious holes in our education plugged to a certain extent by the unlucky academic staff who were having to deal with these rumbustious young men. We were enjoying ourselves enormously but didn't take the whole thing terribly seriously.

'And that put Crap Miers in an interesting position because obviously he had to support his staff and see that we didn't misbehave and waste the time too obviously, but his interest was much more in how we did on the games field.'

Oswald was a promising rugby player and ended up playing for the college teams. 'You couldn't do too much wrong if you played a decent game of rugby,' he said. 'It was terrific having this man who took such a great interest in our performance in games and things like that. Crap was a very loyal supporter and always there on the touchline. Despite the great disparity in our ages and seniority, I got to know him reasonably well. We were always having a beer after a game.'

Of Miers's character, he said: 'He wasn't grabbing of attention. He got it because of the way he behaved. One never had a view of him interested in self-promotion. He seemed to be a very decent sort of fellow. He demanded and he got tremendous loyalty from people because they knew that he would always back them up.'[7]

Miers had a reputation for hospitality, as his nephew, Colonel Douglas Miers, would recall. Colonel Miers – who as a boy of nine had told George VI of his ambition to join the Cameron Highlanders – was a junior officer in the regiment when he found himself in London with an invitation to a party. He arranged to stay at his uncle's quarters in Greenwich.

'I used to see quite a lot of him, particularly when he was at Greenwich,' said the colonel. 'He was always very good to us. I went to this party with four friends and needless to say they ended up with nowhere to stay, so I said you had better come back to Greenwich. I rang and spoke to Pat so that she could tell Tony what was happening. Tony came down for breakfast the next morning and was very friendly. One of the girls was deaf, seriously deaf, and Tony asked her if she would like a fried egg. She couldn't hear, of course. He asked again and there was no reply. Then he shouted at the top of his voice, "Do you want a bloody fried egg?"

'Pat had to take him aside and explain that the girl – called Verity, I think – was deaf. Tony was absolutely mortified. He was like that but terribly kind and generous. Pat was a very good go-between. You could always turn up at any time of the day or night, and he would always respond.'[8]

One night during the summer of 1955 Pat and her husband were in their quarters when a call came through and Miers threw on his clothes and dashed out. Army cadets from Sandhurst were raiding the college. It was not uncommon for the rival military colleges to launch attacks on each other – flags disappeared, things would get painted and cannon ended up being stolen, not something easily done. Far from putting an end to the fun the Captain of the Royal Naval College encouraged his junior officers by organising the defence of Greenwich. Several raiders were caught and imprisoned in coal cellars.

But there had been some damage and the next morning the Admiral President was furious, and he called a meeting of his senior officers. Miers must have found it difficult to keep a straight face. The order went out to find the culprits. Of course, no one was held responsible because Miers himself was one of the ringleaders.

'He did all the organising, arranging the defence, telling people what to do and so on,' said his son John years later. 'Dad was in his element, running around with chaps, having fun.'[9]

On another occasion a group of junior officers from Greenwich descended on Sandhurst in a number of cars and towed away cannon from the front of the main building. Bags of soot were also thrown through windows. Shortly before the raid, the men were questioned by a village policeman, who was told: 'We're just having a car rally, officer.' Of course, a complaint was made to Greenwich, and Miers had the culprits line up on the parade ground. He gave them an 'almighty blasting' but ended by saying: 'And if you ever do anything like this again, I want to be involved.'

It was during his time at Greenwich that Miers went to war with the Civil Service – and ended up being promoted rear-admiral.

Colonel Douglas Miers explained: 'Tony was a very keen tennis player, and the Civil Service used to have their tournament at Greenwich every year. They used to ring up to arrange it. This particular year Tony had been told that a porter at the gate had not been given his long service medal, and the Civil Service were messing about. So Tony said, "I'm not having the tournament here until this has been sorted out". About three days before the tournament they rang up and said, "We haven't had our usual permission". They were told they couldn't come until this man got his medal. They said they couldn't be blackmailed like this, and Tony said, "Well, you bloody well can. You're the Civil Service, sort it out". At the last minute it was sorted out and the tournament took place.

'Anyway this got back to the First Lord [the senior civil servant at the Admiralty] who said that whatever happens Miers must not be promoted any further. But Mountbatten, the First Sea Lord, ignored this.'

After Greenwich Miers was given command of the 17,720-ton aircraft carrier HMS *Theseus*, which was being used as a training ship. *Theseus* had been launched in July 1944 but missed service in the Second World War. She was commissioned in January 1946 and played an active part in the Korean War.

Julian Oswald, the future First Sea Lord, had gone to Portsmouth for further courses and was ready for a ship appointment after being confirmed in the rank of sub-lieutenant. Miers needed a sub-lieutenant in *Theseus* to act as 'sub of the gunroom' – the person in charge of mess arrangements and some training for the most junior officers – and was shown a list of possible candidates.

Oswald said: 'He was asked, "Which of this horrible shower would you like running your gunroom?" Miers said, "I'll have Oswald, he won't be as bad as some".'

Once again the emphasis was on sport, especially rugby. *Theseus* had a lot of good sportsmen on board, though it is not clear whether that was down to luck or design.

'Crap was desperately keen that his ship should do best,' said Oswald. 'He got very wound up about this and gave extraordinary exhibitions on the touchline, especially when things weren't going well.'

Theseus was at Portland with a similar carrier, HMS *Ocean*, as part of the Home Fleet Training Squadron. One of the sporting highlights was a rugby match between the carriers. The team from *Theseus* had a good record and were widely tipped to win. 'It was a miserable, wet afternoon,' recalled Oswald. 'We played so badly it was embarrassing. We lost to *Ocean* by a narrow margin, and we were all hang-dog. Crap had been marching up and down the touchline shouting instructions and cursing. He disappeared just before the final whistle.'

Miers immediately took his launch back to *Theseus*, moored in Portland harbour, and his team followed later.

'When we got back on board the officer of the watch looked at us and said, "You lot are in trouble. You're to go straight to the hangar". So there we were in our rugger kit, holding our boots, dripping with mud, and we went to the hangar. To our amazement the whole ship's company were mustered there – about 1,400 people. There was a stage at one end and we were shuffled on to it. Then Crap walked in and he gave us the bollocking of all time. He told us what an absolute miserable shower we were – that we'd let him down, let the ship down, let the navy down, we'd let everyone down. We just stood there cowering under this tirade. There were an awful lot of people and I could see some of them smiling.'

Laughing at the memory, Admiral of the Fleet Sir Julian Oswald added: 'All that did was to illustrate how enormously seriously he took winning. He was not about losing. It was an exceptional act of an exceptional man to go and tear us up like that. It lasted less than ten minutes but it seemed like five hours.'

Two days later everything was back to normal. 'He never bore a grudge,' said Oswald. 'If you did something wrong you got a jolly good bollocking. Then it was forgotten. But you'd better not do it again.'

Miers sometimes enjoyed a rather unusual form of entertainment after a mess dinner. He would invite junior officers, usually midshipmen or sub-lieutenants, to fight him. 'He was very keen on wrestling in a semi-fun way,' said Oswald. 'It was odd really. A lot of people, myself included, didn't know quite how to take it. We didn't know whether to go all out and thump him or not.

'He'd be in his mess undress and you'd be sent for to go to his cabin and he would say, "Take your jacket off. Right, come on, hit me". And he'd provoke a fight. You didn't want to hit him because you'd been told that you would be keel-hauled for hitting a senior officer. But here he was telling you to do it.

'Whether he did it with ratings, I don't know. I think it was mostly restricted to the gunroom, the junior officers. It was a bit concerning, and I remember exchanging views with one or two friends about this. We came to the conclusion that every great man has a few foibles.

'It wasn't too serious but it was slightly difficult to know how to play it. I often wondered, too, if this wasn't a little bit of a test – "I'll see if Oswald can handle a situation like this. Come on, hit me, Oswald. Come on, I can't feel that".

'Would I eventually give in or run away or sit down? It was an odd business. I think he would have been annoyed if you didn't try but I don't think he used full force. He was in many ways a physical person. You were very conscious of it, even when you were standing and talking to him. He would stand very straight and puff his chest out. By this time he was about 50 and quite heavy. So if you did this wrestling with him and found yourself underneath, it could be challenging.

'In my days as a junior officer he was the only senior officer I had known to behave like that. I knew a lot of funny senior officers who did peculiar things but there wasn't anyone other than Crap who said, "Come and hit me".

'There was no animosity about it. He'd end up putting an arm round your shoulders and saying, "Right, you'd better have a whisky before you go to bed".'

In harbour, Oswald was sometimes a member of the watch-keeping team on board *Theseus*. One morning, doing the watch from 0400 until 0800, he was thinking of breakfast when he saw Miers approaching wearing his medals and carrying his sword. Suddenly, he remembered that the captain had asked for a boat to be ready at 0750 to take him ashore.

'I had completely forgotten,' said Oswald. 'There was a rather short, one-sided conversation and I was told I was under close arrest and to go to my cabin and stay there. So I saluted and disappeared. I went to my cabin and began thinking of alternative employment. I came from a farming family and wondered if they could find a farm for me or something like that.

'It turned out to be a rather unusual day, even on that ship. All the time people would be piped for on the Tannoy system. At about 11.30 that morning a Royal Marine sentry came and said the commander [Commander Geoffrey Carew-Hunt, a gunnery officer who was Mentioned in Despatches five times for wartime service] wanted to see me. So I thought this is when I get the chop, the commander will do the dirty deed.

'I went along to the commander's cabin and it was immediately obvious he had not had a good day. He was a big, powerful man and he looked quite shaken and tired. He said, wiping his forehead, "Oswald, I want you to take the forenoon watch".

'I said brightly, "I'm sorry, sir, I can't. I'm under close arrest". He said, "So are all the other officers".

'That morning Crap had run through the entire watch-keeping team of eight or nine people, and they had all fallen foul of him. They were all under close arrest in various places. The next day it was forgotten. That was what it was like.'[10]

Commander Hugh Boyce, an engineer officer, served in *Theseus*. His son Michael also joined the navy, becoming First Sea Lord in 1998 and Chief of Defence Staff in 2001. Michael Boyce – later Admiral the Lord Boyce – first met Miers in the early 1960s. He was playing squash for the navy and Miers was president of the Royal Navy Squash Rackets Association.

'Miers was always something of an icon,' said Admiral Boyce. 'He had mellowed in later years, and I always got on with him.'

Of Miers's time in *Theseus*, he said: 'He was quite a physical bully. But if you stood up to him he was fine. My father was a good tennis player. Miers liked tennis and squash. He was charismatic, a tough leader and very ruthless.'[11]

Many of the young men who found themselves in *Theseus* were doing National Service. They included upper yardmen, officer cadets from the lower deck, who faced a five-month course. There was not a lot of sympathy from regulars. Miers, however, went out of his way to encourage the National Servicemen.

'We were put under a great deal of pressure on the course,' said David Candlin, who joined the carrier as a 19-year-old upper yardman in the winter of 1954. 'We had little time to relax and never went ashore during the week. We received instruction from senior rates and officers. Some of the petty officers were hard and sarcastic, at times to the point of being almost sadistic. Our course officer seemed to think it necessary to be quick to criticise and never to encourage. Others were less severe, but there was little contact with them away from the classroom unless it was for some misdemeanour, usually trivial.

'It was during this prison-like existence that Captain Miers took command of our ship. Before long he came to make us feel that we could all succeed and become valuable members of the service.'

A badminton competition in the hangar deck was announced and Candlin, who had played a lot during school holidays, put himself forward. 'Miers heard about it and in typical fashion refused to be left out,' he said. 'I had what turned out to be the great good fortune to draw him as an opponent. Apparently, he had not played the game before. At first I started to win quite easily, but after a time he got the idea of the game and proved to be extremely nimble. It was a very close run thing, but in the end he just managed to beat me. I shall maintain to my dying day that I did not give it away. We parted good friends and thereafter it was to my advantage that I was marked as a man who was good at games.'

Theseus spent most of her time swinging around buoys in Portland harbour, but there were occasional trips to sea, including visits to Portsmouth, Brest and Gibraltar. On one of these occasions Candlin found himself on the bridge as upper yardman of the watch 'somewhat bottom of the large pile of officers and cadets' there.

'It was my first duty with Miers in command and he suddenly turned round and said to the assembled company, "Officer of the watch, fuck off, navigating officer, fuck off". Several others were told to fuck off. Then he said, "Upper yardman, take over".

'Suddenly here was I unexpectedly alone in charge of this great monster, but Miers made certain the time was profitably used with various manoeuvres, and I came away feeling quite experienced.'

Later Miers asked: 'Did you enjoy that?'

'Yes, sir.'

'Good, I believe in letting you all have a go.'[12]

Among the National Servicemen in *Theseus* was Nigel Lawson, who served as Chancellor of the Exchequer in Margaret Thatcher's government. 'I am afraid that all I can now recall is that he was known as Mad Miers,' said Lord Lawson of Blaby.[13]

Ten years after the end of the Second World War Miers was given an appointment that would take him to an area of conflict. This time the enemy was terrorism. In January 1956 he was promoted rear-admiral and two months later he became Flag Officer Middle East, based in Cyprus. The terrorist group Eoka had launched its campaign on the island on the night of 1 April 1955, and the Governor of Cyprus, Field Marshal Sir John Harding, wanted 'a fighting admiral'.

Eoka was seeking enosis, the union of Cyprus with Greece. This cause had been rumbling on with various degrees of intensity for decades. By the early 1950s it had come to the fore again. Many Greek Cypriots, who made up the majority of the population, liked the idea. Turkish Cypriots, the minority, did not. The Greek and Turkish governments took up entrenched positions, and a fair solution seemed impossible. In any case, Britain did not wish to give up its crown colony because the island had become an important military base following the withdrawal from Gamal Nasser's Egypt. Cyprus had been part of the Ottoman Empire until Great Britain, the island's administrators since 1878, annexed it in November 1914. Less than a year later the British offered Cyprus to Greece as a condition of entering the First World War on the Allied side. Greece declined the offer, with great irony.

There were two key figures pressing for enosis in 1955 – Archbishop Makarios III, head of the Cypriot Orthodox Church, who was also the ethnarch, leader of the Greek Cypriot community, and George Grivas, a retired Greek army colonel of Cypriot birth who set up Eoka. Makarios supported terrorism, but the extent of his involvement with Eoka remains unclear. Certainly, many people in Britain saw him as a priest with blood on his hands.

On the night of 1 April 1955 bomb attacks were launched at government and military targets, which were largely ineffective. Three days later a bomb was thrown into an army bus carrying servicemen's wives on a shopping trip, but it failed to explode. The pattern for years of violence, with appalling atrocities, had been set.

Miers arrived in Cyprus on 15 March 1956, taking up his post at the headquarters of the Middle East Command in Nicosia. Home was Admiralty House, a fine rented villa on the shore outside Limassol. The new admiral was quickly made aware of the problems. On 17 March a patrol of Royal Marines from 45 Commando was ambushed in the Troodos mountains. At least one Eoka man was killed. The next day a 19-year-old gunner of the Royal Artillery died when a landmine exploded under his vehicle at Yialousa. He had been helping to man a maritime radar battery.[14]

There was a lighter side on Sunday 18 March, when soldiers keeping watch on a monastery at Cape Andreas reported seeing the periscope of a submarine. Several ships were ordered to search the area and an RAF Meteor was involved. Miers had been at a church service and went to his headquarters after being alerted.

'When the situation was explained to me I decided that no submarine could possibly be operating submerged so close inshore off a rocky and not very well charted coast in sight of two of our ships,' he noted. 'The military authorities very kindly allowed me to interview the sergeant in charge of the patrol later in the day and, after hearing his story and receiving a very helpful report from the commanding officer of HMS *Sefton* [a minesweeper], I decided that the patrol had been watching a cormorant swimming on the surface and diving for food in the prevailing flat calm.'

On 21 March there was a clear reminder of the seriousness of the terrorist threat. Miers was at a meeting with Field Marshal Harding at his official residence in Nicosia when it was revealed that a bomb had been found under the mattress of the governor's bed. A Greek Cypriot servant planted it, and suspicions were aroused when he and two other employees failed to turn up for work. The bomb was removed by an army lieutenant, who carried it in a dustpan to the end of the garden where it exploded minutes later. Harding had spent the night sleeping on the bomb. It had not exploded because he kept his bedroom windows open and the explosive was meant to detonate at a warmer temperature. The field marshal insisted he had never slept better.[15]

Miers recognised a face from *Theseus*, David Candlin, when the young midshipman arrived in Cyprus from Malta in HMS *Striker*. The landing craft was carrying the admiral's car and crates of wine for him, which had been stored in an ammunition locker. Miers ignored a large piping party of sailors and Royal Marines standing by on the gangway from the bow ramp to the jetty and 'kept dancing about talking animatedly to people ashore'.

Candlin saluted and said he had the wine. 'You fucking idiot, shut up about that' came the reply. 'I'm supposed to buy it from the Naafi but balls to the Naafi!'[16]

That March was the worst month since the start of Eoka's terrorist campaign. There were 156 bombings, as well as other attacks. Military, police and civilian deaths totalled 16, with 45 wounded.

In his monthly reports to the Commander-in-Chief, Mediterranean, Miers listed all events of significance. In his April report, he told of the murder of assistant superintendent Aristotelis Kyriakos of the Cyprus Police. The 35-year-old officer was killed as he left the maternity wing of Nicosia General Hospital after seeing his young wife and son of four days. Miers reported: 'He was considered the best of the few very good Cypriot police officers and had been responsible for the identification and detention of a large number of Eoka leaders last summer.'

Miers's main task in the fight against Eoka was to ensure that his ships prevented any arms or explosives reaching Cyprus by sea. By May he was able to report: 'A recent intelligence report indicates that smuggling of arms from Greece into Cyprus is now considered impracticable due partly to the virtual impossibility of avoiding naval and air patrols and partly the difficulty of finding ships and crews prepared to undertake such activities. We are not, however, allowing ourselves to adopt a complacent attitude on this account.'

During that month the navy boarded 59 vessels but found nothing suspicious. The British, however, had not made things easy for themselves. After the Second World War the army dumped a large quantity of explosives in the sea off Famagusta. The explosives had washed closer to shore and were being picked up in the nets of fishing boats. Large amounts were sold to Eoka. It was some time before it was realised that this was the terrorist group's 'sole and very successful source of TNT'. Famagusta bay was closed to trawlers and a civilian diver was hired to recover the remaining explosives.

As Flag Officer Middle East, Miers displayed his usual energy. He was always on the move between Admiralty House, Nicosia, Famagusta and Episkopi, as well as other anchorages such as Kyrenia, Larnaca or Paphos. He would work at a desk or a table wherever he happened to find himself, or in the back of his staff car, and was 'totally exhausting to serve'. His secretary, Jimmy Henegan, suffered badly from indigestion, and his driver, an able seaman, 'lived on Rennies'.

Miers was not entitled to have a flag lieutenant, but he decided that his post needed one because of the Cyprus emergency. Rather than pursue the matter through slow channels at the Admiralty in Whitehall, he managed to get a National Service midshipman, John Pode, seconded to his staff. Pode, a good squash player, had been in *Theseus* when Miers was captain. He was promoted acting lieutenant, but whether he received the appropriate pay for that rank seems doubtful. And their lordships probably remained in the dark about the appointment.

Pode turned out to be a rather nervous 'flags', constantly worrying that he might have forgotten something and making urgent phone calls. Like many service personnel during the emergency, he carried a personal sidearm. One day he was sitting in the hall of Admiralty House cleaning his pistol, unaware that it contained a round. The gun went off, with the bullet passing through Miers's study. The story goes that Pode, appalled by what had happened, crept to the study door, opening it slowly. The room was empty and he heaved a sigh of relief, saying: 'Thank God the old bugger's not here.' A roar came from under the desk: 'Oh yes, I fucking well am.' Pode was relieved of his pistol, but he remained flag lieutenant until his National Service ended. After that incident Miers relied on a Royal Marine escort for protection.[17]

Guy Timpson also served as flag lieutenant. For a time he was accommodated in a chalet at the bottom of the garden at Admiralty House. 'Every morning Tony would stalk across the lawn and into the sea for a swim,' Timpson recalled. 'When he had finished he would open the door of the chalet, hurl his wet costume at me with a growled, "Get up you bugger", and then stalk stark naked across the lawn into the main house. From that moment things would start to happen, telephones would ring, people would arrive and everything had to be sorted out before we left for the joint headquarters, which were now in a new complex at Episkopi. Several times I had to keep leaving the breakfast table to sort something out and many times his wife, Pat, would slip a bacon sandwich into my hand as we were about to leave.'

On the day that Timpson started as 'flags' Miers held a lunch for Harding and other important guests. 'Tony had told me with considerable satisfaction that I would have to eat my lunch in the kitchen as every place was taken,' said Timpson. 'As I was parking my car I became aware that a helicopter was taking off and it turned towards Nicosia and disappeared. Everywhere was consternation. Apparently poor Harding had gone upstairs for a wash and had slipped on the marble floor and broken his arm. The helicopter had been summoned and taken him to hospital. With more than a wicked smile, Pat said, "Now there is room for you to eat with us".'

Timpson observed a darker side in Miers's relationship with his wife: 'Sadly, Tony could be thoroughly unpleasant to her in public, a trait for which many never forgave him. However, she gave him her unswerving loyalty for the whole of their life together. I know many people asked her how she put up with his treatment, but all she would say was that other aspects of their life together more than made up for it.

'On one occasion just the three of us were having lunch and he launched into a really beastly tirade at Pat, reducing her to tears. I excused myself from the table and went on to the terrace. After a short time Pat came out on her own, apologised to me for having been embarrassed – which made it worse – and asked me to please come back to the table. All three of us finished a rather quiet meal.'

Pat would say of the relationship: 'Yes, he was hot tempered but he was also romantic and sentimental, and he was always very contrite after any unpleasantness. I knew that he loved me and depended on me very much. We travelled widely together and met many interesting people. Life with Tony was not humdrum.'

Of Miers's character, Timpson said: 'He demanded total loyalty but he gave the same in return. Anyone daring to criticise a member of his staff would find themselves the object of a violent verbal assault. However, as is so often the case with someone with his characteristics, he would always respect anyone who stood up to him. One of his favourite openings was "Isn't it absolutely bloody?" followed by a tirade against whoever or whatever had crossed him.'

When Timpson arrived in Cyprus, he took command of a patrol boat based at Famagusta. At night, patrol boats did not show lights, and navigation was difficult because they usually had to go close inshore without the help of radar. One night Timpson's patrol boat went aground on a reef, and a minesweeper towed it back to Famagusta. Timpson had to make a report to Miers.

'A few months before, another patrol boat captain had had a similar misfortune, but when each of us left the island to go home, Tony told us that these reports had remained in the admiral's desk drawer and were never forwarded to the commander-in-chief.'

One day Miers learned that a patrol boat captain, Will Crutchley, had organised a beard-growing competition. The admiral hated beards and drove to Famagusta to confront Crutchley. 'What the hell do you think you're doing?' he demanded. The officer stood his ground, pointing out that as a commanding officer he had the right to give himself permission to grow a beard. But the beard came off after Miers issued a direct order. Crutchley then received an invitation to spend the weekend at Admiralty House.

Miers was generous with his entertaining, and guests did not have to be high ranking to be on the receiving end. Barbecues would be laid on at Admiralty House for visiting ships. 'He would also go to endless trouble to accept and attend an invitation given by younger members of his staff, believing that they had obviously gone to a lot of trouble and expense and should be supported however inconvenient the timing might be,' said Timpson.

Miers did not forget the army, which was bearing the brunt of the fighting and taking the heaviest casualties. He encouraged ships to forge links with regiments. In June 1956, for example, the minelayer HMS

Manxman was affiliated with the Wiltshire Regiment, the destroyer HMS *Duchess* with the King's Own Yorkshire Light Infantry, the destroyer HMS *Chevron* with the Royal Norfolk Regiment, and the minesweeper HMS *Essington* with the Highland Light Infantry. When crews went ashore, they could expect to be entertained by the soldiers.

Miers reported that 'low-grade' terrorists were responsible for many of the shootings and bombings in June: 'The bad execution may be partly due to the fact that members of the security forces are much quicker on the trigger than they used to be, while the lack of discrimination may be caused by an absence of central direction, since Grivas was known to have lost touch with his organisation.'

Unlike the army and to a lesser extent the air force, navy personnel had not been targeted by terrorists, but that changed on the morning of 14 January 1957. As usual, seaman Philip Bingham rode away from his married quarters in Nicosia on a scooter, heading for naval headquarters. Bingham, aged 23, from Ipswich, Suffolk, was a writer on Miers's staff. Along the route, a gunman stepped out and opened fire several times, killing him. He was buried with full naval honours the next day. Miers discovered that the weapon had been a 9mm automatic pistol 'the property of French forces stationed on the island' [Britain and France had launched Operation Musketeer, the attack on the Suez Canal, on 31 October 1956].

Intelligence reports soon suggested that Bingham's attacker was Nicos Sampson, a ruthless Eoka killer. Sampson worked as a photographer for a local newspaper and got 'scoops' by returning to the scene of his attacks to take pictures. He was arrested two weeks after the death of Bingham and charged with killing two British detectives on 'murder mile', Ledra Street in Nicosia. Sampson was acquitted of murder because of a technicality. He was eventually convicted of other terrorist offences and sentenced to death, but Harding granted him clemency and he was freed from a life sentence after Makarios became president of Cyprus in 1960. Sampson himself briefly became president in 1974 following a coup, which provoked Turkey's invasion of the island. He died of cancer in 2001.[18]

Eoka claimed the lives of many servicemen, but a significant number also died in accidents involving firearms and vehicles.

On the night of 4 February 1957, Miers checked on the effectiveness of his ships' patrols by embarking in the destroyer HMS *Corunna*, under the command of Terry Lewin, the future Chief of Defence Staff who had impressed him at Greenwich. He concluded that *Corunna* was 'a most efficient and enthusiastic' ship. Two trawlers and a drifter were investigated during the night and an exercise with the RAF was carried out in the morning. Lewin found Miers kind and considerate 'in spite of his reputation as the rudest man in the navy'.[19]

Another future Chief of Defence Staff involved in patrolling Cyprus was Edward Ashmore. He was in HMS *Blackpool* commanding the 6th Frigate Squadron. 'I, of course, called on him [Miers] on joining the patrol and was so well received and cheerfully entertained,' recalled Admiral of the Fleet Sir Edward Ashmore. 'Tony's reputation with the navy was excellent and we all trusted and liked him immensely.' In 1977, after becoming Chief of Defence Staff, Ashmore met Miers at a function and found that he was still 'quite a tiger'.[20]

Colonel Douglas Miers discovered that his uncle had an unconventional way of inspecting ships at anchor. 'Tony would insist on swimming out to ships,' he said. 'He would take off all his clothes except his pants. A launch would follow with a towel and his clothes. And the admiral would be piped aboard just wearing a towel.'

Miers liked to visit one particular minesweeper because the captain had a large picture of the singer Petula Clark on display. It is not clear why the officer was such a big fan, but Miers was impressed. 'Tony thought it was very dashing for one of his captains to have Petula Clark on show,' said Colonel Miers. The singer went on to record the songs *Sailor*, *Romeo* and *My Friend The Sea*.[21]

At the end of October 1957, Harding gave up his post as governor. He had taken the job reluctantly, insisting he would do it only for two years. When he arrived back in London, he denied he had disagreed with the Prime Minister, Harold Macmillan, on the way forward in Cyprus. He received a peerage. His replacement was Sir Hugh Foot.[22]

The following year, 1958, was punctuated by further atrocities, Eoka ceasefires and political juggling aimed at finding a solution. Two incidents perhaps summed up the continuing tragedy. On 27 February three sailors drowned when their launch capsized as they went to search two suspicious Greek trawlers. On 2 August Sergeant Reginald Hammond, aged 23, of the Royal Army Ordnance Corps, died after being shot in the back by a terrorist as he bought an ice cream for his 2-year-old son in the centre of Nicosia.

Miers reported that there had been serious allegations of brutality involving the security forces in the Asha, Lyssi and Vatli areas. An investigation was launched and 26 people out of 8,000 inhabitants came forward with complaints. 'The most serious case was a quarter-inch scalp wound,' he pointed out in his September report. 'Other complaints included a case of sunburn, an insect bite and a birthmark which was being passed off as a bayonet wound.'

There was a promising start to 1959. Because of a lull in terrorist activity, restrictions on leave to main towns were partially lifted, although officers and senior ratings still went around armed.

Following an agreement by Greece and Turkey on the future of Cyprus, which was ratified by Britain, Makarios returned to the island on 1 March, three years after being deported. Nine days later Grivas gave an order for Eoka to disband.

Miers reported: 'After four and a half years in Cyprus and after considerable doubt about his intentions, Grivas, dressed theatrically in Eoka guerrilla uniform, quietly left the island on 17th March for Athens in a Greek air force Dakota escorted by two Greek army officers. On arrival in Athens he was received by a guard and band and three members of the Greek cabinet, including the foreign minister, and given a hero's welcome by hundreds of thousands of Greeks. He was subsequently received by the Greek prime minister and the King of the Hellenes. In addition to being promoted to the rank of lieutenant-general, Grivas has been honoured in an exceptional manner with the award of several decorations.'

Miers ended his March report on a happy note, pointing out that the navy had triumphed on the squash court. A team entered by the ships on patrol won the major units championship, beating the Grenadier Guards 5–0 in matches in the final.

By May 1959 it was time for Miers to haul down his flag. 'I await with considerable interest the publication of the memoirs of General Grivas to hear his side of the story,' he wrote. 'I believe, however, that the maritime patrols will come well out of it and will be found to have constituted a considerable deterrent. I would not be surprised if it transpired that not one single consignment of arms or ammunition has, in fact, entered Cyprus across the beaches during this time.'

Grivas did admit that it had been difficult smuggling arms to Cyprus. Some weapons came from Greece using parcel post or couriers, and at one point Eoka resorted to using shotguns. Explosives were often made from materials bought in shops.[23]

Eoka, Makarios and Greece failed to get enosis. Cyprus became independent but since the Turkish invasion of 1974 it has been a divided island, with Britain retaining sovereign bases.

It was Lord Mountbatten, the First Sea Lord, who decided that Miers had reached the top of his promotion pyramid, although he allowed him to remain Flag Officer Middle East for a year longer than planned.[24]

Miers said it had been a wonderful three years. But he was fast approaching the saddest day of his life . . . the day when he would leave the Royal Navy.

Chapter 21

THE SADDEST DAY

Miers was placed on the retired list on 7 July 1959 but he left the navy officially on 9 August after a spell of leave. Reading *The Times* at home one morning, he was stunned to see that he had been given a knighthood, the KBE (Knight Commander of the Order of the British Empire). The previous year he had been made a CB (Companion of the Order of the Bath). The knighthood was on the recommendation of Admiral Sir Charles Lambe, who had been appointed First Sea Lord when Lord Mountbatten became Chief of Defence Staff. 'Charles Lambe thought that Tony had done such a wonderful job in Cyprus that he should get a knighthood,' Pat recalled. 'Tony had no idea of this – no one told him – so he was amazed to read it in *The Times*, and came to me as I lay in the bath and said, "Hello Lady Miers!" I thought he was pulling my leg. He was so pleased I could share the honour with him.'

Miers and his wife experienced a different life when they returned to Britain from Cyprus. They had been too generous with their entertaining at Admiralty House. Now finances were a problem. 'We had no money and two children at school,' said Pat. 'We ended up in a bedsitting room in Queen's Gate. We just sat there because we couldn't see our friends. Most of our belongings were in Harrods depository.'

Miers spent six months looking for a job. Surprisingly, the Victoria Cross hero ended up as the manager of a button factory in Birmingham, but he remained a 'ball of fire', tackling the job with his usual enthusiasm. Women workers on the factory floor, who rarely saw their bosses, were surprised by his visits and friendly manner. 'Tony treated them like his sailors and they adored him,' said Pat. Miers wanted to know everything about the business. He soon came to the conclusion that Buttons Ltd was inefficient. His dose of medicine helped to make the company a success again. During the week he would stay in a hotel in Birmingham, returning to London for the weekend.[1]

In November 1960 Miers was invited to speak at a gunroom dinner in HMS *President*, a Royal Naval Reserve ship moored on the Thames near Blackfriars Bridge. Many of the men there had been in *Theseus*. He was in good spirits, but he said in his speech that the day he retired from the navy had been the saddest of his life.[2]

The following year, along with other executives, he lost his job at Buttons after a takeover. Miers then joined the London and Provincial Poster Group, with an office on the sixth floor of Ingersoll House in Kingsway, central London. By this time he and Pat had moved to a house in Roehampton. From 1971 he also worked for National Car Parks, a business thriving under the guidance of Donald Gosling and Ronald Hobson, who became two of Margaret Thatcher's favourite businessmen and were later knighted. Although Miers had the title of Director for Development Coordination, most people at NCP knew him as 'The Admiral'.

Miers did a lot of entertaining, building up contacts and negotiating deals. 'He was a tower of strength, a remarkable man who reached everyone's life,' said Sir Ronald Hobson. 'But he wasn't always easy. He was impatient, someone who wanted immediate action.'

Hobson remembered being with Miers, who could not abide lateness, at Trooping the Colour one year. They were sitting in the stands on Horse Guards Parade when a ticket holder appeared minutes before the ceremony was due to start. Miers spotted that the man was wearing a Wellington College tie. 'He shouted "You were in such and such house and you were never late then – why are you late now?"'[3]

In 1977 another admiral, Sir John Treacher, joined as chief executive. The former Commander-in-Chief Fleet had reached the rank of full admiral, but he was known in the company as 'Sir John' and Miers continued to be called 'The Admiral'.

Four years later Treacher left NCP to join the Playboy Corporation as chairman and chief executive, with offices in Park Lane. Playboy had been experiencing problems with the Gaming Commission over the running of its casinos. When Miers heard that Treacher was planning to sign on with the colourful Hugh Hefner, he was horrified, got on the phone and 'gave him a lecture', saying: 'You can't do that.' Treacher shrugged off the concern, but he did not stay long.

They had not seen much of each other professionally, but on one occasion their paths crossed in Scarborough, where Miers was entertaining three young executives from a local property company. Treacher recalled: 'He was taking them to lunch in the Grand Hotel, and in the posh American bar asked them what they wanted to drink. They rather hesitatingly asked for beer and Tony, the perfect host, said he would join them and ordered four beers. Whereupon the waiter said, "We don't have beer in this bar".

'Tony responded, "Do you have beer anywhere else in this hotel?"

'"Oh yes, sir."'

'Which brought forth, "So fucking well go and get it". They got their beer.'[4]

In business, as in the navy, Miers emerged as a natural leader. His son John said: 'He had this thing about getting people on his side. He would have an absolute explosion but, generally speaking, apart from the villain who was getting the crap, everyone else standing around would end up agreeing – he would be doing something right rather than wrong. He was a bit naughty.

'Some people are born leaders and he was one of them. He was quite extraordinary. He was the type of person who if he walked into a crowded restaurant and said stand up, everybody would stand up. No one would say why? They would stand up. If I walked into a restaurant and said stand up, half of them wouldn't hear me and the others would say why? He just had this amazing gift to make people do things. He didn't do things, he got other people to do things.'

That included the family. 'For example, when we had the old coal cupboard outside my mother would go and shovel the coal and if it was raining my father would hold the umbrella.'

One day Miers and his wife went to the countryside for a point-to-point meeting. 'They decided to stand by one of the fences because they thought it would be rather fun to see things at first hand,' said John. 'A horse came up through the side of the fence and crashed onto all the people, one of whom was my mother. Dad just managed to get out of the way but my mother was quite badly hurt. Anyone else would have rushed to help her but not my father – he organised everyone else. It was not that he didn't love her. He stood there directing – you help her, you get an ambulance, you get the police. That was his nature. He would stand back, which is, of course, what a leader should do.

'My mother could never win an argument. I always remember when I was young and we were driving to the Black Isle [a peninsula north of Inverness, where Miers's brother Ronald took up farming after retiring from the army in 1952]. Our car had those orange flip-up indicators between the front and the rear door. Because it was a long drive my parents took it in relays and after a couple of hours would pull in to a lay-by. For some reason all naval officers are in a hurry – nothing can be done slowly, you would waste time. When my mother was pulling in to a lay-by she would put the flipper up. Then she would get out and run round the front and my father would run round the back and jump in the driver's seat. But she would forget to put the flipper down and Dad would run straight into it and it would snap off.

'There would be a blazing row. She was stupid enough to leave the flipper up – not that he was stupid enough to run into it. If the reverse happened, she was stupid to run into it. She could never win.'[5]

Miers devoted a lot of time to various associations and good causes. He was a governor of the Star and Garter Home in Richmond from 1970 to 1976, president of the Submarine Old Comrades Association (now the Submariners Association) from 1967 to 1981 and a councillor of the Lawn Tennis Association for many years. During Wimbledon fortnight he would host social and business lunches, making it clear that he expected everyone to arrive on time. A guest turning up a couple of minutes after the stipulated time of say 12.45 would incur his displeasure, even if he happened to be the First Sea Lord.

'He was terribly rude to people if they were late,' said Pat. 'Sometimes people would get stuck in traffic, but he would say, "If you thought you were going to be late you should have spent the night in a caravan in the car park". He was absolutely livid with one couple. The poor wife left and I found her sobbing in the loo.'

Miers also planned well ahead, with military precision. When some friends in the United States told him they intended to visit Britain, he decided they would all go to Rules restaurant in Covent Garden, which had been a favourite haunt of Charles Dickens, John Galsworthy and H.G. Wells. It was January when he phoned to book a table for June, taking the restaurant somewhat by surprise. There was even more surprise when he placed the order for dessert – strawberries and cream for eight.

'Now you or I would give them a chance, say ring up a week beforehand to make sure they would have the strawberries and cream,' said John. 'Dad wanted to see if these people could do what they'd been asked. So we went to this place. We sat down, had the main courses and the waiter came along and said, "Would you like to see the dessert menu?"

'Dad replied, "We've already ordered". The waiter looked a bit confused. "Strawberries and cream. We've ordered strawberries and cream".

'The waiter went off, came back and, with an embarrassing cough, said, "I'm sorry, sir, we've run out".

'Explosion. But I think my father would have been disappointed if they had brought the strawberries and cream.'

Miers was in demand as a public speaker. He gave lectures for RAF officers on moral leadership courses and several times addressed a younger audience at the Cadet Training Centre in Frimley Park, Surrey. He spelled out his own philosophy, stressing the following points in his scribbled notes: 'leadership – art of creating and maintaining high morale and through it directing men to achieve a definite purpose; down to earth; be yourself, study great but don't imitate; loyalty – superiors and subordinates; ability – know your job, personality no substitute for inefficiency; sincerity will overcome frailties, quick temper etc, men don't look for a saint; consistency – harsh but not inconsistent, toughest ships are happiest; dedication – unselfish and enthusiastic, them first you last; trust men – love them; belief in God.'

He told the cadets: 'Nelson was deeply religious and I always feel a lump in my throat at the beautiful prayer he wrote within an hour of his final battle and death. I have never wavered in my belief in God's power. One should never go into any action or contest without praying first and should never forget to thank him at the end. When I have failed in anything I have realised it is lack of prayer that has caused it – I have been trusting in myself.

'I have been a very lucky person – by which I mean God has been very kind to me, and I know that if I go on trusting him – without being anything but a sinner and far removed from saintliness – he will continue to favour my causes, so long as they are worthy.'

Miers ended by emphasising the first principle of leadership: 'Whoever would be the first among you shall be the servant of all.'[6]

Although he did not put any pressure on his son, John decided that he wanted to join the navy. 'My father was 40 when I was born and when I was young I knew him as a captain and an admiral,' he said. 'So my experience of the navy was through my father as a senior officer. I found it all very attractive. It never occurred to me you had to start at the bottom. He encouraged me and I just thought it was something I wanted to do.'

But like his father he had a problem with sight in one eye. It will be remembered that the forceful Mrs Miers persuaded the navy to take her son after it initially turned him down. In a similar way, Miers helped John. He discovered that a leading rugby player had started using contact lenses without any detriment to his game, and he successfully argued John's case with the Admiralty.

'Dad found an eye specialist and I duly learnt how to wear a contact lens that put me well inside the standards,' said John. 'Having passed the eye medical I never wore it again.'

He went to Britannia Royal Naval College, Dartmouth, as a cadet in 1965. Later he resisted the idea of volunteering for the Submarine Service but changed his mind. 'So many of my friends had already joined that it was the only thing to do,' he said. 'I did terribly badly on the basic training course – a mixture of idleness and cockiness – and there were signals concerning how I was to be failed. Somehow, someone senior decided that I should be allowed to scrape through. Perhaps they were still frightened of the wrath of Crap if they failed his son.

'Funnily enough, they never realised that he would have reacted totally differently. He would have given me the bollocking, not them. He was a great believer in supporting those who had the courage to make unpopular decisions.'

John recalled the time when the submarine HMS *Walrus* returned to HMS *Dolphin* at Gosport after an exercise and he was the casing officer. It was a weekend when the Submarine Old Comrades Association was holding a reunion. Standing on the jetty at dawn on the Saturday and watching the submarine come in were Miers – 'slightly the worse for wear after a night of heavy drinking' – and the Captain (S).

'I had always incurred the wrath of my commanding officer as casing officer,' said John. 'Something always went wrong. Inevitably on this day the casing party performed abysmally and at one stage it was too much for the captain, who shouted at the first lieutenant, "Stop Miers's leave for a week". As soon as we were secure the captain leapt ashore to report to the Captain (S). When he reached the top of the jetty he recognised my father, who smiled and said, "I have just come to take my son away for the weekend".

'My captain said, "That will be fine, sir". If only he had known that if he had said he had stopped my leave, my father would have laughed and said, "Jolly good show, do him good".'[7]

John went on to pass 'perisher' and to get his own submarine command. Miers was already a proud father. In August 1979 he went to a ceremony in Portsmouth to see the Commander-in-Chief Fleet, Admiral Sir James Eberle, present John with the Queen's Commendation for Brave Conduct. John was in the submarine HMS *Finwhale* when a Libyan cargo ship and an American freighter collided in fog off Gibraltar. He was praised for ignoring danger and showing skill and initiative during the evacuation of casualties.

'We were right there and closed to assist,' he said. 'I was in charge of the boarding party and we had to search for missing crewmen in the sinking freighter. It involved crawling along flooded passages in the dark to see if there were survivors at the other end, and it also involved tending to badly injured men. It was what anyone would have done in that situation but it was us who were there.'[8]

In 1986 John left the navy in the rank of lieutenant-commander to pursue a business career.

Miers had been out of uniform a long time when one day Pat decided to have a clearout at their home in Roehampton. She thought her husband no longer needed his uniforms and put them in the dustbin. Looking out of the window later, she was horrified to see dustmen walking down the street wearing the uniforms of a highly decorated rear-admiral. She rushed out and retrieved them.

In 1966 Miers had been admitted to the Worshipful Company of Tin Plate Workers Alias Wire Workers. This is a City of London livery company, originally given a royal charter as a trade guild in 1670. The livery companies, still going strong, see themselves as trustees of the City and carry out charity work.[9] The Miers family have been members of the Tin Plate Workers, on and off, for more than three centuries.

In the 16th century the family were yeoman farmers in the Furness district of Lancashire (now part of Cumbria) – not far from Barrow-in-Furness. They were among the earliest Quakers, but they suffered persecution – beatings, fines and imprisonment – and farming proved impossible. So one Nathaniel Miers went to London and in 1681 became an apprentice tin-plate worker, learning how to make such household products as pots, pans, candle-holders and lanterns. He served as the Master of the Tin Plate Workers in 1712 and prospered as a tin-plate merchant. Nathaniel's son John Miers was the Master in 1752, and he spread his business from London to Glamorgan. The family became considerable landowners in South Wales. A large part of their main estate, with important coal areas, was sold in 1914 for £325,000, a considerable sum in those days. But there were many beneficiaries and lawyers' fees swallowed a significant amount.[10]

In 1984 Admiral Miers followed his ancestors as the Master. By this time, however, he was a sick man. The diagnosis was liver cancer. 'He was hugely proud when he became the Master,' said Colin Brough, who was the Master in 1987–8. 'He was following a family tradition. I think he might have died a year or two earlier but for that. I'm sure he said to himself, "To hell with what is happening to my body, I'll become the Master". He was extremely frail but he battled on.'

Senior members hold a court meeting four times a year, and at one of these gatherings Brough, who thought it was time to widen the appeal of the company, proposed admitting women as liverymen. He laughed as he recalled: 'The admiral looked at me like thunder and basically said, "Over my dead body". A vote was taken and I was amazed that someone else put his hand up. There were just the two of us – 18 others refused to defy the admiral.

'Four years later, when I was the Master, it was approved. He would not have liked that. He was traditional and had lived in a male society. I remember him as an extremely kind man, courteous but a bit gruff at times. He was a man of honour.'

Years earlier, one of the court meetings had been told of John Miers's bravery award. 'He was moved to tears about his son,' said Brough. 'He was really a man with a soft heart – a bit of a softy. It was lovely to see it.'[11]

Another honour that Miers cherished was being a freeman of Inverness. The Queen Mother was also a freeman, and when they met at a function Miers pointed out that he was wearing his freeman's ring. The Queen Mother sighed and admitted that she had forgotten to put her ring on. The next time they met she wagged her finger and smiled. 'I've got it on,' she said.

At the end of 1984 Miers underwent 'a series of rather serious internal operations from which, with Pat's marvellous support, I hope in time to make a full recovery'. He left hospital a few days before he and Pat celebrated their ruby wedding anniversary on 20 January 1985.

An event that also pleased Miers was the launch of the nuclear submarine HMS *Torbay*, the fifth vessel to bear the name. At 5,208 tons and with a speed of 32 knots, the Trafalgar class boat, designed for Cold War operations, was a world away from Miers's *Torbay*. The builders, Vickers, invited him to the ceremony at Barrow-in-Furness on 8 March and he went with his wife, but it was a struggle.

One of the guests was Roy Foster, who had served with Miers in the wartime *Torbay*. Foster wanted to speak to him when the platform VIPs walked off to a lunch hosted by the directors of Vickers, but Miers had to go by car.

'I wrote to him saying I was sorry that we did not meet but that I hoped he was pleased with the drill and speed with which *Torbay* sped down the slipway. I had a very nice letter from him saying he was sorry that we did not make contact but how moved he had been by such a memorable day. Seeing him peering over the front of the platform, a thought crossed my mind that I hoped everything would go right. If Lady Herbert, who launched her, had found it necessary to give a push, I think she might have learnt a few new words and I would not put it past Crap to tell the chairman of Vickers to get the thing back up the slipway and do the drill again.'[12]

Miers replied to Foster's letter on 16 March and revealed how ill he had become:

The reason I was in a car is that I am trying to recuperate from several very serious operations which have put me out of action since last October in the course of which I have lost more than four stone and my collar size is down from seventeen and a half to fifteen. I am literally skin and bone and terribly weak, only being kept alive on a non-fatty diet and no alcohol by the marvellous love and care of Pat. I should never have gone but Pat supported the decision and Vickers were wonderful. They flew us up from Northolt, put us up in their guesthouse and even provided breakfast in bed!

I must say the lunch was the worst strain, with me unable to eat most of the courses, but all three speeches by the Vickers chairman, controller and Lady Herbert made very flattering remarks and, where I feared to be a nuisance, it seemed that they all appreciated us making the journey.

By the time he returned home he was 'absolutely exhausted'. The next day, Saturday, he had planned to go to Twickenham to see England and Scotland fight it out for the Calcutta Cup, but he was still very weak and the weather was freezing. For Miers to miss a big rugby match . . .

He spent several months sorting out his finances and compiling lists. One list detailed what wine should be taken from the cellar over the next three years.

In May he was in fighting mood again and appeared to be optimistic about his chances of recovery. Remarkably, at 78, he was still an employee of National Car Parks and wanted to get back to work. But his condition continued to deteriorate.

On 30 June 1985, during his beloved Wimbledon fortnight, he said from his bed at home: 'I'm still the Master [of the Tin Plate Workers] if I die today. If I die tomorrow, I'm a former Master.'

He died that day. His last word was 'Cheerio!'

In 2005 the nuclear submarine *Torbay* was affiliated with the Worshipful Company of Tin Plate Workers. By chance, liveryman Tony Woods met Commander Chris Groves, his godson, who happened to be *Torbay*'s captain. The strong links with Miers and the wartime *Torbay* made it an easy decision. Livery companies have a long tradition of supporting the armed forces.

Miers had joked with his family that it would not be worth holding a memorial service because few people would turn up. On 31 October 1985 the Metropolitan Cathedral of St George, Southwark, was packed for his service of thanksgiving. Admiral of the Fleet Sir John Fieldhouse represented the Duke of Edinburgh.

Rear-Admiral Sir Anthony Miers was buried at Tomnahurich Cemetery, Inverness, near his place of birth. His brother Ronald had died 11 years earlier.

One of the tributes came from Graham Stainforth, Master of Wellington College from 1956 to 1966, who had been at the school with Miers in the 1920s: 'Fierce determination allied to fine intelligence characterised him all his life. He calculated shrewdly and then acted resolutely. When war broke out some of us were discussing our contemporaries and the universal opinion was that the one character who could be guaranteed to get a VC was Tony Miers. Shortly after the investiture, when he was my guest in the common room, true to his image he went up to the Orange [his old dormitory] and challenged them to try to remove his trousers. Later he returned as happy as a sand-boy, with blood on his collar, having lost a shoe and retrieved other garments in a glorious scrimmage.

'But underneath the force and drive and occasional bluster on a short fuse one had many glimpses of a warm and generous spirit, a loyal friend, a devoted and almost docile family man.'

Stainforth had this telling observation: 'It was indeed fun to watch how little aware he was of the skill and patience with which his dear wife, Pat, was managing him.'[13]

Chapter 22

LUDOVIC KENNEDY ACCUSES

Commander Paul Chapman, who had been *Torbay*'s first lieutenant, wrote to Pat Miers soon after seeing her husband's obituary in *The Daily Telegraph* on 2 July 1985. Part of his letter said:

> *I was not all that surprised, having seen Sir Anthony's last to me dated 15/1/85. At his age a major op may well succeed even though the patient dies. But he was tough enough to last a few more months. I hope he was not in pain.*
>
> *These things have to happen sometime, but it is a reminder that we are now 'the older generation', and how best should we spend the evening of life? In Sir Anthony's case, he devoted so much energy and effort into all his activities that it was astonishing that he lasted as long as he did. So many of these activities were, of course, on behalf of others.[1]*

As well as expressing his sorrow, Chapman had another reason for writing. He wanted to warn Pat about Ludovic Kennedy. The previous year, at an hour's telephone notice, the broadcaster and writer had turned up in Chapman's home town of Poole, Dorset, to ask him about *Torbay*'s actions during her third patrol in July 1941 in the aftermath of the Battle of Crete. Chapman wrote:

> *Sir Anthony, with his well-known dislike of the media, had fobbed him off. So Ludovic came to me. His question was in the sense, 'Had not Torbay done things that would have been called war crimes if we had lost the war?'*
>
> *What I remembered, I told Ludovic. This would be incomplete, both from the passing of the years and because as first lieutenant my normal post during*

236

surface action would be in the control room. At least I was able to disabuse him of the notion that we had taken prisoners and then shot them. I also spoke of the unusual circumstances of the Battle of Crete.

Kennedy took notes and indicated that he might, at some stage, publish something about *Torbay*'s actions. The meeting troubled Chapman, and on 1 June 1984 he wrote to Kennedy, stressing: 'I recall no shooting of prisoners, and aver that this did not happen. *Torbay* did machine gun people in rubber boats. The people were uniformed and armed soldiers. At the time I thought that this was wrong, but later I came to agree that, in all the circumstances, it was right. I am glad that it was not I who had to make a snap judgement.'

Chapman sent another letter to Kennedy on 3 July 1984, pointing out that the Battle of Crete had been particularly vicious. The German 11 Air Corps, for example, had inflicted a 'new degree of savagery' on the Royal Navy, which paid a high price in men and ships as it evacuated thousands of soldiers after the island's defeat in May 1941. He wrote: 'I know from personal talk to survivors that if the Stukas had fuel remaining they stooged around machine-gunning anything they could see floating. My friend Dick Yorke, from the *Greyhound* [a destroyer], survived because he could not get out from under the litter of dead and dying on top of him in the bottom of a whaler.'

Kennedy continued to fail to get Miers to talk to him, and by January 1985 he had turned his attention to Pat, knowing that her husband was seriously ill. He admitted that he was probably stirring up trouble for nothing. He wrote to her: 'I would not wish his silence when I wrote a few years ago, and again now, to be misinterpreted. I myself believe that he could, if he wished, convincingly justify his action, and I am sorry for his sake that he has not availed himself of the opportunity to do so.'[2]

Finally he telephoned: 'This is Ludovic Kennedy and I wish to talk to Admiral Miers about a caique incident in the Aegean.'

Pat said she would ask him. The admiral was sitting in the dining room at their Roehampton home feeling extremely weak and said that he could not possibly speak to anyone. Pat went back to the telephone and said: 'Tony cannot speak to you – he is very ill with liver cancer and he is dying.' She put the phone down.[3]

In 1989 Kennedy published his autobiography, *On My Way To The Club*, in which he devoted several pages to 'a submarine atrocity'. He said Captain Stephen Roskill, the official naval historian, had told him of a 'disgraceful' episode involving a British submarine that attacked caiques carrying German troops off Crete. The submarine commander, it was claimed, ordered seven survivors in a dinghy from one of the caiques to be shot. Kennedy described him as 'a much-decorated officer who had risen to high rank . . . his courage and exploits were legendary'. The author compared the officer's actions to that of a German U-boat commander, Heinz-Wilhelm Eck, who was executed in 1945 after a British military court found him guilty of a war crime. Kennedy related how Eck's submarine, *U-582*, had sunk the Greek merchant ship *Peleus* while on patrol off the west coast of Africa on 13 March 1944.[4] In fact, the submarine was *U-852* and she was on passage to the east of Ascension Island, heading for a patrol in the Indian Ocean. Kennedy also placed Eck's execution on Luneberg Heath when it was in Hamburg. Detached observers might decide that it was hardly a reasonable comparison. The British submarine commander was said to have ordered the shooting of seven crack alpine soldiers. According to Chapman, they were still armed and heading 'lickety-split' back to Crete where probably they had been used to hunt down Allied soldiers hiding in the mountains after the island's surrender. It was in the heat of battle and the action was over quickly.

After sinking *Peleus*, Eck – not facing any threat – spent more than five hours in the area, ordering crewmen to use machine guns and grenades on survivors, nearly all of them civilians, who were unarmed and 'helpless'. The U-boat was carrying a doctor and even he joined in the carnage. A total of 36 died. There were only three survivors.[5]

Kennedy pointed out to his readers that he had been unable to get the British submarine commander to give his side of the story. He admitted that he could never have matched his courage 'in a hundred years', and questioned: 'What right had I to tarnish the reputation of an acknowledged war hero and needlessly distress his family?' But he still decided to do it. He concluded: 'Today he is dead . . . And I don't know which has nagged at me most, the lack of courage shown by the brave man in fending me off and declining to discuss what he had done, or my lack of courage in declining to write about it.'

One thing the British submarine commander was not short of was courage. He simply did not wish to revisit the past with Kennedy. The author admitted earlier in his autobiography that, as an adult, he still had a childhood fear of crossing a field with cows in it.[6] He had joined the Royal Naval Volunteer Reserve soon after the Second World War broke out, but there had been a proviso: 'Wherever I went in the war and whatever I did had to be in some outfit where there was the minimum likelihood of personal combat.'[7] Although he served in destroyers escorting convoys, he led a charmed life and for a year of the war acted as ADC to the Governor of Newfoundland, well away from danger.[8]

Kennedy did not name Miers or *Torbay*, but it was not long before they were identified. On 5 February 1989 *The Sunday Telegraph* ran a front-page story written by its defence correspondent, Simon O'Dwyer-Russell, with the headline 'Was Royal Navy VC submariner a war criminal?' The first two paragraphs read: 'The Ministry of Defence is to launch an urgent high-level inquiry into allegations that Britain's most decorated Second World War submarine commander ordered the killing of German prisoners in the Mediterranean in 1942.

'Extensive research by *The Sunday Telegraph* has established that the officer was 36-year-old Lt Cdr Tony Miers, commanding the submarine *Torbay*. He received a Victoria Cross from King George VI at an investiture at Buckingham Palace three weeks to the day after allegedly ordering the killings.'

Those two paragraphs contained five errors of fact: the Ministry of Defence was not having an urgent high-level inquiry; Miers was not the most decorated Second World War submarine commander [Lieutenant-Commander David Wanklyn was awarded the VC and three DSOs]; the Germans were not prisoners; the year was 1941; and the VC investiture took place more than 12 months after the action.

The report went on to say that Miers's order to shoot the enemy 'caused a near-mutiny among the *Torbay*'s crew with the submarine's first officer, Lt Tony Kidd, and an army soldier on board, refusing to shoot the Germans . . .'

There was never a near-mutiny among the crew because most of the men were below and would not have known what was going on during the surface action. The first lieutenant was Paul Chapman, not Kidd whose first name was Hugh but had the nickname Tono.

The reporter gave Kennedy as the source and repeated the author's comparison with the German submarine commander Heinz-Wilhelm Eck, giving the wrong U-boat and place of execution.

The story speculated that the Admiralty had not dealt with Miers at the time because he was a VC winner and it would have been too embarrassing. This was nonsense. The attack that earned Miers the award took place the following year.

Like Kennedy, the report failed to mention that after the caique ostensibly surrendered a German tried to throw a hand grenade at the submarine and another soldier had been about to open fire with a rifle. Both men were shot.

On 6 February *The Daily Telegraph* ran a similar story, but the 'urgent high-level inquiry' was toned down to 'The Ministry of Defence is investigating allegations . . .' Some of the errors resurfaced, and the Germans had become 'helpless prisoners'.

Two days later *The Daily Telegraph* published a letter from Miers's son John in which he told of the family's distress at the allegation. He pointed out that there were 'numerous inaccuracies and omissions' in the stories, and 'no mention is made of the fact that the German soldiers were armed and far from passive'.

He continued: 'I know that if my father ordered German soldiers to be fired upon it was because he had no alternative if he was to safeguard his own men, his submarine and the British soldiers on the nearby shore where the German soldiers would ultimately have landed.' He also pointed out that his father's patrol report had made no attempt to disguise what had happened, and that Admiral Cunningham, the Commander-in-Chief, Mediterranean, had commended him.

There was also a letter of support from the naval author John Winton, who wrote: 'In the luxury of peace we can criticise men like Miers. In wartime we desperately need them. If the Ministry of Defence really are conducting an inquiry, they should drop it.'

On 9 February the *Daily Mail* weighed in with a two-page spread highlighting the 'armchair campaign to massacre a war hero's reputation'. But a few days later *The Sunday Telegraph* produced another story by its defence correspondent headlined 'Miers killings storm grows'. It said that an investigation by Rear-Admiral Clarence Howard-Johnston had led to Eck's trial, and quoted him as saying: 'If Miers had been German and we investigated the shootings off Crete, I have absolutely no doubt that he would have been tried and probably executed for what he did.' The admiral appeared to have been told that the soldiers were prisoners and unarmed.

According to a third *Sunday Telegraph* story, 'The *Torbay*'s bloody night', George Bremner, one of the folbot commandos, who had been approached by Kennedy, 'shepherded' seven alpine soldiers from the caique on to the submarine's casing so that they could be held as prisoners. But Chapman said that a witness 'in a prime position to see' had insisted no such thing happened.

The Sunday Telegraph continued to receive letters on the subject and published six of them, all in support of Miers. The leading letter was from Roy Foster, who wrote: 'I was the third officer of *Torbay* and was present on the gun platform throughout the night action against the three caiques. Various reports have stated that the German soldiers aboard the second caique were made prisoners. This was not the case. These men, like many soldiers, sailors and airmen, were unfortunately in the wrong ship, the wrong place, at the wrong time. *Torbay*'s instructions were to prevent the landing, in Crete, of troops, ammunition, stores and fuel. This was war. All war is brutal. It is unfortunate that submarine warfare does not allow the rescue of survivors.'

Vice-Admiral Sir Ian McGeoch pointed out: 'The *Torbay* was close inshore in the German-dominated Greek waters from which the Mediterranean Fleet, lacking adequate air cover, had been driven with heavy losses by the Luftwaffe.

'To have remained on the surface while embarking survivors would not only have hazarded the *Torbay* and her crew, but prejudiced the achievement of her vitally important mission.

'To leave German combatants to be rescued by their own side would have been to add gratuitously to the enemy's fighting power. Miers accepted full responsibility for his action, while submitting it to the judgement of his superiors. As we know, he was vindicated. Let us not lose, in peacetime, what the celebrated naval historian Mahan called "the sentiment of what war requires".'

A poignant note was sounded by a reader who wrote: 'I have just watched my wife set off for the market in her wheelchair to which she is confined as a result of injuries received when her [fully illuminated] hospital ship was sunk during the Sicily landing. I have never heard any mention of that particular crime.'[9]

In the House of Commons on 21 February, Conservative MP Cyril Townsend asked whether the Ministry of Defence 'is going to carry out an internal inquiry into the actions of the late Rear-Admiral Sir Anthony Miers VC DSO, when in command of the submarine *Torbay* in the Mediterranean in 1941'.

Defence Minister Archie Hamilton replied: 'No.'[10]

Five days later *The Sunday Telegraph* returned to the subject, publishing a letter from Bremner in which he gave his version of events on 9 July and also on August 18, when *Torbay* was trying to rescue Allied soldiers from Crete.

He complained: 'Miers was always very generous with bravery awards to his officers and crew . . . As far as I know, none of the folbot section who sailed with him were recommended for bravery which may be due to his great dislike of the army . . .'

This was not true. Miers was proud of his family's extensive service with the army, and at the end of his report on the special operation to rescue soldiers from Crete he singled out Bremner for praise in risking his life on several occasions. Bremner was subsequently awarded the Military Medal.

Bremner's letter ended: 'Miers was brave, and deserved all his honours and awards, but I will never forgive him for his actions in the shooting incident, which I have had to live with on my conscience for the past forty-seven years.'

But the troubled conscience was not in evidence when he wrote to Miers in 1981 asking for help with a book he planned to help write called *Submarine Soldiers*. He ended his letter: 'I should like to take this opportunity to say thank you to you and the crew for all your bravery and skill in taking us out of so many tight spots during my patrols with *Torbay*.'[11]

Miers replied explaining that he had not kept records 'as I have always been mainly interested in the future' and that Chapman was probably the best person to contact. Bremner may have taken exception to Miers's typical bluntness: 'I would much rather not become involved in any interviews or further correspondence.'[12]

In 1989, the year that *On My Way To The Club* was published, Chapman also had a book out, *Submarine Torbay*, in which he added a piece in the wake of the controversy caused by Kennedy's accusation. Chapman wrote: 'The writer's opinion, for what it may be worth, is that there is more of a resemblance to a publicity stunt than to an unburdening of conscience. He who inspired the story was in home waters on the date in question, and had known of the matter for some years.'

Vice-Admiral Sir Ronald Brockman, who had been on the personal staff of the First Sea Lord, Admiral of the Fleet Sir Dudley Pound, at the time of *Torbay*'s exploits, read Chapman's book and congratulated him on it. Brockman had known Miers since about 1930 and knew 'full well how tough he was and what a magnificent leader'. He added: 'War is a very nasty business and personally I cannot remember any adverse comment in the Admiralty about Tony's actions off Crete in dealing with the German soldiers. I felt very much for Pat . . . what a swine that Ludovic is.'[13]

Pat received many letters of support. Typical was a message from a Royal Naval Reserve officer, John Briggs, who had served under Miers in *Theseus*. He sent copies of two highly critical letters he had written to *The Sunday Telegraph* in the hope that they would 'ease the pain and insult to your family'. The newspaper declined to publish the letters.[14]

In 2005 Ludovic Kennedy had little to say about the controversy he had provoked. Referring to his autobiography, he said: 'I note that in that I have not named Commander Miers or Rear-Admiral Miers as he later became. I must have written about it somewhere else, but I don't recall where or when.'[15]

What Kennedy could not remember was a lengthy article in *The Telegraph Magazine* in 1991 under a large headline, 'War Crimes'. This time he named

Miers and again compared him with Eck. Kennedy corrected some of his earlier errors but went on to make others. Describing Miers's character, he pointed out that as a young officer he had been court-martialled for striking a rating. Actually, the charge was attempting to strike a rating. The fact that Miers reported himself was not mentioned. Moving on to the events of 9 July 1941, Kennedy said the caiques that were attacked had been carrying a cargo of bay leaves and raisins. According to Miers, one of the vessels was ferrying petrol and a second had ammunition and oil. A schooner that also came under fire was 'quickly ablaze from stem to stern' because it was 'filled' with explosives and petrol.

Kennedy went on to give Bremner's version of the seven mountain troops from the second caique being on the casing of the submarine, all of them unarmed – which Chapman has already disputed. This is what Miers put in his patrol report:

> **0357** *Opened fire on the second caique whose crew took to the water whilst those remaining on board made signals of surrender, shouting, 'Captain is Greek'. The submarine was put alongside, the berthing party on the casing being accompanied and covered by one of the embarked soldiers with a tommy-gun, with which he shot an obviously German soldier as he was about to hurl a grenade.*
>
> *After a brief pretence at being Greek, the whole party when addressed in German by the navigating officer, replied in German, 'I am German'. They were all forced to launch and jump into a large rubber float (which was the only form of lifeboat) and the demolition charge was then laid and fired. The navigating officer (who was fortunate to use his pistol first against a lurking German who was about to fire a rifle at point-blank range) reported that the caique was filled with ammunition, oil and petrol. She was of about 100 tons, was fitted with a spark W/T transmitter, wore the German flag and had LV painted on her side.*
>
> **0427** *Submarine cast off and with the Lewis gun accounted for the soldiers in the rubber raft to prevent them regaining their ship . . .* [16]

The action against the second caique had lasted 30 minutes. Unlike Eck, Miers had not spent hours looking for people to kill. A folbot commando and Chapman had refused his order to open fire on the soldiers in the raft, which was apparently carried out by a rating.

So were seven alpine soldiers killed in this way? Although Miers said he 'accounted for' the soldiers, he could not have known for certain that they had all died. This was a night action and, according to Chapman, they were at least 100 yards from the submarine. And the Germans never made such a claim. The only source putting the number at seven appears to be Bremner, which Kennedy readily accepted. Bremner, of course, did not witness the incident.

Kennedy went on to say that Miers's action caused 'consternation' among his superiors. He wrote: 'What Admiral Cunningham, the Commander-in-Chief Mediterranean, and the Board of Admiralty were most concerned about were reprisals . . .'

There is no evidence that Cunningham or the Admiralty expressed any concern. The admiral wrote: 'This was a brilliantly conducted offensive patrol which inflicted severe damage on the enemy. These results are not obtained by chance, but by sound appreciation and careful planning, which together with his offensive spirit, render Lieutenant-Commander ACC Miers, Royal Navy, an outstanding submarine commander.'[17]

Miers was very much a man in the mould of Cunningham, who was 'brutally ruthless' and famously issued the order, 'Sink, burn and destroy. Let nothing pass'.[18] With years to reflect, there was only praise for Miers when Cunningham's autobiography, *A Sailor's Odyssey*, appeared in 1951, and there was no criticism in John Winton's 1998 biography, *Cunningham, The Greatest Admiral Since Nelson*.

Pound, the First Sea Lord, had long ago made up his mind about the enemy. In 1936, when Admiral Erich Raeder, commander-in-chief of the Germany navy, refused to attend the funeral of Admiral of the Fleet the Earl Beatty because of the humiliation of the surrender at Scapa Flow at the end of the First World War, Pound commented: 'Who wants these sinkers of hospital ships and machine-gunners of sailors in the water at Admiral Beatty's funeral anyway?' (German U-boats had targeted British hospital ships during the First Wold War.)

But Kennedy claimed: '. . . the Admiralty sent a letter instructing him

[Miers] in the strongest terms not to indulge in such practices again.' Kennedy was asked if he had seen a copy of this letter but he declined to answer.

A book called *Waves Of Hate, Naval Atrocities Of The Second World War* appeared in 2002, and the author, Tony Bridgland, devoted a chapter to Miers and *Torbay*, making claims similar to Kennedy's. He wrote: 'Privately, Miers received a strong letter from their Lordships instructing him to desist with such tactics on future patrols.' Bridgland was also asked if he had seen a copy of this letter, and he replied: 'I am certain that I never saw the letter you mention.'

The author also wrote: '. . . in 1989, the official naval historian, Captain Stephen Roskill, said in an interview with broadcaster Ludovic Kennedy, "It was a submarine atrocity. It was disgraceful".'[19] In fact, Roskill had died six years earlier.

Bridgland increased the number of men killed to ten, giving the captain of the caique *LV*, Fritz Ehlebracht, as the source. But in its story headlined 'The *Torbay*'s bloody night', *The Sunday Telegraph* carried an interview with Ehlebracht in which he said he saw only two sailors killed 'trying to get away as fast as possible from the enemy'. He and other survivors were rescued by a German flying boat later that day and taken to Athens.[20]

Only one senior officer appears to have expressed concern about *Torbay*'s attacks and that was Admiral Sir Max Horton, Flag Officer Submarines. The Board of Admiralty only became involved because he asked for its guidance.

Horton wrote: 'The action taken by *Torbay* at 1450 on 4th July and at 0427 on 9th July 1941 raises an important question of policy. There is reason to believe that the incidents referred to have become known to the enemy and that his propaganda has made much of them. The possibility of reprisals clearly exists and such reprisals may not only affect submarines but also the crews and passengers of any ship sunk by enemy action. As far as I am aware, the enemy has not up to now made a habit of firing on personnel in the water, on rafts, or in open boats, even when such personnel were members of the fighting services; since the incidents referred to in *Torbay*'s report, he may feel he is justified in doing so. In my opinion it would be wise for Admiralty to issue a clear statement of the policy to be followed in this matter and, in this connection, looking at it from the material as opposed to the ethical point of view, it appears that we have more to lose than the enemy by following the policy adopted by *Torbay*.'[21]

Horton sent his letter on 25 September 1941 and received a curt response on 14 November: 'Their lordships are satisfied that commanding officers of HM submarines can be trusted to follow the dictates of humanity and the traditions of the service in matters of this kind and that it is unnecessary to promulgate general rules which might give the impression that commanding officers were in the habit of taking action not in accordance with the accepted custom.'[22]

Horton's point about the enemy being handed a propaganda coup was checked by naval intelligence, which found that the Germans had not made that much of *Torbay*'s actions. The first reference came as late as 7 September, when there were several broadcasts in different languages, including English. There was only one German newspaper report. In a memo, the director of naval intelligence pointed out: 'No mention of reprisals has been made and the incident had only a single day's interest for the wireless section of the German ministry of propaganda.'

This is what the Germans broadcast: 'The British have once more perpetrated an outrage. Three small Greek sailing boats in the eastern Mediterranean were attacked by a British submarine. Two of the Greek craft were shelled from close range and set on fire. The submarine then approached the two sinking boats and took their crews under machine-gun fire, whereby four of the sailors were killed. After the survivors were taken ashore by the third sailing boat, they made the following statement under oath. The person who navigated one of the sailing boats described how a shell hit his boat. He ordered his crew to jump overboard. An officer from the submarine called out to the men remaining on deck to take to their rubber boat. While his men were scrambling into the lifeboat and trying to get away from the burning craft, the submarine opened fire on the lifeboat from only twenty yards. Four sailors were killed and two severely wounded. The bullet-ridden rubber boat sank. The submarine machine-gunned the swimming men. By skilfully dodging the machine-gun fire, none of the survivors were hurt. After a time the submarine disappeared.'[23]

There was no mention of the fact that the caiques were carrying soldiers. One reason why the propaganda broadcasts ended so quickly could have had something to do with the atrocities being carried out by German forces in Crete. They had met fierce resistance from day one of their invasion on 20 May 1941, with one New Zealand battalion wiping out 155 paratroopers near Maleme 'like a duck shoot' and civilians outside Perivolia killing Germans with axes and spades.[24] North of Daratsos, the enemy used hospital patients as human shields. After Crete's surrender around 900 civilians and resistance fighters were executed as reprisals – for example, 60 at Kondomari and 200 at Kastelli Kissamou. Entire villages were destroyed.[25]

At sea, German pilots found it hard to show mercy. Horton's letter led to the involvement of M Branch, the Admiralty's secretariat, which pointed out that HMS *Kingston* had been fired on while picking up survivors from the destroyer HMS *Greyhound*. This ship was hit by Stuka dive-bombers and sank in the Kithera Channel, north west of Crete, on 22 May.[26]

Crewmen from the sinking cruiser HMS *Gloucester* were machine-gunned and bombed in the water. A total of 722 lost their lives. Dive-bombers also attacked survivors from Mountbatten's doomed destroyer HMS *Kelly*.[27] There were cases of attacks on lifeboats from merchant ships. And the enemy were not averse to attacking their own men, as Cunningham discovered in July 1940. British destroyers were bombed as they picked up 545 survivors from the stricken Italian cruiser *Bartolomeo Colleoni* and during the voyage back to Alexandria.[28]

M Branch noted: 'The navy has been criticised in some quarters for being over careful of the lives of enemy sailors. In all the circumstances and in view of the fact that the enemy have much more to answer for in this respect than we have, it is not proposed to take any further action.'

Horton had emerged from the First World War as a distinguished submarine commander, and went on to achieve great distinction as Commander-in-Chief Western Approaches. In that capacity he is widely recognised as the principal architect of victory in the Battle of the Atlantic. It is surprising that in 1941, as Flag Officer Submarines, he seems to have been unaware of the ferocity of the fighting in and around Crete. He could not have been more wrong when he wrote: 'As far as I am aware, the enemy has not up to now made a habit of firing on personnel in the water, on rafts, or in open boats . . .'

On the subject of Crete, Kennedy ignored Chapman's plea to consider Miers's actions in the context of that fighting.

It is worth recalling that on several occasions Miers made a point of sparing Greek crews of sailing vessels which were carrying supplies for the Germans, and on 9 August 1941 off Benghazi he did not torpedo an Italian vessel almost certainly masquerading as a hospital ship, noting: 'In view of the enemy's shameful record of abuse of every known privilege of war among civilised peoples the temptation to fire was great and, in the main, the spirit of the ship's company seemed to favour no quarter being given, but in the end the dictates of humanity traditional to the Royal Navy prevailed and I reluctantly broke off the attack.'

Towards the end of his article Kennedy indulged in speculation for which he offered no evidence: 'Should he [Miers] have been brought to trial by court martial for the second time in his career? On strictly legal grounds, yes. But to have removed from his command one of the most courageous and successful of British submarine captains at a time when our fortunes in the Mediterranean were at a low ebb was to ask the Admiralty too much.

' . . . there was later reason to suppose that the reprisals the Admiralty and Admiral Cunningham feared eventually took place . . . Miers must bear some responsibility for the murder of British commandos captured in the Aegean in 1942.'

In fact, an order to execute British commandos was issued by Hitler in October 1942 – some 15 months after Miers's attacks on the caiques – and it stemmed largely from his anger over the success of raids by special forces and in particular an attack on the Isle of Sark in the Channel Islands when German prisoners were shot while trying to escape.

Kennedy went on to point out that Miers continued to enjoy a successful naval career, becoming Admiral President of the Royal Naval College at Greenwich, a post he never held.

In his autobiography and the magazine article, Kennedy stressed that his main source had been Captain Roskill, whose books included *The War At Sea 1939–1945*. The distinguished historian, he insisted, had described Miers's action as an 'atrocity'.

This has been disputed by Roskill's eldest son, Nicholas Roskill, who revealed: 'I was puzzled that my late father could have encouraged Ludovic Kennedy to write about the alleged shooting incident or, indeed, referred to it without qualification as "disgraceful" and an "atrocity". My father was always exceptionally careful about the dangers of over-dramatisation of wartime events. I felt that it was wholly uncharacteristic of him to have positively encouraged Kennedy to publicise an episode, the facts for which must be uncertain . . .

'My father was always meticulous about his facts.'

Nicholas Roskill did his own checking: 'I was able to establish with some certainty that, far from encouraging Kennedy, my father had urged him to act with the greatest caution in publicising the episode, about which he was himself very unsure. Indeed, he could not remember for certain which submarine was involved. He warned Kennedy about the dangers of publication, the need to check facts and not to rely on memory. Most important of all, he evidently felt the episode was potentially so delicate that he insisted Kennedy should never mention his name in this connection. Kennedy promised to honour this request.'

Nicholas Roskill continued: 'I have had an extensive and unsatisfactory exchange of letters with Kennedy, who has accused me of many things, including being impertinent, seeking to protect Lady Miers, trying to exercise censorship over him, disagreeing with my own father, knowing nothing about the subject and acting with effrontery! My own view is that he has taken this aggressive attitude because he has unwisely trodden in a sensitive area, has broken his word and has sought to gain personal publicity from an episode about which no one can now be certain . . .

'I have been in touch with Lady Miers and I have endeavoured to persuade Kennedy to apologise to her and her family. Whatever the facts may be, it is surely wrong that the wife and family of a distinguished holder of the Victoria Cross should be greatly upset by a publicity seeking television personality.'[29]

The Miers family remain angry about Kennedy's accusation. 'To do something like that is unbelievable,' said John Miers. 'It had nothing to do with the facts. Here were men who were the enemy, with guns, in uniform. The shore was two miles away, they could swim, let alone go in a boat. They could go and kill some of our soldiers. That's war. We're not sitting in armchairs. Kennedy was trying to make it into something it wasn't. I thought it was disgraceful.

'My mother was very upset. The thing that upsets all our family is that as a result of this man putting something in print my father is now an alleged war criminal. He's not an alleged war criminal. Just because someone decides he wants to accuse him doesn't mean he's an alleged war criminal. It's like saying he's probably innocent but he might not be. He is innocent.'[30]

Lieutenant-Colonel Christopher Miers, John's cousin, said: 'Ludovic Kennedy is a sanctimonious shit. If he had published before Tony's death he would have been sued for libel. When the allegations appeared in the press, supporters of Tony offered to put up whatever amount might be necessary to fight a case. But Pat had to tell them that the laws of libel no longer apply after death.'[31]

In 1994 Ludovic Kennedy was knighted for services to journalism.

Appendix 1

Awards of Rear-Admiral Sir Anthony Miers

Victoria Cross (*London Gazette*, 7 July 1942).

Knight Commander of the Order of the British Empire (1959).

Companion of the Order of the Bath (1958).

Distinguished Service Order (*London Gazette*, 7 October 1941). For courage, enterprise and devotion to duty in successful submarine patrols.

Bar to DSO (*London Gazette*, 7 April 1942). For courage, skill and coolness in successful submarine patrols.

Mention in Despatches (*London Gazette*, 1 January 1941). For general good service.

1939–45 Star.

Atlantic Star.

Africa Star bar North Africa 1942–43.

Pacific Star bar Burma.

Defence Medal.

War Medal (with MiD oak leaf).

Naval General Service Medal 1909–62 bars Cyprus, Near East.

George VI Coronation Medal 1937.

Elizabeth II Coronation Medal 1953.

Elizabeth II Silver Jubilee Medal 1977.

Legion of Merit, Officer, United States (*London Gazette*, 28 May 1946). For distinguished service to the Allied cause throughout the war.

APPENDIX 2

HMS TORBAY, THE T (TRITON) CLASS SUBMARINE

T class submarines were built to replace the Oberon, Parthian and Rainbow classes. The first boat, *Triton*, was ordered by the Admiralty in 1935 and completed in 1938. Fifty-three of the submarines were completed between 1938 and 1946, and they were built in three groups. *Torbay* was one of the 15 boats of Group One, 9 of which were lost during the Second World War, including *Triton*.

Specification – HMS *Torbay*
Pennant number: 79
Laid down: 21 November 1938
Launched: 9 April 1940
Completed: 14 January 1941
Builder: HM Dockyard, Chatham
Normal displacement: 1,325 tons
Length: 275ft
Beam: 26ft 7in
Draught: 12ft
Speed: 15.25kts on the surface, 8kts submerged
Engines: diesel engines and electric motors
Batteries: 336 cells weighing c.150 tons
Diving depth: 300ft
Watertight compartments: 6
Main armament: 10 x 21in torpedo tubes, 1 x 4in gun
Complement: 61 in wartime
Patrol duration: up to 42 days

When Japan surrendered, *Torbay* and *Trident* were the only Group One boats still operational. *Torbay* was sold in December 1945 for scrap, a sudden and sad end for a submarine that had given such valuable service. In a final tribute the breaker's yard cut her name from the metal and presented it to Anthony Miers. It remains in the family's possession.

APPENDIX 3

MAPS

THE MEDITERRANEAN THEATRE 1941/42

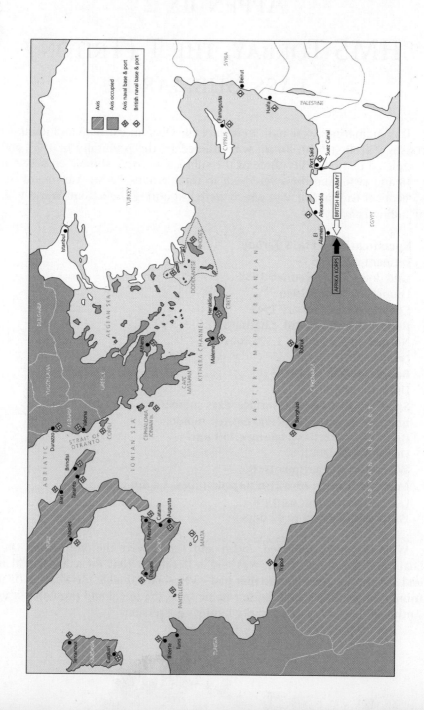

THE CORFU HARBOUR RAID

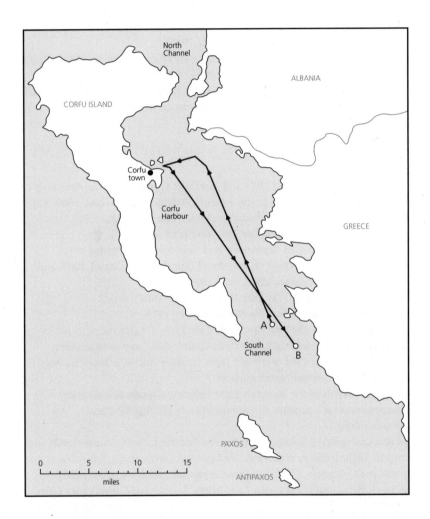

The attack that won Miers the Victoria Cross. (A) At 19:42 on 4 March 1942 Torbay entered the Corfu Channel from the south. (B) At 11:20 on 5 March the submarine finally emerged from the channel after torpedoing two supply ships in the harbour and evading patrol vessels, a destroyer, a plane, 40 depth charges – and a boom defence schooner.

NOTES AND SOURCES

Chapter 1

1. Miers's character: obituary, *The Times* (2 July 1985).
2. All naval postings and promotions and their dates are taken from Miers's service record.
3. Harry Oram's teaching and the collision of *L12* and *H47*: Wendy Harris, *The Rogue's Yarn, The Sea-going Life Of Captain 'Joe' Oram* (Leo Cooper, 1993), ch. 10; A.S. Evans, *Beneath The Waves, A History Of HM Submarine Losses 1904–1971*, pt 3 (William Kimber, 1986).
4. *Thetis*: Harris, *The Rogue's Yarn*, ch.17.

Chapter 2

1. Leaving for war on 12 August 1914 and arrival in France: *Historical Records Of The Queen's Own Cameron Highlanders*, seven volumes (William Blackwood, 1909–62).
2. Captain Douglas Miers and the Sudan and Boer War campaigns: ibid.
3. Lance Corporal Richard George: *The 79th News* (October 1914).
4. Letter from Captain Miers: 23 September 1914: *The 79th News* (October 1914).
5. Family background: interviews with Colonel Douglas Miers, April 2007, and Lieutenant-Colonel Christopher Miers, July 2007.
6. Marriage of Captain Miers: *The 79th News* (January 1902).
7. Bandsman Henry Rosher: *The 79th News* (January 1915).
8. Captain Ewen Brodie: *The 79th News* (April 1915).
9. Regimental casualties: *Historical Records Of The Queen's Own Cameron Highlanders*.
10. Regimental Records of the Somerset Light Infantry and War Diary for July 1917: death of Lieutenant-Colonel Maurice Miers.
11. Regimental Records of the Somerset Light Infantry: Captain Ronald Miers.
12. Unnamed corporal's account of Captain Miers's killing: *The Times* (29 November 1901).
13. Trial and execution of Solomon van As: *The Heidelberg News* (27 June 1902) and the Somerset Light Infantry magazine, *The Light Bob Gazette* (n.d.).
14. Superstitions: interview with Lieutenant-Commander John Miers, May 2007.
15. Margaret Miers: interviews with Lady Miers, Lieutenant-Commander John Miers, Colonel Douglas Miers and Lieutenant-Colonel Christopher Miers, 2007/8; Margaret Miers's letter to the War Office, n.d. but probably sent in October 1914.
16. William Wyamar Vaughan and F.B. Malim: David Newsome, *A History Of Wellington College 1859–1959* (John Murray, 1959).
17. Love of sport: interviews with Lady Miers and Lieutenant-Commander John Miers, 2007/8.
18. Commander Richard Compton-Hall: *The Submarine Review* (July 1997).

19. Graham Stainforth: *Wellington Year Book* (1985).

20. Eyesight and VC prediction: interviews with Lady Miers and Lieutenant-Commander John Miers, 2007.

Chapter 3

1. Court martial: report in newspaper, unknown (17 February 1933). Probably a Plymouth newspaper.

2. Rugby injury: note on service record, 3 March 1933.

3. Origin of Gamp and Crap: various sources.

4. Hong Kong posting: interview with Lieutenant-Commander John Miers, May 2007.

5. Paddy Dale and Sub-Lieutenant Grace: written reminiscences of George Pickup, n.d.

6. Hugh Mackenzie: *The Sword Of Damocles, Some Memories Of Vice Admiral Sir Hugh Mackenzie* (The Royal Navy Submarine Museum, 1995), ch. 6.

7. Richard Dyer: letter from Lieutenant-Commander Dyer to Commander Paul Chapman, 26 August 1990.

8. Loss of *Rainbow* and *Triad*: Evans, *Beneath The Waves*, pt. 4.

9. *L54*'s sporting prowess: interview with Lieutenant-Commander John Miers, May 2007.

10. Miers's driving: interview with Colonel Douglas Miers, April 2007.

11. Horton and young captains: Vice-Admiral Sir Arthur Hezlet, *British And Allied Submarine Operations In World War II, vol. 1* (The Royal Navy Submarine Museum, 2001), ch. 2.

12. Alexander McCulloch: written reminiscences, 12 October 1983.

13. Frederick Rumsey: written reminiscences, n.d.

14. Obituary, Paul Chapman: *The Daily Telegraph* (January 1994).

15. Collision with tanker in Loch Long and other mishaps: Commander Paul Chapman, written reminiscences, n.d.

16. Loss of *Sahib* and *Cachalot*: Evans, *Beneath The Waves*, pt 4.

Chapter 4

1. Loss of *Odin*, *Grampus* and *Orpheus*: Evans, *Beneath the Waves*, pt. 4. Hezlet, *British And Allied Submarine Operations in World War II*, ch. 5.

2. Torpedo shortages: Hezlet, *British And Allied Submarine Operations in World War II*, ch. 9.

3. Miers: report of 1st Mediterranean war patrol, 23 April–13 May 1941.

4. *Kingston*: Paul Chapman, *Submarine Torbay* (Robert Hale, 1989), ch. 4.

5. Report of Captain 1st Submarine Flotilla to Commander-in-Chief, Mediterranean, 3 June 1941.

6. Miers: report of 2nd Mediterranean war patrol, 28 May–16 June 1941.

7. Greece and Crete and the Royal Navy's losses: Andrew Cunningham, *A Sailor's Odyssey, The Autobiography Of Admiral Of The Fleet Viscount Cunningham Of Hyndhope* (Hutchinson, 1951), chs 25, 28 and 30.

8. Report of Captain 1st Submarine Flotilla to Commander-in-Chief, Mediterranean, 4 July 1941.

9. Cunningham: message dated 21 July 1941.

Chapter 5

1. Miers: report of 3rd Mediterranean war patrol, 28 June–15 July 1941.
2. Chapman: *Submarine Torbay*, ch. 6.
3. Miers: report of 3rd Mediterranean war patrol.
4. Report of Captain 1st Submarine Flotilla to Commander-in-Chief, Mediterranean, 29 July 1941.
5. Cunningham: message dated 13 August 1941.
6. Ludovic Kennedy: *On My Way To The Club* (William Collins, 1989).

Chapter 6

1. Miers: report of 4th Mediterranean war patrol, 2–22 August 1941.
2. Kennedy: *On My Way To The Club*.
3. Chaos on Crete beach: letter from Paul Chapman to George Bremner, 12 June 1981.
4. Major Ray Sandover: Antony Beevor, *Crete, The Battle And The Resistance* (John Murray, 1991), ch. 21.
5. Report of Captain 1st Submarine Flotilla to Commander-in-Chief, Mediterranean, 17 September 1941.
6. Crete holiday: letter from Miers to Commander Richard Compton-Hall, 17 January 1985.
7. Bremner: *The Sunday Telegraph* (26 February 1989).

Chapter 7

1. Roy Foster: written reminiscences, 25 August 1987.
2. Miers: report of 5th Mediterranean war patrol, 6–28 September 1941.
3. Report of Captain 1st Submarine Flotilla to Commander-in-Chief, Mediterranean, 12 November 1941.
4. Cunningham: message dated 15 December 1941.

Chapter 8

1. Philip Le Gros: written reminiscences, n.d., and an interview arranged by the Royal New Zealand Navy Museum, December 1994.

Chapter 9

1. Miers: report of 6th Mediterranean war patrol, 7–18 October 1941.
2. Information on Captain (later Lieutenant-Colonel) John Haselden supplied by his son, Gerald Haselden, and the Long Range Desert Group Preservation Society.
3. Report of Captain 1st Submarine Flotilla to Commander-in-Chief, Mediterranean, 2 December 1941.
4. *Proteus* and Miers's character: written reminiscences of Commander Jeremy Nash and interview, February 2007.
5. Commander Philip Francis: obituaries in *The Times* and *The Daily Telegraph* (October 2000).

Chapter 10

1. Miers: report of 7th Mediterranean war patrol, 10–24 November.

2. Report of Lieutenant-Colonel Robert Laycock on Operations Copper and Flipper, 10 February 1942.

3. Lieutenant Tommy Langton: Elizabeth Keyes, *Geoffrey Keyes VC Of The Rommel Raid* (George Newnes, 1956), ch. 23.

4. Report of *Talisman*'s 4th Mediterranean war patrol.

5. Background of Lieutenant-Colonel Geoffrey Keyes: Keyes, *Geoffrey Keyes VC*, chs 11, 12, 14, 16, 17, 20.

6. Girlfriend Pamela: Keyes, *Geoffrey Keyes VC*, ch. 22; Michael Asher, *Get Rommel* (Weidenfeld and Nicolson, 2004), ch. 19.

7. Rommel attack: Keyes, *Geoffrey Keyes VC*, ch. 24; Asher, *Get Rommel*, ch. 27.

8. Keyes: *Geoffrey Keyes VC*.

9. Death of Keyes: Asher, *Get Rommel*, ch. 28.

10. Report of Captain 1st Submarine Flotilla to Commander-in-Chief, Mediterranean, 10 February 1942.

11. Row over *Talisman*: Chapman, *Submarine Torbay*, ch. 9.

12. Rommel's whereabouts and British intelligence: Asher, *Get Rommel*, ch. 29.

Chapter 11

1. Augustus Armishaw: Miers, report, 3 December 1941.

2. Miers: report of 8th Mediterranean war patrol, 9–27 December 1941.

3. Captain Robert Wilson: report of Folbot Operations.

4. Report of Captain 1st Submarine Flotilla to Commander-in-Chief, Mediterranean, 15 January 1942.

5. Miers's torpedo blunder: Chapman, *Submarine Torbay*, ch. 10.

6. Miers: report of 9th Mediterranean war patrol, 8–31 January 1942.

7. Report of Captain 1st Submarine Flotilla to Commander-in-Chief, Mediterranean, 26 March 1942.

8. Miers: report on 'Organisation and Training of Folbot Section', 31 January 1942, and sent to Captain 1st Submarine Flotilla.

9. Cunningham: *A Sailor's Odyssey*, ch. 34.

10. Jeremy Nash: letter to the author, 20 February 2009.

11. Castelorizzo raid: Cunningham, *A Sailor's Odyssey*, ch. 25.

Chapter 12

1. VC prediction: interview with Lady Miers, February 2007.

2. VC boast: interview with Lieutenant-Colonel Christopher Miers, July 2007.

3. Report of Captain 1st Submarine Flotilla to Commander-in-Chief, Mediterranean, 2 April 1942.

4. Miers: report of 10th Mediterranean war patrol, 20 February–18 March 1942.

5. Report of Captain 1st Submarine Flotilla to Commander-in-Chief, Mediterranean, 2 April 1942.

6. Interview with Philip Le Gros, arranged by the Royal New Zealand Navy Museum.
7. Cunningham on Miers: Cunningham, *A Sailor's Odyssey*, ch. 34.
8. Pridham Wippell: Order Of The Day No. 2, 12 May 1942.
9. Leslie Philips: *Ilford Recorder* (8 November 1945).
10. Philips's ashes: Chapman, *Submarine Torbay*, ch. 15.
11. Chapman on Miers's VC: letter from Paul Chapman, recipient unknown, 2 July 1984.

Chapter 13
1. Miers: report of 11th Mediterranean war patrol, 2–24 April 1942.
2. Leslie Philips: *Ilford Recorder* (8 November 1945).
3. Chapman: *Submarine Torbay*, ch. 15.
4. Report of Captain 1st Submarine Flotilla to Commander-in-Chief, Mediterranean, 1 May 1942.
5. Interview with Philip Le Gros, arranged by the Royal New Zealand Navy Museum.
6. Miers: report of *Torbay*'s passage home, 8 June 1942.
7. Robert Clutterbuck: comments made in 1958.

Chapter 14
1. Buckingham Palace investiture: information supplied by Sir David Miers and Lieutenant-Colonel Christopher Miers.
2. Honor Miers: letter to her husband Ronald, 29 July 1942.
3. Tribute from the Cameron Highlanders: *The 79th News* (October 1942).
4. *Daily Mirror* (8 July 1942).
5. Miers's attack on the press: report, newspaper unknown (6 August 1942).
6. Miers's assessment of Chapman: report covered the period from 8 January 1941 to 22 August 1942.
7. Chapman's career: obituary, *The Daily Telegraph* (January 1994).
8. Chapman's comments on Miers and submarine operations: interview arranged by the Imperial War Museum, September 1993.
9. Chapman's comments on Midshipman Drake and Lieutenant Kidd: written comments made to Gus Britton (1981) and Commander Richard Compton-Hall (1986) of the Royal Navy Submarine Museum.
10. Miers's assessment of Kidd: report covered the period 13 April 1941–27 October 1942.
11. Miers's assessment of Verschoyle-Campbell: report covered the period 22 March 1941–27 October 1942.
12. Miers's assessment of Melville-Ross: report covered the period 22 March 1942–27 October 1942.
13. Career of Melville-Ross: obituary, *The Daily Telegraph* (17 February 1993).
14. Miers's report on Leslie Jones, 5 August 1942.

Chapter 15

1. Miers: report on 'HM Transport *Queen Elizabeth'*, dated 17 December 1942 and sent to the head of the Admiralty delegation, Washington DC.

2. Hitler's reward offer to U-boat captains: Daniel Allen Butler, *Warrior Queens, The Queen Mary And Queen Elizabeth In World War II* (Leo Cooper, 2002), ch. 6.

3. Miers: letter to Honor Miers from a San Francisco hotel address, 21 January 1943.

4. Ibid.

5. Ibid.

6. Ronald Miers and the North Africa campaign: *Historical Records Of The Queen's Own Cameron Highlanders*.

Chapter 16

1. Miers: report of *Cabrilla's* first patrol, dated 25 January 1944, and sent to Rear-Admiral Herbert Pott at the British Embassy in Washington, with copies to the Commander-in-Chief, Eastern Fleet, the First Naval Member, Australian Commonwealth Naval Board, and the Flag Officer Submarines.

2. Douglas Hammond: report of *Cabrilla's* first patrol, n.d.

3. Assessment of *Cabrilla's* patrol: Captain John Haines, commander of Submarine Squadron Sixteen, 12 November 1943.

4. Assessment of *Cabrilla's* patrol: Rear-Admiral Ralph Christie, commander of Task Force Seventy-One, 24 November 1943.

5. *Guardfish* and *Extractor*: Clay Blair Jr, *Silent Victory, The US Submarine War Against Japan*, vol. 1 (J.B. Lippincott, 1975), pp. 804–5.

6. Details of Douglas Hammond's career and death: information supplied by the US Submarine Force Museum and the US Naval Academy Alumni Association.

7. Sir Robert Knox: letter, 19 June 1944.

Chapter 17

1. Miers: letter to Rear-Admiral Barry, 11 November 1943.

2. Ibid.

3. Admiral Barry's letter on X-craft, 12 January 1944.

4. Admiral Barry's letter criticising Miers, 12 January 1944.

5. Visits to Solomon Islands and New Guinea, and PT boat missions: Miers produced a lengthy report.

6. American torpedo fiasco: various sources, including US submarine historian Clay Blair Jr in *Silent Victory*.

7. Sir David Miers: comments to the author, January 2009.

Chapter 18

1. Miers's word was law: Vice-Admiral Sir Arthur Hezlet, *HMS Trenchant At War, From Chatham To The Banka Strait* (Leo Cooper, 2001), ch. 11.

2. David Blamey: written reminiscences and conversation with the author, May 2007.

3. Donald Douglas: written reminiscences, n.d.

4. Vice-Admiral Sir Anthony Troup: conversation with the author, March 2007.

5. Patricia Millar and Miers: interview with Lady Miers, February 2007.

6. Commander Jeremy Nash: interview, February 2007.

7. Miers's challenge to a Scouser: written reminiscences of Albert Gillespie, n.d.

8. *Trenchant*'s silent reception: Hezlet, *HMS Trenchant At War*, ch. 11.

9. Antony Rowe: written reminiscences, n.d.; obituary, *The Daily Telegraph* (11 December 2003).

Chapter 19

1. Albert Gillespie: written reminiscences, n.d.

2. Submarine casualties: Hezlet, *British And Allied Submarine Operations in World War II*, ch. 33.

3. Aces and claims: ibid., ch. 34.

4. Vice-Admiral Sir Ian McGeoch: letter to *The Sunday Telegraph*, 19 February 1989.

5. Lieutenant-Commander Richard Raikes: letter to Gus Britton of the Royal Navy Submarine Museum, 31 October 1986.

6. Sir David Miers: comments to the author, January 2009.

Chapter 20

1. *Orion*: interview with Lady Miers, February 2008.

2. Postings: Miers's service record.

3. Pat's meeting with her mother in law: interview with Lieutenant-Commander John Miers, May 2007.

4. *Blackcap* and anecdotes about Miers: *Royal Naval Air Station Stretton, HMS Blackcap* (Antrobus Heritage, 2004).

5. Cini: interview with Lady Miers, February 2008.

6. Terry Lewin: Richard Hill, *Lewin Of Greenwich, The Authorised Biography Of Admiral Of The Fleet Lord Lewin* (Cassell, 2000), ch. 4.

7. Julian Oswald at Greenwich: interview with Admiral of the Fleet Sir Julian Oswald, November 2007.

8. Miers at Greenwich: interview with Colonel Douglas Miers, April 2007.

9. Sandhurst raid: interview with Lieutenant-Commander John Miers, May 2007.

10. Julian Oswald in *Theseus*: interview with Admiral of the Fleet Sir Julian Oswald, November 2007.

11. Michael Boyce on Miers: author's conversation with Admiral the Lord Boyce, April 2007.

12. David Candlin: written reminiscences of Lieutenant-Commander David Candlin, 2007, and conversation with the author.

13. Lord Lawson: letter to the author, 30 November 2007.

14. Terrorist attacks 1956–8: Miers's monthly reports to the Commander-in-Chief, Mediterranean; Richard Stiles, *Mayhem In The Med, A Chronicle Of The Cyprus Emergency 1955–1960* (Savannah, 2005).

15. Plot to kill Field Marshall Harding: Michael Carver, *Harding Of Petherton* (Weidenfeld & Nicolson, 1978), ch. 13.

16. David Candlin: written reminiscences of Lieutenant-Commander David Candlin, 2007, and conversation with the author.

17. John Pode and character of Miers: written reminiscences of Lieutenant-Commander Guy Timpson, 2007.

18. Philip Bingham's death and Nicos Sampson: Miers's monthly report, 12 February 1957; Stiles, *Mayhem In The Med*; written reminiscences of Lieutenant-Commander Guy Timpson, 2007; Sampson, obituary, *The Independent*, 11 May 2001.

19. Miers: *Corunna* and Lewin: Hill, *Lewin Of Greenwich*, ch. 5.

20. Edward Ashmore and the 6th Frigate Squadron: Admiral of the Fleet Sir Edward Ashmore, letter to the author, 18 November 2007.

21. Colonel Douglas Miers: interview, April 2007.

22. Departure of Field Marshal Harding: Carver, *Harding Of Petherton*, ch. 13.

23. Eoka's problem with arms smuggling: George Grivas, *Guerrilla Warfare*.

24. Mountbatten's decision on Miers's future: interview with Lady Miers, February 2007.

Chapter 21

1. Miers's knighthood and job with Buttons Ltd: interviews with Lady Miers, February 2007 and February 2008; Lady Miers, letter to the author, 22 October 2007.

2. *President*: written reminiscences of Lieutenant-Commander David Candlin, 2007.

3. NCP: interview with Sir Ronald Hobson, April 2008.

4. Sir John Treacher: letter to the author, 24 May 2008.

5. John Miers on his father: interview, May 2007.

6. Miers's lectures: personal notes.

7. John Miers's naval career: written reminiscences, 2008.

8. Rescue off Gibraltar: John Miers, *Portsmouth Evening News* (9 August 1979).

9. Information supplied by the Worshipful Company of Tin Plate Workers Alias Wire Workers.

10. Family history: information supplied by Lieutenant-Colonel Christopher Miers.

11. Colin Brough on Miers: conversation with the author, November 2007.

12. Roy Foster at the launch of *Torbay*: written reminiscences, 25 August 1987.

13. Graham Stainforth: *Wellington Year Book* (1985).

Chapter 22

1. Paul Chapman: letter to Lady Miers, 2 July 1985.

2. Ludovic Kennedy: letter to Lady Miers, 1 January 1985.

3. Ludovic Kennedy's phone call: information supplied to the author by the Miers family, January 2009.

4. Submarine 'atrocity': Kennedy, *On My Way To The Club*, ch. 19.

5. Sinking of *Peleus* and trial of Eck: John Cameron (ed.), *The Peleus Trial*.

6. Afraid of cows: Kennedy, *On My Way To The Club*, ch. 2.

7. Kennedy joins the navy: ibid., ch. 5.

8. ADC to Governor of Newfoundland: ibid, ch. 9.

9. *The Sunday Telegraph* and *The Daily Telegraph* stories and letters (February 1989).

10. House of Commons statement: Hansard, 21 February 1989.

11. George Bremner: letter to Miers asking for help with a planned book, 30 May 1981.

12. Miers's reply to Bremner, 8 June 1981.

13. Vice-Admiral Sir Ronald Brockman: letter to Paul Chapman, 8 March 1990.

14. John Briggs: letter to Lady Miers, 9 February 1989.

15.'I did not name Miers': Kennedy, letter to the author, 18 June 2005.

16. Miers: report of 3rd Mediterranean war patrol, 28 June–15 July 1941.

17. Admiral Cunningham: comments on *Torbay*'s third patrol, message dated 13 August 1941.

18. 'Ruthless' Cunningham: John Winton, *Cunningham, The Greatest Admiral Since Nelson* (John Murray, London, 1998), ch. 17; 'Sink, burn and destroy': ibid., ch. 19.

19. Tony Bridgland: *Waves Of Hate, Naval Atrocities Of The Second World War* (Leo Cooper, 2002), ch. 5: letter to the author, 18 February 2008.

20. Fritz Ehlebracht newspaper interview, 'The *Torbay*'s bloody night', *The Sunday Telegraph* (February 1989).

21. Admiral Sir Max Horton's concern: message SM 4051, 25 September 1941.

22. Admiralty reply: M 013843/41, 14 November 1941.

23. German propaganda translation, 6 September 1941.

24. 'Duck shoot' and Perivolia killings: Beevor, *Crete*, ch. 9.

25. Executions: ibid., ch. 21.

26. M Branch: message, 17 October 1941.

27. Attack on *Gloucester* and *Kelly* survivors: Beevor, *Crete*, ch. 14.

28. Attack on survivors of *Bartolomeo Colleoni*: Cunningham, *A Sailor's Odyssey*, ch. 22.

29. Nicholas Roskill: letters to Paul Chapman, 25 September and 8 October 1990; letter to the author, 1 June 2008.

30. Lieutenant-Commander John Miers: interview May 2007.

31. Lieutenant-Colonel Christopher Miers: interview July 2007.

BIBLIOGRAPHY

Akermann, Paul, *Encyclopaedia Of British Submarines 1901–1955* (Maritime Books, 1989).

Allaway, Jim, *Hero Of The Upholder, The Story Of Lieutenant Commander MD Wanklyn VC, DSO**, The Royal Navy's Top Submarine Ace* (Airlife, 1991).

Asher, Michael, *Get Rommel* (Weidenfeld & Nicolson, 2004).

Ashmore, Edward, *The Battle And The Breeze, The Naval Reminiscences Of Admiral Of The Fleet Sir Edward Ashmore* (Sutton Publishing, 1997).

Beevor, Antony, *Crete, The Battle And The Resistance* (John Murray, 1991).

Blair, Clay Jr, *Silent Victory, The US Submarine War Against Japan*, vol. I (J.B. Lippincott, 1975).

Bridgland, Tony, *Waves Of Hate, Naval Atrocities Of The Second World War* (Leo Cooper, 2002).

Brodhurst, Robin, *Churchill's Anchor, The Biography Of Admiral Of The Fleet Sir Dudley Pound* (Leo Cooper, 2000).

Butler, Daniel Allen, *Warrior Queens, The Queen Mary And Queen Elizabeth In World War II* (Leo Cooper, 2002).

Bryant, Ben (Rear Admiral), *Submarine Command* (William Kimber, London, 1958)

Cameron, John (ed.), *The Peleus Trial* (William Hodge, 1948).

Carver, Michael, *Harding Of Petherton* (Weidenfeld & Nicolson, 1978).

Chalmers, W.S., *Max Horton And The Western Approaches* (Hodder and Stoughton, 1954).

Chapman, Paul, *Submarine Torbay* (Robert Hale, 1989).

Courtney, G.B., *SBS In World War Two, The Story Of The Original Special Boat Section Of The Army Commandos* (Robert Hale, London, 1983).

Cunningham, Andrew, *A Sailor's Odyssey, The Autobiography Of Admiral Of The Fleet Viscount Cunningham Of Hyndhope* (Hutchinson, 1951).

Evans, A.S., *Beneath The Waves, A History Of HM Submarine Losses 1904–1971* (William Kimber, London, 1986).

Fairrie, Angus, *Queen's Own Highlanders, Seaforth And Camerons* (Queen's Own Highlanders Amalgamation Trustees, 1998).

Grivas, George, *Guerrilla Warfare*.

Harris, Wendy, *The Rogue's Yarn, The Sea-going Life Of Captain 'Joe' Oram* (Leo Cooper, 1993).

Heathcote, T.A., *The British Admirals Of The Fleet 1734-1995, A Biographical Dictionary* (Leo Cooper, 2002).

Hezlet, Arthur (Vice-Admiral Sir Arthur Hezlet), *British And Allied Submarine Operations In World War II, vol. I* (The Royal Navy Submarine Museum, 2001).

——, (Vice-Admiral Sir Arthur Hezlet), *HMS Trenchant At War, From Chatham To The Banka Strait* (Leo Cooper, 2001).

Hill, Richard, *Lewin Of Greenwich, The Authorised Biography Of Admiral Of The Fleet Lord Lewin* (Cassell, 2000).

Historical Records Of The Queen's Own Cameron Highlanders, seven volumes (William Blackwood, 1909–62).

Ireland, Bernard, *The War In The Mediterranean* (Arms & Armour Press, 1993).

Jameson, William, *Submariners VC* (Peter Davies, London, 1962).

Keegan, John, *The First World War* (Hutchinson, 2001).

Kemp, P.K., *HM Submarines* (Herbert Jenkins, London, 1952).

Kennedy, Ludovic, *On My Way To The Club* (William Collins, 1989).

Keyes, Elizabeth, *Geoffrey Keyes VC Of The Rommel Raid* (George Newnes, 1956).

Preston, Anthony, *The Royal Navy Submarine Service, A Centennial History* (Conway Maritime Press, 2001).

Macintyre, Donald, *The Battle For The Pacific* (B.T. Batsford, 1966).

Mackenzie, Hugh, *The Sword Of Damocles, Some Memories Of Vice Admiral Sir Hugh Mackenzie* (The Royal Navy Submarine Museum, 1995).

Mars, Alastair, *Unbroken, The Story Of A Submarine* (Frederick Muller, London, 1953).

——, *British Submarines At War 1939-1945* (William Kimber, London, 1971).

Newsome, David, *A History Of Wellington College 1859-1959* (John Murray, 1959).

Potter, E.B., *Nimitz* (Naval Institute Press (US), 1976).

Royal Naval Air Station Stretton, HMS Blackcap (Antrobus Heritage, 2004).

Roskill, S.W., *The War At Sea 1939-1945*, volumes I and II (Her Majesty's Stationery Office, 1956).

Stiles, Richard G.M.L., *Mayhem In The Med, A Chronicle Of The Cyprus Emergency 1955–1960* (Savannah, 2005).

Thomas, David A, *Submarine Victory, The Story Of British Submarines In World War II* (William Kimber, London, 1961).

——, *Crete 1941, The Battle At Sea* (Andre Deutsch, 1972).

Treacher, John (Admiral Sir John Treacher), *Life At Full Throttle, From Wardroom To Boardroom* (Pen & Sword Maritime, 2004).

Trenowden, Ian, *The Hunting Submarine, The Fighting Life Of HMS Tally-Ho* (Crecy Books, 1994).

Warren, C.E.T., and James Benson, *Will Not We Fear, The Story Of HM Submarine Seal* (George G. Harrap, London, 1961).

Wingate, John, *The Fighting Tenth, The Tenth Submarine Flotilla And The Siege Of Malta* (Leo Cooper, 1991).

Winton, John, *The Victoria Cross At Sea* (Michael Joseph, 1978).

——, *Cunningham, The Greatest Admiral Since Nelson* (John Murray, London, 1998).

ACKNOWLEDGEMENTS

First my thanks must go to George Malcolmson, the archivist at the Royal Navy Submarine Museum. George was enthusiastic about this project from the start and went out of his way to provide material. I am also grateful to the museum's former director, Commander Jeff Tall, and to Debbie Corner, who did picture research.

I am indebted to Admiral Miers's family, especially Lady (Pat) Miers, Lieutenant-Commander John Miers, Colonel Douglas Miers, Sir David Miers and Lieutenant-Colonel Christopher Miers.

Reminiscences and papers of some of the men who served in the wartime submarine HMS *Torbay* were invaluable – Commander Paul Chapman, Lieutenant-Commander Roy Foster, Philip Le Gros, Alexander McCulloch, Frederick Rumsey and Leslie Philips.

My thanks also to Admiral of the Fleet Sir Edward Ashmore, David Blamey, Admiral the Lord Boyce, Colin Brough, Lieutenant-Commander David Candlin, Lieutenant-Colonel Alaistair Cumming, Lieutenant-Colonel David Eliot, assistant regimental secretary of The Rifles, Taunton, Lieutenant-Colonel Angus Fairrie, Stephen Finnigan, supervisory curator of the US Submarine Force Museum, Michael Henderson-Begg, Gerald Haselden, Sir Ronald Hobson, Kelvin Hunter, curator of the regimental museum of The Highlanders, the Imperial War Museum, Lieutenant-Colonel George Latham, director of the regimental museum of The Highlanders, Lord Lawson of Blaby, Michelle Mazanec of the US Naval Academy Alumni Association, Commander Jeremy Nash, the National Archives, Kew, the National Archives, University of Maryland, Admiral of the Fleet Sir Julian Oswald, Allen Packwood, director of the Churchill Archives Centre, Churchill College, Cambridge, and his staff, Captain Christopher Page, head of the Naval Historical Branch, Ministry of Defence, George Pickup, Nicholas Roskill, Lieutenant-Commander Guy Timpson, Admiral Sir John Treacher and Vice-Admiral Sir Tony Troup.

Guidance given by my agent, Duncan McAra, and the editorial team at Haynes has been much appreciated.

INDEX

270